W9-CMF-210

THE IDEA OF POPULAR SCHOOLING
IN UPPER CANADA

The Idea of Popular Schooling in Upper Canada

Print Culture, Public Discourse, and the
Demand for Education

ANTHONY DI MASCIO

McGill-Queen's University Press
Montreal & Kingston · London · Ithaca

ISBN 978-0-7735-4045-3 (cloth)
ISBN 978-0-7735-4046-0 (paper)

Legal deposit third quarter 2012
Bibliothèque nationale du Québec

Printed in Canada on acid-free paper that is 100% ancient forest free
(100% post-consumer recycled), processed chlorine free

This book has been published with the help of a grant from the
Canadian Federation for the Humanities and Social Sciences, through
the Aid to Scholarly Publications Program, using funds provided by
the Social Sciences and Humanities Research Council of Canada.
Funding has also been received from Bishop's University.

McGill-Queen's University Press acknowledges the support of the
Canada Council for the Arts for our publishing program. We also
acknowledge the financial support of the Government of Canada
through the Canada Book Fund for our publishing activities.

Library and Archives Canada Cataloguing in Publication

Di Mascio, Anthony, 1975–

   The idea of popular schooling in Upper Canada : print culture,
public discourse, and the demand for education / Anthony Di
Mascio.

Includes bibliographical references and index.
ISBN 978-0-7735-4045-3 (bound). – ISBN 978-0-7735-4046-0 (pbk.)

   1. Education – Ontario – History – 19th century. 2. Education –
Social aspects – Ontario – History – 19th century. 3. Education –
Political aspects – Ontario – History – 19th century. 4. Public schools
– Ontario – History – 19th century. 5. Ontario – Intellectual life –
19th century. I. Title.

LA418.06D54 2012   370.971309'034   C2012-902102-4

Typeset by Jay Tee Graphics Ltd. in 10.5/13.5 Sabon

For my father, Raffaele Di Mascio

Contents

Acknowledgments

This book began as a dissertation at the University of Ottawa, where my supervisor, Chad Gaffield, was the most influential person both in the development of its writing and in my personal development as an academic. His enthusiasm and passion for scholarly research and ideas are infectious, and his concern for his students is nothing short of remarkable. The special care he took in guiding me through the scattered thought behind what would become this book is something I will never forget, and I owe him more thanks than I can express here.

Before moving to Ottawa, I completed an MA under the supervision of David Levine in the Theory and Policy Studies in Education program at the University of Toronto. He challenged me to think more deeply about the history of education and provided me with the support and encouragement to do so. While there, I was also encouraged and intellectually stimulated by Harold Troper. His Origins of Modern Schooling seminar introduced me to the debates and issues on this topic.

At the University of Ottawa, a number of colleagues and friends contributed to the development of my research and writing. Members of the "Research Group" not only provided comments and suggestions for revision, but also offered the type and quality of friendship that made my work even more rewarding. I am grateful to Adam Green, Betsey Baldwin, Ivana Caccia, Jessica Van Horssen, Jo-Anne McCutcheon, Katie Rollwagen, Linda Fitzgibbon, Lucie Lecomte, Nic Clarke, Ruth Dunley, Samy Khalid, Stacey Loyer, and Tim Krywulak.

The members of my doctoral examination committee, Elizabeth Jane Errington, Richard Connors, Ruby Heap, and Timothy J. Stanley, provided valuable comments and suggestions that have enhanced the manuscript significantly. I was fortunate to have had a comprehensive field course in British history with Professor Connors. The meetings and conversations I had with him had an enormous impact on my writing and on the ways in which I approach the study of history. I also had a comprehensive field course in Canadian history with Professor Stanley. I have benefited immensely from his ideas and especially from his challenge to rethink Canadian history and the various ways in which it is imagined.

Over the years, others have commented on my work, have offered insight through conversation, or have provided intellectual stimulation, moral support, or encouragement in equally valuable ways. They include Bruce Curtis, Carl Kaestle, Carlo Ravenna, Crystal Sissons, David Gamson, David Williams, Frederick Augustyn, Genevieve Bonenfant, Giulio Silano, Jan Grabowski, Jean-François Lozier, Jeffrey Mirel, John Stephens, John Willis, Kim Tolley, Martin Barlosky, Martin Hubley, Michael Charles, Michael B. Katz, Michel Duquet, Nancy Beadie, Patrice Milewski, Paul Reale, Rhonda Hinther, Robert D. Gidney, Sharon Anne Cook, Teva Vidal, Wayne Urban, and Wyn Millar. I would also like to thank my new colleagues and friends at Bishop's University, Avril Aitkin, Betty Kreuger, Catherine Beauchamp, Christopher Darius Stonebanks, Corinne Haigh, Darren Millington, Eva Mary Bures, Linda Leblanc, Lisa Taylor, Marge Heggison, Sunny Man Chu Lau, and Trevor Gulliver, for welcoming me into such a collaborative and supportive environment. My family, from Toronto to Lettomanoppello, has been a constant source of support.

Kyla Madden, at McGill-Queen's University Press, has taken much time and effort to see the manuscript become a book. I hope that every new scholar can find as able, encouraging, and supportive an editor as she. To her, the anonymous readers, and the entire staff at McGill-Queen's University Press, I owe special thanks.

This book has been published with the help of a grant from the Canadian Federation for the Humanities and Social Sciences, through the Aid to Scholarly Publications Program, using funds provided by the Social Sciences and Humanities Research Council of

Canada. Additional financial assistance has been provided through a publication grant awarded by Bishop's University. Financial support was provided in earlier stages by the University of Ottawa, the Ontario Graduate Scholarship Program, the Fonds de recherche sur la société et la culture Québec, and the Canadian Museum of Civilization. Parts of this book have previously appeared in *McGill Journal of Education* and in *History of Education Quarterly*. I am grateful to the editors for permission to republish that material here.

The one who deserves most to be singled out for her contribution to this book is Leigh. It is to her that I ultimately owe everything, both in the writing of this book and life in general. From the moment I met her, Leigh has continually given to me and has asked nothing in return. Thank you, Leigh, for all that you've provided me with over the years. Thank you for encouraging me throughout the writing of this book, for reading it, for critiquing it, and for sharing your ideas. Thank you for sticking with me through all of the ups and downs. I couldn't have done it without you. Thank you.

THE IDEA OF POPULAR SCHOOLING
IN UPPER CANADA

Introduction

"Backwater," "backwoods," "the bush," "howling wilderness." If you consider some of the words that have been used to describe Upper Canada, it would seem unlikely that a region with such depictions, as well as a lingering reputation in our historical imagination as a nascent society devoid of culture, the arts, and an intellectual elite, would be a maverick in the development of popular schooling. Yet it was. Within six years of the region's founding, Upper Canadians drew up legislation that made provisions for a university and a relatively complex system of grammar schools. Only a decade later, with a non-Aboriginal population of roughly 75,000 scattered throughout 6,000 kilometres of bush, Upper Canada established a network of grammar schools supported in part by the state and began pushing, both in government and through the popular press, for a common system of schooling available to all inhabitants. And nine years later, in 1816, the roots of that system took form. In that year, Upper Canada became one of the first jurisdictions in the modern world to pass a common school act with provisions for the publicly aided schooling of the entire population. Why did popular schooling begin in such earnest in Upper Canada?

The research behind this book began with a question: what do we know about the origins of popular schooling in Ontario? The answer to this question is not clear-cut and often depends on what sources we choose to help us make sense of the past. Scholars of Upper Canada have typically focused on official archival records. Prior to the 1960s, the historiography characteristically represented the development of popular schooling as the triumph of great men, such as John Strachan and Egerton Ryerson, who designed a universal system of education aimed at providing equality of opportunity to all.[1] Benevolent school promoters, in this Whig interpretation, advocated a state-supported school system with a common curriculum aimed to place the children of the rich and poor on equal footing.

Beginning in the 1960s, scholars began virtually to rewrite history and challenged the linear and progressive narrative of schooling's origins. Schooling in the early nineteenth century, they pointed out, was *ad hoc* and sporadic, and the drive to initiate a system of education was instead located within the context of the systemic social and political changes of the mid-nineteenth century. They also challenged the notion that history, as a field, should be about the commemoration of great men. Scholars began to heavily criticize the Whig narrative that focused on school promoters as advocates of the lower classes and proponents of liberal democratization. Revisionists challenged these assumptions and brought to light the oppressive nature of bureaucratized schooling. The "great men" who built the school system were now characterized as socially conservative "school promoters" involved in the construction of a school system that taught the specific values of an emerging urban and middle class.[2] Further revisionist history and neo-Marxist theory in the 1980s and 1990s held that prominent school promoters, in an effort to secure political hegemony for the social and political elite, built a large and powerful system of schooling centralized in the office of education.[3] In an attempt to excavate the voices of the anonymous, many of these scholars examined and extracted correspondence between the political elite at the head of education departments. The bulk of these scholars, therefore, narrowed the time period of schooling's origins in the mid-nineteenth century and pinpointed the years around 1841 to 1876 – in which an educational bureaucracy was built – as those in which our modern system of schooling began.[4]

Certain other scholars have focused their attention on the development of schooling at the local level.[5] Their research has demonstrated the influence that local administrators, school trustees, groups of parents, teachers, and other school advocates had in the creation of a school system. Such studies have suggested that central authorities themselves often reacted to local decisions. With official archival records as their main source of research, their concentration has inevitably been centred again in the middle years of the nineteenth century, where the bulk of the archival material is found.

For at least two good reasons, historians of education in Upper Canada have concentrated on this period and these sources. First, the historical record on education in this period is bountiful. The establishment of a department of education in Canada West in 1841, an office that would be controlled by Ryerson and his assistant J. George Hodgins for roughly thirty years, provides the historian with a ready collection of official state documents related directly to the making and expansion of a school system in Ontario. Ryerson and Hodgins, to their credit, kept meticulous records, and the archival material on education that they left behind provides more than a lifetime's worth of work for any scholar. Second, the major school administrators of the nineteenth century – and in this regard Ryerson certainly stands out – were prolific writers who put, it would seem, virtually every thought they had about the direction of schooling in the province onto paper.

In the early nineteenth century, however, there was no official department of education, and thus very little archival material to draw from. Official documentation on education in early Upper Canada is sporadic, and a central department of education was not established until 1822, under the name of the General Board of Education. That board itself, however, was an afterthought to the Common School Act passed in 1816, and although its records provide a great deal of information concerning the administrative and institutional developments of the time, they tell us very little about the idea of popular schooling and its advocates. Certainly, the major school promoters in early Upper Canada left behind a good deal of writing concerning education and the idea of school expansion in the province. For the most part, however, scholars have concluded that we know very little about the context of educational development in this period, especially the earlier period prior to 1820. Thus, answering the question of why popular schooling began in such earnest in Upper Canada becomes increasingly challenging. As two of the most prominent scholars in the field have put it, "We know almost nothing about the political context of the attempts to secure and preserve that appropriation except what the barebone record of the legislative journals tells us."[6]

We are thus left with a two-pronged conundrum in what we know about the origins of schooling in Ontario. First, we know much more about the administrative and bureaucratic developments, and reactions to those developments, in the middle to late nineteenth century than in the earlier period. Second, and related to the first, the available historical record encourages us to concentrate on the origins of the school *system* – or on the various school laws and regulations that put the system in place. What about the origins of the *idea* of popular schooling? How was it imagined and by whom? We know that parents were sending their children to school even before the compulsory school laws of the middle to late nineteenth century. Why?

The problem with tracing the origins of an idea through official state records is that you can only go back so far. The passing of the school act of 1846 under Egerton Ryerson, who would spearhead the department of education into Confederation and establish the province's school system, stands out as a watershed in the writing of the history of education in Upper Canada. That act itself, however, was based on the school act of 1843, which was based on the act of 1841. If you keep tracing the official records backwards like this, you will find a number of proposed school bills in the 1830s and two common school acts in the 1820s, before you come to a dead stop at the Common School Act of 1816 (Upper Canada's first legislated universal school act) and the District School Act of 1807 (which established grammar schools). These earlier acts seem to be a reasonable place to locate the origins of the idea of popular schooling, but the problem with these earlier acts, as previously mentioned, is that there was no department of education in Upper Canada at the time of their passing, and so there are very few official records that help us contextualize the ideas behind them. Using what is there, we know that John Strachan, the Anglican bishop of Toronto and leader of the Family Compact, pushed for classical grammar schools for the children of prominent landholders and government officials. Strachan wrote a report on education – presented to the House of Assembly and the Legislative Council after the War of 1812 – that served as the blueprint for the Common School Act of 1816.[7] Still, we don't have a clear sense of why Strachan did this and why Upper Canadian parents went along with the idea.

But what if we change the sources? And what if we begin to ask not what the major school advocates were promoting, but what a broader representation of the population wanted? What if we shift our concentration away from the official discourse surrounding popular schooling in Upper Canada and move toward sources that tell us more about the *unofficial* discourse among a variety of Upper Canadian inhabitants? Recent scholarship on Upper Canada has certainly suggested that by changing both the sources and the objects of our inquiry, we can learn much more about the making of official public policy in Upper Canada.

The shift in research on Upper Canada away from the narrative of prominent individuals who controlled the social, political, and economic development of the colony and toward a "deliberative democracy" model of colonial development suggests new avenues of exploration in the history of Upper Canadian education. In his study of public opinion and deliberative democracy in Upper Canada, Jeffrey McNairn argues that public opinion emerged as a new form of authority in Upper Canada. Through a meticulous and thorough review of colonial newspapers, McNairn suggests that the public was exposed to, and involved in, the theatre of politics through the press and that the increased publication of newspapers in Upper Canada resulted in public dialogue that not only influenced but also shaped the political development of the province.[8]

Carol Wilton has also examined popular political participation in a study of petitioning movements from 1800 to 1850.[9] Wilton suggests that "ordinary Canadians" were much more involved in the political process than previously believed. She convincingly argues that political outsiders often challenged established patterns of paternalism and notions of hierarchy and promoted the development of an expanded public sphere in Upper Canada.[10] Politics, in this sense, was not the exclusive domain of the elite, but rather a more open arena in which many ideas were exchanged. This book builds upon the deliberative democracy model and explores how print culture during the late eighteenth and early nineteenth centuries enabled the emergence of popular schooling as a central discourse in Upper Canada.[11]

This book differs from typical histories of schooling in Ontario in two ways. First, it concentrates its attention on early Upper Canada.

On what is now a tucked-away corner of Ryerson University just off Yonge Street in downtown Toronto stands a commemorative statue of the university's namesake, Egerton Ryerson, with the label to that monument proclaiming him the "Founder of the School System of Ontario." To what extent should we accept this statue's label? We cannot lose sight of the fact that when Ryerson took office in 1844, three common school acts had already been passed in the colony. The first dated back to 1816, when Ryerson was only thirteen years of age and possessed little influence in the institutional foundations of Upper Canada. The first aim of this book, then, is to shift attention back to Upper Canada and ask why this early legislation was drawn up when it was and what the significance of common schooling was both at the time and in later developments in Canada West and Ontario.

The second differentiating feature of this book is that it reconsiders who was advocating for schools in this earlier period. At first glance, educational history can clearly identify its champions. John Strachan, the would-be Anglican bishop of Toronto who boarded a ship from Scotland to Quebec in 1799 upon the request of the Upper Canadian legislature to secure an agent ready to promote the interests of schooling in the province, is commonly considered the architect of the Common School Act of 1816; but in what context was this act drawn up? After all, Strachan was called from Scotland for the purpose of promoting education and initiating a system of schooling, but from where did the impetus of this request derive? The point I am making is that the *idea* of popular schooling came before the man. There is a context here that must be considered if we are to understand the origins of the idea of popular schooling in the colony.

This book, then, is about the history of an idea – the idea of popular schooling in Upper Canada. I believe that in order to understand the origins of popular schooling in Ontario, we have to begin earlier than the period in which school laws and bills were made, and we have to consider more than the rhetoric and discourse of the politicians who drew up those school laws and bills. The two men most credited with drawing up legislation for popular schooling in Upper Canada were themselves latecomers to the idea. It was the idea itself that created space for them in the political arena to consider the shape and form of educational legislation. Assertions that the idea of popular schooling came from these men, and a few others, who had a bold new vision for the people of Upper Canada, are not satisfying. They presume that these politicians were the shepherds of public education, for good or bad, and that the masses were a following herd. When we consider, however, that these men were not universally popular – that they in fact were the objects of much public anger and disdain – then the idea that they convinced thousands of Upper Canadian parents to follow them into the unknown land of government-aided schooling is even less satisfying. Indeed, no single political figure in this era of fragmented politics and divided loyalties could have sold his or her vision to an entire population in so short a time. How, then, did so many divided men and women – divided by politics, religion, ethnicity, and class – agree upon sending their children to "common" schools in the nineteenth century?

To be sure, a number of scholars have grappled with these questions. In his study of family economies in late nineteenth-century Ontario, Chad Gaffield argues that the appetite for schooling was both motivated and constrained by the political and economic realities of the times.[12] By looking at family economies, Gaffield explores the ways in which parents strove to provide material security and survival for their children. As limited land inheritance made outmigration common in Ontario, families sought to provide for sons and daughters who would not inherit land. The provision of schooling, in this sense, became a form of inheritance. If major school promoters were restructuring society and making schooling a common experience of growing up, then parents welcomed the intrusion as a material benefit to their families. The centrality of the family remained consistent as societies were being reorganized. Families could take advantage of societal reorganization in ways that benefited them and posterity. In this regard, the desired ends of the ruled could converge with the desired ends of the rulers and provide for an agreement – albeit for different reasons – on the necessity of a common system of schooling. Gaffield's study raises the possibility for explorations concerning how multiple ideas and desired ends converged and allowed for different people to utilize schooling for their own reasons. Did different ideas converge even earlier in the century? How can we examine the ideas and intentions of those who willingly sent their children to school prior to the compulsory school attendance laws of the late nineteenth century and even prior to the major school developments of the mid-nineteenth century?

Elizabeth Jane Errington explores these questions, among others, in her study of schoolteachers and female labour in early nineteenth-century Upper Canada.[13] Despite being excluded from official colonial politics, wives and mothers played a significant role in the development of Upper Canada. Parents often sought educational opportunities for their children, but those children too often faced the demands of life in a frontier society. Daughters especially were expected to attend to the duties of the household, which too often took time and energy away from their studies. Parents, especially those with modest incomes, were often left regretting that they could not provide an adequate education for their daughters, one that would allow them to sustain a modicum of material comfort independently. Their solace lay, as in the case of Frances Stewart in 1833, in their daughters' at least acquiring skills that would be useful after marriage.[14] Errington demonstrates that an appetite for schooling was clearly alive among certain Upper Canadian parents in the early nineteenth century and that efforts were often made to provide an education for their children. Indeed, in her meticulous examination of previously overlooked notices in the colonial newspapers, Errington demonstrates that private individuals often led the way in the provision of schooling.

By contemplating the variety of possible motivations that made both major school promoters and parents seek the construction of a formal system of schooling, Paul Axelrod builds the central argument of his survey of nineteenth-century educational histories. He suggests that both groups had their own reasons for advocating a system of schooling and that we might better conclude that a mix of circumstances accounted for its growth, particularly from the 1840s to the 1870s. "Compulsory-school legislation," he argues, "tended to follow, not precede, large-scale participation in public schooling."[15] Axelrod's study raises a host of questions that offer new possibilities for further research. Indeed, both parents and major school promoters had their own reasons for advocating schooling, but did the two operate in isolation? That is, did they discuss the formation of a school system independently of one another? To what extent did their discourses overlap? Did groups outside of political circles contribute to the development of educational legislation? Must we insist that one group was leading the movement for schooling, while the other was following? Or, can we speak in terms of a symbiotic relationship that contributed to the formation of a school system in Upper Canada?

What role did parents, teachers, and other individuals with little or no political authority play in affecting educational legislation? Was it coincidental that school acts emerged from the offices of public leaders at the same time that private individuals were writing about the regrets of inadequate schooling in a frontier society and providing themselves with forms of education where there were none provided by government? That is, did private individuals keep their educational ideas to themselves, or did they play an active role in the development of educational legislation? In what ways were private thoughts and writings made part of the official public debate concerning educational development? An exploration of print culture can help broaden our understanding of the idea of popular schooling in Upper Canada. Through print media, private thoughts and ideas could be made part of a broader public discourse.[16]

Communication through print was central to Upper Canadian discourse, as it was to public discourses throughout the world. The invention of the printing press in the fifteenth century that spawned print culture and accelerated the deliberative process of its predecessor, manuscript culture allowed individuals separated by geographical space to communicate with each other at an accelerated pace through the medium of print. Whereas manuscript culture allowed writers to add to or alter the text, creating a discourse between writer and audience, there was very little, if any, back-and-forth or immediate exchange of ideas between writers.[17] Moreover, the intended public audience was vague and unclear and absolutely limited in size. The invention of newspapers and their subsequent multiplication revolutionized public discourse and shifted it, as Marshall McLuhan argues, from "a private confessional form that provides a point of view" to "a group confessional form that provides communal participation."[18] The significance of communal participation through print media to the inhabitants of Upper Canada was immense. Separated from one another by great distances of geography, print media, and especially the regular printing of newspapers, allowed distant individuals to participate in the social, political, and economic life of Upper Canada that was otherwise centred in the capital. By contributing to print culture discourse, print media allowed for a centre of exchange between the individual and a broader public. Participants in the print culture were given a forum of self-expression where their voice was situated within the many other voices of the community.[19] In this way, geographic space was collapsed in Upper Canada, enabling numerous settlements to interact and its individual members to participate in an accelerated and widespread public discourse.[20]

Jurgen Habermas postulates that the press institutionalized regular contacts and regular communication and shifted the hegemony of information from "insiders" to the "general public." The decisive mark of the new domain of the "public sphere" was the published word.[21] Benedict Anderson considers the rise of print culture central to the concept of the "imagined community" and the creation of modern nation-states. The reading of newspapers, he argues, gives rise to a "mass ceremony." Although the newspaper is often read in silent privacy, each reader is aware that the ceremony is being replicated simultaneously by many others. This assures the reader of the existence of a community of participants, despite never having met many of them. The availability of print media in its physical form, such as newspapers, serves to reassure the reader that the imagined world indeed is real. The reader is a member of a public that is not tangible but explicably real.[22]

Seen in this light, print media offered Upper Canadians a way to identify themselves as members of the same community. Upper Canada was only recently settled, with few roads and a simple transportation infrastructure. Print media provided individual voices with a "unified and ready-made public address system"[23] in which ordinary inhabitants could raise ideas of importance that affected the social, political, and economic development of the region. In Upper Canada, this "public address system" allowed inhabitants, as remote from one another as neighbouring colonies and states in North America, to share a common dialogue concerning Upper Canada's interests. In this context, the press provided a platform for central discourses in the colony such as that concerning the schools.

An analysis of print culture also allows us to situate Upper Canadians in their transatlantic and international context. As members of the British Empire, the inhabitants of Upper Canada were involved in an imperial community in which ideas, institutions, and socio-cultural practices were shaped and reshaped through a complex process of interaction between the British Isles and the new settlement societies.[24] As members of North America, the Loyalists and late-Loyalists who arrived in a steady stream from the United States were ensured that their cross-border relationships and ties of community would continue to see an exchange of ideas flowing back and forth across the permeable Upper Canada and United States border.[25] The expansion of the press throughout the eighteenth and nineteenth centuries facilitated this exchange and afforded Upper Canadians a central space in an international discourse.

At the same time, Upper Canadians were not passive participants in the exchange of ideas with either the United States or the British Isles. As the development of popular schooling in the colony demonstrates, they were leaders in that exchange. They began exploring, debating, and framing the structure of popular schooling before the first major wave of British migration to the colony, which came after 1815. By that time, the development of common schooling in Upper Canada had already reached its first climax, and plans were drawn up by colonial leaders, who recognized the will of "the people" on this issue, for the legislation that would mark the beginning of government involvement in the publicly funded education of the entire population. The British metropolis itself would not see a similar development until the second half of the century.[26] The influence of British imperialism in the development of popular schooling through its colonial administrators is a common part of the narrative in studies of the origins of popular schooling. In Upper Canada, however, the movement for popular schooling began in earnest through public discourse. In this regard Upper Canadians were influenced by their North American neighbours, who recognized the potential of popular schooling to strengthen the republic and create a national consciousness. By no means, however, were the popular or official debates regarding common schooling in Upper Canada tantamount to those taking place in the republic to the south. Upper Canada's educational discourse included as well the ideas of those committed to the British link, and the possible use of schooling for maintaining that link was indeed a central feature of educational discourse in Upper Canada.[27]

To what extent did Upper Canadians exchange ideas about education, and to what extent did they bring those ideas into the public sphere? To what extent did the public discourse affect official educational reform? As McNairn and Wilton demonstrate, the growth of a deliberative democracy in Upper Canada allowed ordinary inhabitants to utilize public discourse in ways that gave them authority in the political process. To what extent, then, were they involved in the creation of the educational legislation that led to popular schooling? What can the exchange of educational ideas in the public arena tell us about the influence of public opinion on the official making of the school system?

Print culture sources offer much to broaden our understanding of the origins of popular schooling. These sources also have their limits. We must use terms such as "the public," "the people," and "public discourse" very carefully when examining late eighteenth- and early nineteenth-century Upper Canada. Who exactly do we mean by the public? Who were the people? Who participated in the public discourse? Or, more importantly perhaps, who were excluded? The public in Upper Canada was not a public of equals, and public discourse in Upper Canada, by extension, was not a discourse among equals.[28] Race, gender, and class were major determinants of one's social status and ability to participate in Upper Canadian print culture. A study of print culture and education in Upper Canada must therefore not purport to examine the entire population. Aboriginals and Upper Canadians of African descent were no more than minor participants in public discourse. William Lyon Mackenzie, editor and proprietor of the *Colonial Advocate*, reported Mississauga Aboriginals at Credit River among his subscribers,[29] yet the participation of Aboriginal people in Upper Canadian print culture appears to have been limited to reading, at least for a small minority. For those with the means, participation in print culture discourse through letters to the editor could be done anonymously. It is safe to suppose that the number of non-white participants was low, as literacy levels and schooling among non-whites was low.[30]

Women were excluded from official politics throughout Upper Canada's existence. Errington points out that age, location, marital status, and class all had an impact on what was expected of women, what they did, and how they did it.[31] Thus, some classes of women had better means of participating in the print culture discourse than others, if indirectly through their affluent husbands or community circles and voluntary associations. In addition to indirect influence, the evidence analysed by Errington and McNairn does suggest that women often made themselves a direct part of the print culture discourse. The goods and services advertised within the colonial newspapers certainly acknowledge women as readers as well as consumers.[32] Moreover, some wives also managed newspapers during the absence of their editor-husbands, and others retained ownership of newspapers as widows.[33] While women were excluded from the official legislative political process, the evidence suggests that a significant number of them were not systematically excluded from Upper Canadian print culture and public discourse.

We might reasonably assume that participation in print culture discourse was limited to affluent Upper Canadians because they were the most likely to be literate. Still, the evidence suggests that there was no direct correlation between one's material prosperity or social status in Upper Canada and one's ability to read and write. Harvey Graff, in *The Literacy Myth: Cultural Integration and Social Structure in the Nineteenth Century*, indicates that literacy and illiteracy rates among the poor and wealthy were relatively the same.[34] Despite acknowledging the limitations of his research, namely the limited evidence drawn from nineteenth-century census data, Graff successfully challenges the literacy myth and calls into question established assumptions concerning the hegemony of literacy among the quintessential upper echelons of society.[35]

While literacy might have been more widespread than generally assumed in Upper Canada, class could still place limitations on one's ability to participate in print culture discourse. One needed money, after all, to subscribe to Upper Canadian newspapers or purchase the pamphlets and books available. In the early nineteenth century, most Upper Canadian newspapers charged approximately four dollars for a year's subscription.[36] This number represents roughly three days' wages for the average artisan and some journeymen.[37] A general profile offered by McNairn suggests that subscribers included professionals, clerks and shopkeepers, skilled artisans and journeymen, and most relatively established farm families. Subscribing to a newspaper in Upper Canada represented a considerable investment, or a luxury, for many of these subscribers.

A newspaper subscription, however, was not necessarily out of reach, even for the poorer classes. Many subscribers were constantly in arrears and paid only what and when they could. Newspapers would threaten to stop sending copies, but only when subscribers were more than a year behind in payment, which meant many individuals could receive newspapers without incurring the expense.[38] Moreover, payment could take the form of wheat, flour, and other produce, thus expanding the scope of potential subscribers.[39] Participation in Upper Canadian print culture discourse was limited by class, but it was not confined to the wealthy alone.

Considering the extent to which newspapers were passed on to subsequent readers in the eighteenth and nineteenth centuries, the number of participants might be significantly higher than the number of subscribers. In 1825, Mackenzie was informed that a number of non-subscribers were reading copies of the Colonial Advocate that had "made the tour of Brockville half a dozen times."[40] Access to newspapers was made possible in Upper Canada through the subscriptions of family and friends; at local stores, inns, and taverns; through voluntary associations; and through libraries, newsrooms, and Mechanics' Institutes. Domestic servants could find newspapers to read in the homes of their affluent employers. Boarders could find newspapers there as well, as they were more likely to stay in the homes of the affluent than in the homes of the poor.[41]

Readership is not the only indication of the extent of public discourse. To what extent did print media reflect public discourse, and to what extent did print media shape it? This two-sided question is central to understanding the importance and the complexities of print media and print culture discourse in Upper Canada. In The Transformation of the Public Sphere, Habermas raises the example of London coffee houses and other public spaces as mediating centres of public discourse.[42] Private people could meet in public spaces where they shared and debated ideas. This interaction was shaped by, and itself shaped, the print culture discourse. In this way, participants in the "mass ceremony" of private newspaper reading, as described by Anderson, moved into a public space where they and non-readers alike could discuss the information drawn from the print media. Once the written word entered the public space, literacy was not a prerequisite for participation in the public discourse. Such was the case in John Howison's *Sketches of Upper Canada*, where the author recounts an Upper Canadian landlord entering his tavern and reading newspaper articles to a group of seamstresses. Rather than being passive recipients of this performance, the landlord's audience actively commented upon and critiqued the articles in a lively public discourse.[43]

Such accounts serve to suggest that many more inhabitants were influenced by and influenced print culture discourse than any observation of subscription rates or interpretations of class might suggest. Print media collapsed space in Upper Canada and allowed literate persons in Upper Canada to participate in centralized public discourse; but illiteracy did not prevent individuals from taking part in this discourse. Print culture was influenced by public discourses through participants not directly involved in the making of the content of the print media but certainly involved in the making of public ideas. Julia Roberts's recent study of tavern culture in Upper Canada demonstrates, for example, that taverns afforded Upper Canadians a "public space" where ideas were exchanged between inhabitants of all stripes, including Aboriginals and non-whites, rich and poor.[44] This very real space, like the virtual space of print media, allowed those with no political power to have influence in the direction of public policy.

Still, there were the serious inequalities in Upper Canada that remind us that public discourse in Upper Canada, even if widespread, was not a discourse among equals. Aboriginals, Upper Canadians of African descent, women, the poor, and other minority groups consistently faced obstacles to participation in Upper Canadian print culture discourse.[45] The majority of the participants were those who had access to newspapers and the time to engage with them; and this was usually, but not always, men of British origin. It is in this sense that the public in Upper Canada was not a public of equals. McNairn is surely right in suggesting that many of the editors of Upper Canadian newspapers exaggerated and assumed a community of interest when they spoke of "the people" rather than "the public of newspaper readers."[46] Any study of the public through print media cannot purport to enumerate the educational ideas of the entire population. What it does offer, however, is an important step toward a broader understanding of the intellectual underpinnings of schooling in Upper Canada.

Race, class, and gender were not the only divisive elements in Upper Canadian society. Religion divided the people of Upper Canada. The Church of England might have been perceived to have privileges that the status of an established church would have within the empire, including rights to land and political power, but in reality such privileges were never absolute and were in fact the stuff of much contention within the public discourse. Even within a group of white and wealthy males, loyalties would often be divided. A number of historians of Upper Canada have demonstrated that identity was, to a greater or lesser degree, based upon religious affiliation, and one's conception of Upper Canadian society was often drawn from the articulations of social order found within one's religious community, both inside and outside of the church.[47] In a nascent society composed of individuals who paid serious attention to the world they were making, religion was a key concern and source of contention.[48]

The main sources for this study are newspapers, pamphlets, petitions, and proceedings and reports published in the *Journal of the House of Assembly of Upper Canada* and the *Journal of the Legislative Council of Upper Canada*. Extant copies of Upper Canadian newspapers printed in the period from 1793 to 1832 have been systematically analysed.[49] Of the hundreds of surviving pamphlets from this period, I have analysed all pamphlets dealing with the educational and political developments of Upper Canada. These pamphlets typically include travellers' observations, political writings by both prominent and anonymous inhabitants, civic and religious writings, and statistical and geographical accounts.[50] Print culture often morphed into and manifested itself as participatory democracy through petitioning. In addition to those found in the newspapers, many of the petitions cited in this study have been gathered from the *Journal of the House of Assembly of Upper Canada* and the *Journal of the Legislative Council of Upper Canada*. Inhabitants generally petitioned the House of Assembly directly on educational matters, such as requests for school funding. They also very often petitioned the lieutenant governor directly. Surviving petitions sent to the civil secretary of Upper Canada, housed at Library and Archives Canada, were thus also examined.[51] In order to link print culture discourse with the political developments of the day, I have juxtaposed my print media analysis with an examination of the *Journal of the House of Assembly of Upper Canada* and the *Journal of the Legislative Council of Upper Canada*. The *Documentary History of Education*, compiled between 1894 and 1910 by historian and former assistant superintendent of education for Canada West J. George Hodgins, remains a valuable resource for documents pertaining to educational development in Upper Canada.[52] In particular this collection provides complete reproductions of educational reports and House of Assembly and Legislative Council committee reports.

Historical research in the last one hundred years has left a debate among historians of education in Ontario about what were the intentions and desired consequences of those who imagined the school system in nineteenth century Upper Canada. This debate has left a puzzling complexity in the history of attitudes about schooling's potential to change society. Schooling certainly has two faces. On one side, it can be used by political rulers as a means of societal organization and control; on the other, it offers a promise to those ruled of liberation from the constraints of societal organization and control. Schooling means and promises many different things to many different people. Since the nineteenth century, conservatives, radicals, liberals, socialists, religious fundamentalists, and secularists, among others, have all held deep convictions about the capacity of schooling to bring about desired social, political, and economic changes. To bring about, that is, the ideal society. How did these different groups, with different goals and ends in mind, create a common system of schooling for all? How and why did these different groups all come to share the same hope that this monolithic system could be used to bring about their own specific conception of the ideal society?

Between Vision and Impetus:
The Deep Roots of Schooling, 1784–1799

Studies of the history of Upper Canada usually begin with the arrival of Loyalist settlers in the western portion of Quebec in 1784 and the creation of the colony of Upper Canada through the Constitutional Act of 1791, which divided Quebec into Upper Canada, with a predominately Protestant and English-speaking population, and Lower Canada, with a predominately Catholic and French-speaking population. The central theme in the early history of Upper Canada is usually considered to be the transformation of a "howling wilderness" into fruitful settlements and towns containing most of the comforts of modern life as it was understood in the late eighteenth century. The central figure in this history is John Graves Simcoe, the colony's first lieutenant governor.[1]

Much has been written about Simcoe and other prominent political leaders of late eighteenth-century Upper Canada. This writing has contributed to a deep understanding of the social, political, and economic development of the colony in its earliest years. The history of education, however, is usually not considered a relevant theme in eighteenth-century Upper Canada. In 1797, land was set aside for a university and grammar schools, but little else was done in the political arena to promote schooling. What was said and done by those outside of the political arena has received much less attention. Typically, the early Loyalist settlers are regarded as having been indifferent to the idea of popular schooling. Schooling in this period is generally represented as a private matter, taking place in the home and administered through family or local community ties, such as those with the local church, and as something that was pursued when other demands of frontier life were not pressing. People "were preoccupied with living, and making a living," historian Paul Axelrod writes. While schooling might have mattered, survival mattered more, and children were expected to do their part in helping the family work the land, care for the household, and contribute generally to the family economy. When there was time, and where there were resources, children might attend a common, private, or denominational school, but these were usually children from the more privileged families, who could afford it.[2]

Yet, the historical record does provide some evidence of interest among these early settlers in a more expansive system of schooling. As early as 1787, settlers from present-day Kingston straight through to Niagara petitioned the governor general of Quebec, Lord Dorchester, for government aid in the establishment of a few schools stretching along the western limits of the St Lawrence.[3] Moreover, evidence from the available newspapers after the founding of the colony and prior to the nineteenth century indicates that educational discourse as it related to the establishment of government-aided schooling was nascent but also certainly growing in these early years. The participants in this discourse, and the audience for much of what appeared in print, were more varied than we typically assume, and the colonial elite, who have received the lion's share of attention in the writing of Upper Canadian history, were not leading much of this discourse. In fact, they were often hostile to what was appearing in print.[4]

To be sure, before arriving in Upper Canada, Simcoe had insisted upon the necessity of making immediate provision for "the education of the superior classes of the country." He warned the British government, in fact, that without provisions for schools in the colony, the elite in Upper Canada would be forced to send their children to the United States, where British principles would be "totally undermined and subverted."[5] In the view of colonial officials, the idea of government-aided schooling carried the intention of educating the elite in Upper Canada with values conducive to the successful creation of a British ethos in Upper Canada. Their conception of the public, or at least the public that they wished to aid, we should keep in mind, was a restricted one. Their idea of schooling was not an idea of popular schooling, but rather one that provided a classical grammar-school education to the children of prominent landholders and government officials.

We can see, however, that a few years before the arrival of Simcoe the idea of government-aided schooling was already alive to some extent. In 1787, as noted above, some settlers collectively petitioned the governor general of Quebec for schools. They insisted, in fact, upon a relatively comprehensive network of schools funded directly through the government coffer.[6] In that year, Governor General Lord Dorchester appointed William Smith to head a special committee to report on the state of education and literacy throughout the entire province. Smith had been chief justice of New York State. When Guy Carleton (later Lord Dorchester) had arrived there as head of the British forces during the American War of Independence, the two men established a political friendship and "conversed frequently about ideas of empire and imperial management."[7] In the writing of the origins of schooling in Upper Canada, this report has not received much attention.[8] The report of 1789, however, offers a glimpse into the earliest views and philosophy of education in the territories that would become Upper and Lower Canada, and so it is worth a closer examination. We know through the petition of 1787 that certain inhabitants were calling for government-aided schooling, but would the government agree to this?

The special committee headed by Smith first assembled on 31 May 1787. In an address from Dorchester that was read to those assembled, the members of the committee were curtly told that the system of education throughout the entire province was defective and it was therefore their duty to find a remedy.[9] Thus, the presupposition of the report was, as many educational reports throughout history have been, that the educational system was lamentable and needed improvement. Smith and his committee, composed of five English-speaking and four French-speaking appointed officials, drafted three questions that were to be posed to religious leaders throughout the province. The first question aimed to unveil the present condition of education. A list of the parishes and incumbents was to be drawn up, detailing the number of parishioners, the number of schools, and the "kinds" of instruction theretofore offered. Of most importance to the committee were the literacy levels: "Can it be true," the committee asked, "that there are not more than half a dozen in a parish, that are able to write or read?" The second question posed by the committee reinforced the first, as it addressed "the cause of the imperfect state of instruction"; thus, whether perceived illiteracy rates were valid or unfounded, the system was in any case presupposed to be "imperfect."[10] The second question also provided the basis for the third, which sought the system's remedy.

In addition to the three questions of inquiry, the committee wanted to know if there would be support – from the public generally, but from the Catholic Church especially – for the idea of a unified system of schooling available to all inhabitants. The committee believed that if the main object of schooling was "the cultivation of knowledge" for all inhabitants, then it proposed a union of Catholic and Protestant students attending free schools in every district, with a bilingual university to cap off the system. The plans for a unified and bilingual school system were extremely ambitious, and indeed the hidden yet overarching question in the report has continued to hover above the heads of Canadians for two and a half centuries: can English and French be raised together, live together, and educated together within a unified and shared system? Put more generally, could the entire population, regardless of differences in class or culture, attend the same schools? The committee believed the answer was yes, and in order to achieve its ambitions, it was determined to find "men of learning for the professors chair, free from narrow prejudices."[11]

The committee has been characterized as a "commission" and even as a type of early "royal commission" on education.[12] While the committee had a clear mandate to make recommendations, those recommendations were not binding, nor would the committee's findings have obliged Lord Dorchester and his council to implement a system of education. Real authority would be exerted only by government and, in particular, by the governor general himself. The committee, therefore, knew that if its recommendations were going to be acted upon, the committee itself would need to be taken seriously in the public arena and would therefore need broader support. Thus, before it recommended steps to the colonial government that would fundamentally transform the nature of schooling as it had theretofore existed, it sought that broader support from religious leaders across the province.

The bishop of Quebec, Jean-François Hubert, provided the answers from French Catholic Quebec to the committee's questions, and these answers were incorporated into the final report in 1789. Hubert agreed that "[n]othing is more worthy of the wisdom of the Government under which we live, than the encouragement of Science by every possible means."[13] He immediately began his assessment of the committee's purposes by addressing the university question: "At the name of an University in the province of Quebec, my *native* country, I bless the Almighty for having inspired the Design, and my prayers are offered for the execution of it."[14] He cautioned, however, that undertaking the task of building a university in a frontier society might be a premature idea: "It is very doubtful whether the Province can, at present, furnish a sufficient number of students to occupy the masters and professors that would necessarily be required to form an University. While there remains in Canada so much land to clear, it is not to be expected that the country inhabitants will concern themselves about the liberal arts."[15] Every nation in the world, Hubert was sure, had proven that schooling flourished only when demographic changes occurred resulting in a population with an abundance of labourers no longer needed to work the land. This was not yet the case, he thought, in eighteenth-century Quebec. The *habitant*, he believed, was not ready for popular schooling.

Hubert did concede, however, that the appetite for elementary schooling was alive and well among the *habitants*. In addition to the Jesuit schools run by the church, he told the committee, private schools could be found in Montreal, Quebec City, and Trois Rivières. With the basic curriculum of reading and writing, the "schools are regular and daily, and pretty well frequented."[16] Moreover, the parents, he believed, were satisfied with the education provided. The Jesuit's Montreal seminary, he further noted, had always supported an additional free school in which reading and writing were provided to children "of all ranks." The school was, he thought, "remarkable for its extreme regularity, [and] has had 300 children at a time."[17] Even among young women, he observed, the appetite for education was bursting. Both the sisters of the Congregation at Montreal and the Ursuline nuns at Quebec City and Trois Rivières oversaw some type of formal schooling; in addition to these schools, other institutions could also be found in these towns, with the schools supported by the "communities at their own charge."[18]

Moreover, the quality of education, Hubert argued, was not as defective as the committee presupposed. He insisted that literacy levels in the province were not as low as reported. Whereas the committee suggested that barely a dozen people in each parish across the province could read and write, Hubert insisted that the minimum literacy levels represented at least double that number. The "English" government either misjudged literacy levels in the province or were badly misinformed. While the committee asked how widespread ignorance was, Hubert suggested that the presupposition of ignorance was itself unfounded and, in fact, objectionable.

The bishop's acknowledgment that an appetite for elementary education existed, and in certain cases thrived, begs the question: was his earlier assessment, claiming that Quebec was not yet ripe for the expansion of a system of education, accurate? Was he mistaken? Did he fail to appreciate the appetite for higher education, despite his confession that a clear appetite for elementary instruction was present and expanding? The final report of the committee implies that it thought Hubert's pessimism was not well-founded. Rather than accepting the inability to carry out its plans, the committee insisted upon a scheme that it believed was as crucial to the intellectual growth of the colony as it was to the growth of a united national character in British America.

The committee was bent upon a system composed of three levels. First and foremost, it believed that "certainly there could be no division of sentiment, respecting that elementary instruction, necessary to the lower classes in all countries," must be provided for.[19] Thus, parish free schools with a basic curriculum of reading, writing, and arithmetic would comprise the first level of instruction. At the secondary level, county free schools would also be established with the addition of subjects such the languages, grammar, bookkeeping, and elements of the sciences and mathematics. Third, despite the perceived opposition from French Quebec, the committee proposed a university. On this point there was some caution. The chairman "concurred with the venerable Bishop, that the erection of an University, measuring it by European scale, would be extravagant."[20] Still, the committee would not back down. Once children received an elementary and secondary education, its members believed, the appetite for further schooling would be insatiable and it was better, they thought, that Quebec children seek a higher education within Quebec. It was therefore "to be wished," the committee reported, "that the youth of the province might not be estranged from it, by an Education in foreign parts, but find *at home* sufficient means to qualify them for the trusts, offices and honors of their native *community.*"[21]

The committee had a national vision indeed, and it suggested that Quebec could prove to be the cornerstone for all of British America. "A College under one Rector and four tutors, dividing the labour between them, would, in its opinion, be sufficient, for instructing the students to be expected from all the provinces on this Continent, now remaining to Great-Britain, in Grammar, Logic, Rhetoric, Mathematics, Natural Philosophy, Metaphysics and Ethics."[22] Students, the committee believed, "may be expected from all the provinces under the Governor General residing in this; and the advantage of acquiring one of the most universal Languages of Europe, may be a motive, even in remote countries, for taking the whole circle of the sciences, in a College projected for the commencement of an University in Canada, for His Majesty's American Dominions."[23]

The committee believed that it was crucial to establish a university because only with a university could a locally born body of social and political leaders be cultivated. Without one, it feared the colony would remain "indebted to Emigrants from other Countries" for social and political leadership, thus hindering the unity of the province.[24] The committee's vision, to be sure, was of an educational system that fostered a self-sufficient province. Although alert to the trepidation from corners such as that of Bishop Hubert's, the committee believed that there was no reason to insist that a university project was inevitably doomed. Moreover, since the university would be built through funding from the British crown, it would not prove a financial burden to the people of the province.[25]

Furthermore, and perhaps more importantly, the committee believed it had public support, which made its plan legitimate. "Abstract from the encouragement of public Bodies," it argued, "there are instances of private opulence in many places." Should the government assist by providing "a generosity equal to that opulence," then the school system could prosper and be devoted "to enterprises for advancing the honor of the Nation, in interest of learning, and the welfare of the Human Race."[26] It was better to try building a school system, the committee thought, lest the people of the province remain subject to imported social and political leaders for years to come.

In the end, the committee could not convince Dorchester to implement the ambitious plan, and as it failed to acquire enough support at the level of the political elite, its report was shelved and the proposed system was not initiated. Was Dorchester, like Hubert, concerned that a bilingual university would not succeed? Did he also agree that schooling could only flourish when demographic changes occurred resulting in a population with an abundance of labourers no longer needed to work the land? Whatever the answers to these questions, their relevance was essentially nullified with the political death of the report. As shall be discussed, however, policy in the political sphere was not always in line with ideas in the public sphere. While the report suffered a premature political death, its ideas lingered in public debate for years to come.

A decade later, in 1799, an anonymous traveller and pamphleteer from the United States, reflecting on schooling in Upper and Lower Canada, found a system that was "out of repair."[27] Although a college with a library and good accommodations had been established in Lower Canada, it had been converted into barracks for soldiers and a prison. In conversation with those he met during his travels, this traveller learned that, from the first settlement of the province, large reservations of lands had been made for the promotion of education and that "excellent colleges" and seminaries had been immediately erected but had never been fully cultivated as a result of political discord. When he became acquainted with the report of 1789, he expressed grief over its dismissal.[28] The inability of colonial leaders to act upon proposed school initiatives, he believed, had set back educational development in Quebec and, as a consequence, in all of British North America.

The American observer echoed the conclusions of the 1789 report when he emphasized the necessity of an educated population in the civic life of the Canadas. Turning his attention specifically to Upper Canada, he asserted that "[a]n extensive field is opened for men of letters in every profession. Destitute of colleges, academies and schools, and confiding in the qualifications of the clergy ordained by the bishops in the States, governor Simcoe wished to have introduced such, but an act of the British parliament disconcerted his design."[29] Why, he asked, were school initiatives disconcerted? The efforts for school expansion in Canada were thwarted by British colonial policy, he answered, because the majority of teachers would have had to have been recruited from the United States, thus threatening the supremacy of British leadership in the colony. "The object of the British nation, is to people and cultivate this country, and to make it as perfect a part of the empire as possible. Dreading revolutions, they are cautious in receiving republicans from the States, and wish to encourage husbandmen and labourers only. – Clergymen, lawyers, physicians, and school masters from the States, are not the first characters who would be fostered. Many congregations would have been formed, and schools opened, if the policy in this particular had been different."[30] The American traveller concluded that colonial leaders ultimately chose not to erect a school system in order to maintain a firm grip on the professional leadership of the colony through imported British officials.

In sum, the American observer, like the committee of education a decade before him, concluded that education was in a lamentable state. Professionals and "[m]en of distinguished talents and acquirements" were not being cultivated locally, to the detriment of those born in Upper Canada who would not receive the type of training they needed in order to advance to positions of leadership in their native land. "Pension, place, and favor are reserved for the English and Scotch adventurers, and the sons of Oxford and Cambridge."[31]

The evidence from the newspapers suggests that the American traveller's observations reflected a central theme in educational discourse in late eighteenth-century Upper Canada: government-aided schooling was increasingly considered central to the colony's development and ability to survive on its own. In some ways, the establishment of the press itself served as an informal outlet for mass education. One of the first actions of government was to aid in the establishment of a printing press in Upper Canada. The result was the *Upper Canada Gazette*, established in 1793. The printers of the *Upper Canada Gazette* often emphasized the newspaper's utility as "the Vehicle of Intelligence" in the province and in "the advancement of useful learning."[32] Moreover, as the newspaper grew in popularity and circulation, articles on education and advertisements for schools began to appear regularly. On 2 November 1796, a notification regarding a shipment of books, "including School material and prayer books," was even important enough to be printed on the front page.[33] This is interesting because the front page was usually reserved for government proclamations and other important official notices. The notice for this book sale appeared for several weeks following its initial printing. Two weeks later, the *Upper Canada Gazette* informed its readers that it was preparing "The Upper Canada Calendar For The Year 1797," containing astronomical calculations, lists of the legislative, executive, and military officers, the times when and places where courts were to be held, and so on. Ideas for additional content and involvement in the publication of the almanac was solicited. An analysis of the *Upper Canada Gazette* in the 1790s indeed lends support to the idea of an intellectual culture thriving in Upper Canada. In 1796, for example, the newspaper began to publish literary works such as stories, poems, and the works of William Shakespeare.[34]

But for whom was this outlet for education intended? McNairn suggests that the content of the early newspapers, with some articles frequently using Greek and Latin, reveals much about the assumed readership of the early colonial press.[35] But while much of the newspaper's content was aimed at a small segment of Upper Canadian society, the newspaper also increasingly served a broader population. In addition to putting a growing emphasis on literature and the arts, the *Upper Canada Gazette* began to print articles and essays directly addressing the topic of education common to all. In "A Word to Parents and Masters," an article appearing in the *Upper Canada Gazette* in November 1796, the author urged his readers to begin the training of children at a young age so that the lessons they learned would remain with them as they grew.[36] Focusing on virtues and morals, the article echoed the spirit of Upper Canadian culture that had Simcoe promoted in his legislative speeches at the beginning of the decade. In this sense, the broader public was still a restricted one in which the idea of education was related to the teaching of virtues, morals, and the classics. The idea of practical and useful learning was also promoted in the *Upper Canada Gazette*. In 1797, it began to print self-help essays and articles on topics such as agriculture and "The importance of Punctuality" in the social and commercial life of the province.[37] These articles contained subject matter that was clearly important to the wealthy landowners and government officials, but their tone and almost shameless condescension suggests that they were directed toward a different audience, and social class, altogether.

Who were the authors of such articles? This is a rather important question because, indeed, we cannot assume that the writers were even residing in the colony. Much of the content of these early newspapers was imported from the United States and to a lesser extent from Britain.[38] While the editors included such articles because they saw them as applicable to the social and commercial life of Upper Canada, they were also often pressed in finding local stories and contributions, and in this sense borrowed from foreign newspapers in order to fill the columns of the newspaper. That said, we should be careful not to dismiss these articles as mere fodder for an otherwise thin news industry in Upper Canada. While editors borrowed much of their content, the evidence indicates that they could be very selective in what they borrowed, for there was an abundance of content emanating from the newspapers of the American colonies and from across the Atlantic. Thus, the printing of articles such as these demonstrates what editors deemed to be topics of interest to the readers of Upper Canadian newspapers. That they continued to be printed for many years should also suggest that they were well received by the readers.

At the same time that literary works, self-help essays, and articles containing "useful knowledge" were appearing, Upper Canadian newspaper readers began to see advertisements for formal schooling in Upper Canada. Mr Rich Cockrel announced in 1796 that he would be opening an evening school with the basic curriculum of writing, arithmetic, and bookkeeping.[39] In March of 1797, Mr Arthur offered a further option for parents with the creation of a boarding school in Newark (present-day Niagara-on-the-Lake).[40] Like Cockrel's evening school, Arthur's would emphasize "an useful and ornamental education" in addition to attention to "behavior, religious instruction, and literary improvement of all his pupils."[41] These early schools, as advertised, emphasized the practical utility of schooling for the growing literary and commercial life of the province. The audience for this education was not the elite alone. Indeed, scholars have demonstrated that the colony's elite clearly favoured a more classical education modelled upon the grammar schools of England. We can suppose, then, that the private schools advertised in the 1790s were intended for a broader population, including more ordinary inhabitants – those who had settled Upper Canada seeking financial independence in an unpredictable frontier society and those for whom a practical education at a modest expense could prove a valuable commodity.

Why was a practical education so valued? Again, a reading of the press provides some answers. A practical curriculum, certain writers argued, was a necessity for those who hoped to prepare themselves for pioneer life in Upper Canada. On 10 March 1798, an article entitled "Education. Instructions from a Parent to the Tutor of his Son. A Scrap" was printed in the *Upper Canada Gazette* with this idea in mind. The article outlined the type of education that its author, a parent, believed was desired by the majority of inhabitants. According to this parent, a practical education was favoured over a classical one: "I would not have you, through any zeal or attachment to me, think of pushing my boy into learning of the languages, beyond his own pleasure." Above all, this parent wanted his child to learn what "is necessary or useful to man."[42] Preparing the child for a useful station in life was, it seems, a common theme in articles concerning education in late eighteenth-century Upper Canada. In August 1798, the *Upper Canada Gazette* further emphasized this point in another article concerning the rearing of youth. Tying education to the practical commercial interests of the ordinary inhabitant, the writer of this article reflected upon a recent job advertisement in which individuals with a "bad character" were told that they need not apply. The teaching of virtues and morals thus had an additional benefit, including the attainment of suitable employment. The financial utility of obtaining a good character at an early age, he emphasized, was crucial to achieving financial independence.[43]

The growing appetite for schooling was itself the subject of a sarcastic manuscript appearing in the *Upper Canada Gazette* under the title "An Oration in *praise of* Ignorance." In this article, the author jeered at the growing demand for educational institutions. After

suggesting that the growing number of schools, academies, colleges, and universities "erected for the purpose of encreasing [*sic*]
knowledge" were in fact increasing "sorrow" and that the education received in such schools afforded the student only to learn that
"water will not run up hill" or that "the wind blows sometimes one
way, and sometimes another," the author made clear that his "little
shots" were intended as humour "in an age where the pressure of
science and knowledge is clearly a burden among the people. Education is seen as so important, that it occupies much time in the
psyche of the individual to attain it, or to at least get their children
to attain it." He wanted to offer "comic relief in the midst of that
pressure" to reassure readers that an education was not worth the
present "hysteria" for its attainment. "Men of education are continually haranguing on the advantages of learning; and in many
parts of the world, have had much success," he wrote, and pointing
out the shortcomings of education in North America in a sarcastic
tone, he suggested that "it must give infinite satisfaction on to every
lover of his country, to see that the good sense of America will battle their attempts among us."[44] Whether it was hysteria or not, what
was clear was that the appetite for education was alive and well.

Again, such articles should be read with caution. The above sat-
ire probably originated from the United States, where the public discourse concerning popular schooling was already more expansive.
What is important to note, however, is that the United States–Upper
Canadian intellectual border was a permeable one. Ideas disseminated in the American press found their way into Upper Canada, and
while it might have been premature to speak of a wave of education
mania sweeping the colony, the people of the colony were certainly
well aware of the discourse surrounding that mania in the United
States. At least until there were more dependable and frequent transatlantic crossings, print media imported from the United States
remained the choice of editors and, by extension, readers.[45] Moreover, with a population overwhelmingly of American origin and
with kinship and friendship ties across the border, these early Upper
Canadians brought with them the educational discourse and practices that they had been used to in the former colonies to the south.
The above author's viewpoint is supported by the increasing number
of boarding school announcements that can be found in the Upper

Canadian press throughout the later years of the decade, while articles on education, morality, learning, and literature proliferated.

Indeed, Upper Canadians were increasingly concerned with erecting the type of institution that would promote widespread education. Certain inhabitants also formed networks to further promote
their educational goals. Charitable organizations were instrumental
in strengthening the discourse concerning the need for schooling,
and especially schooling for those who could not afford it through
their own means. On 28 June 1797, the *Upper Canada Gazette*
reported that Philanthropy Lodge No. 4, at a meeting in Newark,
had resolved to establish a fund for, among other things, "*the education of orphans & indigent brethren's children.*"[46] Education,
according to this network of individuals, was a right that should
be extended to all classes. This article is important, as it suggests a
growing concern for school expansion and the belief that schooling
should be made available to a broader population of children and
not only to those wealthy few with the resources to pay for it; it suggests a desire, that is, for *popular* schooling.

What was once a private matter was clearly becoming a public
issue in late eighteenth-century Upper Canada. By the end of the
1790s, the public discourse was reflected in the political arena. In
July 1797, the Legislative Council (Upper Canada's appointed upper
house of parliament) and the House of Assembly (Upper Canada's
elected lower house of parliament), although disagreeing on the
scope and form of government-aided schooling, adopted a joint
address to the king requesting him to set apart land for the establishment of schools and a university in Upper Canada. Within their
request was a proposal for a system of free grammar schools in each
district (or, the "district schools") and also for a college or university.[47] The response from Britain, arriving several months later, was
favourable to the cause, requesting only a report from the Executive
Council outlining the costs and measures of the proposed system of
education.[48] As a result, funds and land were set aside in 1797 for
a government-aided system of education. The shape and form of
the school system, however, was yet to be determined and was open
for debate.

David McGregor Rogers, a reform-minded member of the House
of Assembly, sensed that, whatever the case, the atmosphere was

conducive to school legislation, and so he brought in an additional bill aimed at providing technical education to orphaned children.[49] On 29 June 1799, "An Act to Provide for the Education and Support of Orphan Children" was passed.[50] The bill provided for the first publicly funded and regulated form of educational oversight in Upper Canada. Later in 1799, the *Upper Canada Gazette* reported that the legislature solidified its commitment to government-regulated education by introducing the certification of teachers. The newspaper applauded government efforts in regulating teaching and relayed the news: "We are happy in being informed that no person will be [*illegible*], or permitted, by the government, to teach school in any part of this province, unless he shall have passed an examination before one of our missioners, and receive a certificate from under his hand specifying, that he is adequate to the important task of a tutor."[51] Such a measure was seen as essential, as it acted as a check upon "itinerant characters" who preferred the sedentary life of a teacher "to a more laborious way of getting thro' life," and also, and more importantly, it acted as a check upon the potential influence of foreign morals and values in the schools of Upper Canada: "[T]he rising generation will reap infinite benefit from it," the *Upper Canada Gazette* read, "as it will tend to stimulate and encourage men of literary character to make permanent residence among us." Finally, in order to support and promote the law, the *Upper Canada Gazette* encouraged its readers to "patronize so laudable an institution" as that of Mr William Cooper, who was the first "certified" teacher in the history of Upper Canada.[52] Before the dawn of the nineteenth century, then, the wheels of government-regulated schooling were already in motion.

At the end of the eighteenth century, the idea that the community, and not the individual alone, should play a role in the establishment of schooling for Upper Canadian children was significant enough to effect legislation. An essay on the necessity of education published on 13 July 1799 reflected the idea that the community had a role to play. Echoing earlier articles stressing the importance of providing an education early in life, the author emphasized that early impressions were often the leading traits "by which his future conduct and character will be shaped."[53] This being the case, the importance of an early education could not be too forcibly emphasized. More importantly, the author stressed the growing sentiment in the province that education was a matter of public concern. "It is a matter of the greatest moment," he wrote, "and he who has the superintendence of the education of a family of children, should consider it an employment of the greatest importance that could devolve upon him.– He is not only acting for himself, but for the community at large, and probably for many generations yet to come. He is forming them for action on the great theatre of the world, where they will undoubtedly act in conformity to the precepts and examples received in their infancy."

Education, this author stressed, laid the foundation for what makes "a man a valuable member of society." So valuable was the education of children to society at large that its custodianship could not be trusted to parents alone. In fact, the author suggested that the growing level of crime was directly connected to the neglect parents showed in educating their children: "And I am bold to assert, that it is chiefly owing to the neglect, and misconduct of parents, and those whose duty it is to form and fashion the tender minds of youth, that prisons are so crowded with criminals, and courts of justice have the culprit so often arraigned before them. Wherever I see a person receiving a punishment, inflicted upon him for a crime committed against the community, I consider him less guilty than those who had the superintending of his education." Most Upper Canadian children, the author lamented, received a horrible education at home, "learn the most impious language," and "practice every impiety which we should expect to find in the most abandoned character of mature age." The community, therefore, should provide for the education that certain parents either could not or would not.

The extent to which the colonial government would support a system of schooling in Upper Canada, and the determination of to whom the schools would be made available, however, was yet unclear. In the summer of 1799, Richard Cartwright and Robert Hamilton of the Legislative Council, reflecting the anxiety to develop a system of education in the province, were granted authority to procure an agent to organize and take charge of schooling in Upper Canada. They applied to their friends at St Andrews in Scotland, and after a Mr Duncan and a Mr Chalmers declined, John Strachan "was induced, after some hesitation, to accept the appointment."[54]

Strachan arrived in Upper Canada on 31 December 1799. Neither he nor those who had sent for him knew what action he would take in advancing the idea of a school system for Upper Canada or how they would make sense of the many ways that it was being imagined; but they were all eager to continue the work.

2

From Educational Expansion to
Educational Deadlock, 1800–1811

In the first issue of the year 1800, the editors of the *Canada Constellation*, Gideon and Sylvester Tiffany, after having aroused "official displeasure" as editors of the government-sanctioned *Upper Canada Gazette* by beginning a newspaper of their own in 1799, offered a short review of the progress of Upper Canada in the last century.[1] The editors rejoiced in the transformation of "howling wildernesses" into populated settlements and towns, and an air of optimism blanketed the editorial. "In 1700," the newspaper read, "the quarter of the globe which we inhabit was scarcely known; in 1800, we see an extensive and populous nation existing, beside almost well settled and almost boundless territories of other nations, on the same continent: if so rapid has been population in the last [*sic*], what may our rational calculations be for the ensuing 100 years!"[2]

The non-Aboriginal population expanded from approximately 14,000 in 1791 to between 25,000 and 46,000 in 1800.[3] Most of this population was scattered throughout farms in isolated communities, with Newark, York, and Kingston being the three major towns. It was a nascent society, but as the optimism of the *Canada Constellation* suggests, the future was ripe for expansion. Tied into that optimism was the prospect of school expansion. On 16 May 1801, the *Niagara Herald*, in announcing the opening of the provincial legislature, pointed out that school legislation was among the subjects that were to be discussed in the upcoming year, thus making the upcoming session, in its opinion, one of the "more interesting sessions than that of any former."[4] In fact, the legislative developments of the late eighteenth century cooled down in the first few years of the nineteenth. It would not be until 1807 that school legislation would come into effect.

The District School Act of 1807 is commonly characterized as the result of efforts by the political elite to establish grammar schools for Upper Canada.[5] Houston and Prentice, however, point out that the act was met with a mixed reception. It was immediately questioned by critics who saw the establishment of grammar schools as a benefit to those who were already privileged in the colony. "Certainly the 1797 legislation envisaging free grammar schools," Houston and Prentice conclude, "had been ignored."[6] Although Houston and Prentice note the opposition to the District School Act and draw a connection to the legislation's origins in 1797, the writing of educational history in Upper Canada has tended to look at the making of the act in isolation and not in terms of developments after 1797. For the most part, this is because little was done to promote schooling in the legislature during the intermediary period between 1797 and 1807, as J. George Hodgins points out, and very few records pertaining to the making of the 1807 act itself are extant. Thus, by focusing on legislative developments we can assume that not much, in fact, happened. What was going on, though, outside of the legislature between the 1797 granting of school lands and the passing of the 1807 District School Act? In what ways did the idea of popular schooling continue to live and breathe within the social and intellectual culture of Upper Canada?

In its customary annual reflection, an open letter "To the public" in the *Upper Canada Gazette* in 1801 reflected upon the religion, morality, and social order of Upper Canada and vowed to serve as a literary agent promoting the connection between the "Literary Character" and good government.[7] There was growing optimism, moreover, that government-supported schools could cement this connection. In a series of lectures on the necessity of mass education printed in the *Niagara Herald* that year, the author espoused a curriculum in which civic education was at the core.[8] History, the study of statistics, and the politics of modern states were touted as the backbone of education, "for the first accounts of any country or people, make the strongest impressions on our minds." Civic education was suggested as imperative to any curriculum that might be developed in schools. Moreover, civic education, the author believed, offered justification for school expansion.

Indeed, the connection between civic education and the successful development of society was a key theme of the early nineteenth century. On 24 July 1802, an extensive article was printed in the *Upper Canada Gazette* outlining what the author believed to be a maturing philosophy of education. In it, the link between religion, education, and the advancement of civic loyalty was extolled. "The Romans," the author claimed, "made it a primary object of attention to educate their children in the principles, ceremonies and practices of their religion; and some of their most distinguished statesmen having declared, that the strength and glory of the commonwealth was owing, in a great measure, to this important circumstance."[9] The strength of the Roman Empire, according to this writer, was in its insistence on indoctrinating children at a young age with the values and culture of the society. Their children were "trained up" with the values of Rome, and this being done, the values and culture "took root and grew up with them." The success of Roman education was contingent upon the "religious" values promoted in that curriculum.

By contrast, the author pointed to the contemporary French republic, under the leadership of Napoleon Bonaparte, which the author believed was neglecting religious values and thus promoting atheism. France stood "as an awful beacon to warn the world." Wherever religious values were neglected, the social order was destroyed. It was therefore necessary "to rear children for excellence and usefulness, as citizens, and in the various social and domestic departments." In an age when the world was saturated with new political and religious ideas, this article suggested that children be indoctrinated with values supportive of monarchical government and Christianity.[10] A good education, seen in this light, provided for good government.

Still, others offered different reasons for the expansion of education. In an 1802 message to mothers, of a kind typically found in the newspapers of the period, mothers were called upon to be attentive to the first impressions they made upon their children, as these impressions would last for their entire lives. The idea of raising respectable and properly mannered children was touted.[11] Indeed, a number of such writings tended to promote the educational function within the household. As Prentice and Houston argue, such writings "make it clear that education was not by any means equated with schooling in early British North America."[12] What these writings do point out, however, is that ideas of child rearing and education were increasingly becoming a focus of public debate. In eighteenth-century Western societies, the rearing of children was considered to be the responsibility of the family and close community members, but by the early nineteenth century, we begin to see that in Upper Canada many individuals had much to say about what went on inside the homes of those they never met.

Writings in the Upper Canadian press concerning such issues at the turn of the century overwhelmingly emphasized the public benefits of education. As such, education was increasingly advocated as a public concern. While child rearing was still considered largely a private matter, the idea that a broader community should be involved in the process was intensifying. There was also a growing belief that children should be reared not only for the individual but also for the public good. To what extent did this burgeoning idea manifest itself within the public arena of official politics and colonial governance?

Government leaders could hardly ignore the growing discourse in the public arena concerning the expansion of education and the development of a school system. While the progress of schooling was sluggish, the appetite for it was growing. On 16 February 1804, a petition from inhabitants of the county of Glengarry was read in the House of Assembly. Notwithstanding "the wise exertions of the Legislature to promote public prosperity," these inhabitants decried, "they still contemplate anxiety, the ill consequences that may result from the want of schools, both to the present generation and to posterity." For this reason, they petitioned for publicly funded schools in "the most central places" in the colony, under the control and regulation of government.[13] In 1804 and 1805, it was proposed in the House of Assembly that such schools be established in the province, but such proposals failed to pass.[14] In 1806, a bill for "the more general dissemination of learning throughout the Province," initiated by the political dissenter William Weekes, went through the House of Assembly, but the legislature was prorogued before the Legislative Council was ready to vote on it and the bill was dropped.[15]

Political insiders like Weekes, who tended to dissent from mainstream and official government lines, were indeed instrumental in the development of schooling during the early nineteenth century. Together with Robert Thorpe, a judge serving in Prince Edward Island who had been appointed to the Court of King's Bench in Upper Canada and who had entered the political arena in 1805, Weekes formed a group of associates who were, and have been, characterized by both contemporaries and historians as anything from a group of mild reformers to extreme radicals. However their personalities are characterized, their ideas certainly did put them in direct opposition to the executive government. To be sure, the development of popular schooling was not at the top of their agenda. For Thorpe's part, his main objection in Upper Canada concerned land policy. Like D'arcy Boulton, a lawyer and entrepreneur who came to Upper Canada in 1802 from New York State and published a pamphlet in 1805 that decried the corrupt patronage of the executive government and their friends, Thorpe warned Upper Canadians that the unfair distribution of land could eventually lead to political upheaval.[16] Unlike Boulton, however, Thorpe's scathing attacks on the executive government did not end at the tip of his pen. Thorpe became extremely active in cultivating political upheaval. In 1805, both Thorpe and Weekes came to form a friendship based upon their hostility to the established political order, and they began a campaign aimed against the executive government. "Within a year these two men and their small group of associates became identified as champions of 'the people' against the tyranny of the government."[17] Other prominent members of their group included Joseph Willcocks, the home district sheriff from 1804 to 1807; Charles Burton Wyatt, the surveyor general from 1805 to 1807; and John Mills Jackson, who arrived in Upper Canada from England in 1806 and would later write an important pamphlet outlining the grievances of the group.[18]

On 30 August 1806, the *Upper Canada Gazette* reprinted correspondence between William Weekes and the new lieutenant governor, Francis Gore, that suggested that reformers had indeed brought in a new tone for politics in Upper Canada.[19] Weekes presented Gore with a petition signed by a number of inhabitants who pressed for changes in the political culture of the province. In a forceful tone, they insisted that "prerogative and privilege have been indiscriminately sacrificed at the shrine of arbitrary imposition." Weekes warned of retribution if action was not taken, but Gore refused to acknowledge the clarion call. Weekes's complaints were not universal, and Gore's stance was supported by many inhabitants. Pledges of loyalty proliferated in the press.[20] Whether or not the petition signed by Weekes and his associates represented the opinions of only a small group, what was clear was that the debate on political reform was open in Upper Canada. In this context, a burgeoning culture of reform divided Upper Canadians, however unevenly, between those who envisioned increasing powers for the elected branch and those who saw little problem with the status quo.[21]

Speeches and public addresses were the primary means used to disseminate reformist ideas. Petitions were also used, and although they were often ineffective because of the modesty of the petitioners' efforts and the unresponsiveness of the British government, they continued to proliferate and became part of the political culture of the province.[22] Petitions, speeches, and public addresses from anti-establishment voices received considerable attention in the press but were ultimately portrayed in a negative light in the government-sanctioned *Upper Canada Gazette*, which eventually refused to print them altogether. To overcome this obstacle, reformers relied upon the support and resources of Joseph Willcocks and established a printing press of their own. The *Upper Canada Guardian; or Freeman's Journal* was first published in 1807 with Willcocks as its founding editor.

The establishment of this newspaper was a watershed in the history of print culture in Upper Canada. That it was able to thrive and remained in print until 1812 is also very telling of the type of welcome reception it received from a good number of Upper Canadian newspaper readers. The existence of the reform press suggests that the voices of opposition were alive and well. According to historians Carol Wilton and Bruce Wilson, it was a valuable weapon in "the struggle to forge an effective local opposition to the mercantile-official elite of the Niagara district."[23] The threat, however, extended beyond Niagara. Indeed, the press was apparently so threatening that in 1812 the newspaper was bought by supporters of the executive just to shut it down.[24] With the powerful engine of a newspaper, the reform group became, as an anonymous pamphleteer commented in 1807, "the rallying point for all the disaffected and turbulent spirits in the Province, and gained strength daily."[25] It was in this political climate that Upper Canadian legislators would begin building the first forms of government-aided schools.

The educational ideas of these reformers are summarized best in an 1809 pamphlet that attacked the colonial administration, written by John Mills Jackson. Among other abuses, he pointed toward the lack of common schooling as an attempt by the political elite to incapacitate the lower classes. What was worse, he thought, was that they had established eight district schools, modelled upon the grammar schools of England, as preparatory academies for the children of the colony's prominent families. Jackson proposed that although a "laudable attempt" was made in the House of Assembly in 1806 for a more general system of education, it faced resistance from the establishment, which instead "voted eight hundred a year for eight schools [the district schools], as an inducement for protestant clergymen to settle in Canada." While the students in these elite schools received a proper education, Jackson complained, the rest of the population was left with limited choices of private schools run by "unfit" teachers.[26] The district school system, according to this view, was an elite one, providing limited education for those with above average resources. That system, anti-establishment reformers like Jackson argued, should be abandoned and replaced with a system of common schooling.

The extent to which anti-executive pamphleteers, the radical press, and political reformers in the House of Assembly influenced the population is, of course, debatable. Nevertheless, evidence does suggest that their calls for common schooling were representative of a growing movement in favour of publicly aided common schooling. What is also clear is that the material distributed by radicals in the anti-establishment press increasingly opened up the debate.

When on 10 March 1807 "An Act to establish public schools in each and every District of this Province" was passed, it was clear that the act would be far from universally acclaimed. The act, although finally allocating public funds toward a system of schools, did not pass unanimously in the House of Assembly. Among its dissenters was Thorpe, who had taken Weekes's seat in the House after Weekes's untimely death in 1806. Dissenters considered the District School Act elitist and argued that the funds being applied to district schools would be better utilized toward a common system of schooling available to all inhabitants. The District School Act nevertheless passed without causing much further public debate. The act was, of course, a culmination of the efforts of the late 1790s. At the same time, however, it marked a renewal of political involvement in education. On 25 April, the entire act was reprinted for the public eye. The *York Gazette* had made a habit of printing the acts passed in each session of the legislature, and it is interesting to observe that although the District School Act was not the first act passed that year, it was the first to be published in the newspaper, suggesting its importance in the public arena.[27] Although the dissenters in the House of Assembly considered the act elitist, it still represented the first time that public funds were granted for educational initiatives, and perhaps for this reason there was no immediate widespread rejection of the act as it was drawn up.

Later that year, the *York Gazette* printed an address from John Strachan to his students at Cornwall at their public exam. Strachan certainly took some time adjusting to colonial life, and he did not aggressively take hold of educational matters in Upper Canada as one might have expected after his services were procured in 1799. Nevertheless, grand educational ideas were clearly percolating, as his address indicates, and with the success of his school in Cornwall, he was well on his way to establishing himself as Upper Canada's most prominent educator. The school had become one of the first government-aided grammar schools since the passing of the school act earlier that year, and his address says much about what elite leaders like Strachan and his friends at the top of the Upper Canadian political ladder considered the utility of the district schools to be. "One of the greatest advantages you have derived from your education here," Strachan told his students, "arises from the strictness of our discipline." The undisciplined person, he insisted, quickly becomes ungovernable. Strachan's students, however, were governable. An elitist order of society was promoted in Strachan's Cornwall school. Strachan made it clear that he was educating a body of students who would enter positions of leadership in the province, and in so doing, he attempted to instil "a mildness of treatment, a condescension to inferiors, a ready obedience to the just commands of superiors" in order to make them "content and useful in society."[28]

Strachan was slowly becoming a relevant public voice with considerable influence within government circles. As such, there was a growing audience for what he had to say. His first pamphlet was printed in 1807, and it concerned the place of religion in education.[29] Although Strachan considered himself a liberal thinker and a proponent of practical Scottish educational values, one of his fundamental aims, as he made clear in his pamphlet, was to curb secular Enlightenment ideas in favour of Christian theology. Although pragmatic and well schooled in the practical subjects, Strachan insisted upon indoctrinating the elite of Upper Canada with more conservative values. He warned that in the present age of political revolution, dissenters "attempt to inculcate the young" with anti-religious values.[30] His solution was to provide inculcation of his own. Christianity, he told his students, was the culmination of moral and intellectual thought, from the Greeks and Romans, to the Jews, to the thinkers of the Middle Ages, and then to the philosophers of the Enlightenment, many of whom – Bacon, Newton, and Locke – he reminded them, were Christians.[31] Christianity, he thought, should be the backbone of education. This pamphlet situated Strachan among other conservatives in the province, such as the anonymous writer in the *Upper Canada Gazette* in 1802 who argued for the dissemination of Christianity as a means of fortifying the empire. What seemed to differentiate Strachan, however, was his increasingly narrow conception of Christianity, which tended to favour the Church of England over the religions of others. So while Strachan was in line with those imperialists who, according to historian Christopher Bayly, attempted to reaffirm Britain's aristocratic rule after the French Revolutionary Wars, he departed in thought with them by suggesting that the Church of England be the sole dominate religion in the political life of new settler societies and that tolerance of other religions be curbed or limited.[32] That is, this seems to be how he thought Upper Canada should be cast in the empire.

After the passing of the District Schools Act in 1807, elite politicians continued to steer the direction of school expansion despite opposition from a well-supported reform group. In Gore's speech from the throne in 1808, he echoed Strachan's religious sentiment and clearly drew the connection between morality, loyalty, and education that he wished to see achieved in the schools of Upper Canada.

"Since the last session of this Legislature," Gore told the House, "the necessary measures have been taken on my part, and on that of the Trustees appointed by me, for the establishing of Public Schools; institutions which I trust will be the means, not only of communicating useful knowledge to the youth of the Province, but also of instilling into their minds the principles of Religion and Loyalty."[33] Gore was very direct in asserting his position: a fundamental aim of government-aided schooling was to instil loyalty to the crown and, by extension, the British metropolis. So, while the schools had been advocated for practical reasons by certain inhabitants in the press since the late eighteenth century, they were also advocated as vehicles of indoctrination by the government elite. Whatever the case, government-aided schooling was being advocated in Upper Canada, and even if the majority of children remained schooled at home or at the local parish, the idea that government should accept a major role in the expansion of schools on a larger societal scale was being cemented in the minds of Upper Canadian of all political eanings.

Considering their shared interest in education, however, the lower and upper houses of the legislature were not so cooperative in developing school legislation. And, in fact, as quickly as it had been passed, certain individuals led a charge to see the District School Act either altered or wiped off the record. In 1808, Willcocks, seconded by fellow dissenter David McGregor Rogers, who had in 1799 effectively put forward legislation providing education to orphaned children, moved for leave to bring in a bill to repeal parts of the District School Act.[34] In 1810, they attempted it once again.

The movement for common schooling, however, should not be misunderstood to be an exclusively reform cause. It was not dissenters alone who took to the cause of common school promotion. For their own reasons, conservatives also pushed for the expansion of schooling. A pro-establishment anonymous pamphleteer who challenged Jackson's charges agreed that the privately funded schools were run by unfit teachers. The condition of Upper Canadian schools, he acknowledged, was "an evil loudly complained of by every well-wisher of the country" and was the greatest contributor to political instability.[35] The threat posed by these schools, as he saw it, however, was that they were run by mostly American teachers who introduced "a system of discipline not only repugnant to decency and common sense, but highly injurious to morality, and inimical to our form of government."[36] For their own reasons, pro-establishment inhabitants, such as the anonymous pamphleteer, also supported common schooling.

On 3 February 1810, a common school bill was introduced by more conservative members of the House of Assembly.[37] The act would have appropriated funds for common schools in every district while maintaining the district schools. Conservative support of the bill was based on the assumption that it would pacify those members of the House of Assembly calling for common schools while quelling their desire to abolish the district schools.[38] The bill, however, did not have such an effect. It faced resistance among the more reform-minded members still bent upon repealing the District School Act. Only through a shared system of common schools, some of them believed, would the real advantages of education be shared by the poor and rich alike. There was a clear division in the conception of government's role in education. On the one hand, both the Executive and the Legislative Councils, supported by conservative members of the House of Assembly, favoured the idea of a system of district schools where only certain inhabitants could receive an education aimed at preparing them for leadership roles within the province. Such a system, however, would work to perpetuate the social and political hierarchy that radicals wanted to subvert, and it did not address the concerns of certain members of the House of Assembly who hoped to see all inhabitants, rich and poor, educated alongside each other in a single common school system.

The inability to reach a compromise in the legislature gave rise to a division concerning the shape and form of government-aided schooling. Nevertheless, we should be careful to remember that although the shape and form of government-aided schooling was a matter of debate, the need for it was not. For different reasons, and with different ends in mind, both establishment and anti-establishment inhabitants agreed upon government-supported schooling. Which schools would receive support, how much support those schools would receive, and to whom those schools would be open were, by the second decade of the century, still issues that needed to be resolved. What was not an issue, however, was whether government should be involved at all.

What needed to be sorted out now, however, was whether government's role in schooling should be expanded. A pro-executive newspaper, the *Kingston Gazette*, was established in 1810, and in its very first issue, for its own reasons, it took up the cause of promoting common schools. The importance of educating children, the newspaper suggested, had been admitted by many inhabitants in Upper Canada but was not yet fully realized by government.[39] Schooling, according to the *Kingston Gazette*, was required for the indoctrination of common values and thereby the fostering of a cohesive identity and stable society in which not only the intellectual, but also the moral character was elevated. "Habits of subordination acquired in well disciplined schools essentially aid the administration of civil government," the *Kingston Gazette* read. "They introduce a certain uniformity of manners, sentiments and characters, which is a desirable object in any state of society and under any form of government, and peculiarly important to this province, now in its youth, and not yet ripened into national manhood." The idea of a young nation in need of a common identity was at the core of the system of education advocated here. "Our population is composed of persons born in different states and nations, under various governments and laws, and speaking several languages. To assimilate them, or rather their descendants, into one congenial people, by all practicable means, is an object of true policy. And the establishment of common schools is one of those means."[40]

Moreover, the newspaper offered another justification for common schooling when it suggested, as political dissenters had been suggesting, that Upper Canada required trained and homegrown leaders to fill the influential offices in the colony. A democratic, elected House of Assembly, the administration of justice that "calls men in the common walks of life to act as jurors," and the "various subordinate offices" requiring an informed mind gave rise, they believed, to an additional motive "to train up the rising generation in such a manner as to fit them for the performance of civil duties and the enjoyment of civil rights." Upper Canada's system of education had theretofore failed to produce such an educated population, and so it was the intent of the newspaper "to awaken the public attention to this most interesting subject." In sum, the *Kingston Gazette* entered into the public debate on education by promoting a common system of schooling intended to assimilate foreigners, indoctrinate children with the value of subordination to government, and train a generation of locally born provincial leaders. For both different and similar reasons, this conservative newspaper found common ground with dissenters in promoting a common school system.

The conservative press proved to be a valuable forum for educational discourse. In an article on morality and education in the *Kingston Gazette*, "A friend to improvement" suggested that "no subject, of so much importance, has been treated with so much neglect, as the proper education of children."[41] Once again, the call for school expansion was made. "A small part of the community," this writer admitted, "need to prepare themselves for the learned professions, for a small proportion only can be useful, as *divines, lawyers,* or *physicians*; yet every person ought to be able to read and write his own language with propriety, and to have that knowledge of arithmetic, which will enable him to transact all necessary business with ease." Moreover, it was the responsibility of government to provide this education because the demands of a frontier society offered very little time and resources for parents to attend to the education of their children. Were education to be expanded, "we should not see so many taverns and tippling houses crowded as we now do." Moreover, "few broils or disturbances would exist; and the community at large would become enlightened, loyal, and happy." Education was touted by this inhabitant as the panacea for peace, order, and loyalty.

On 13 November 1810, an inhabitant of Kingston provided his reasons for supporting a system of common schools. When the province was first settled, he argued, the demands of a frontier society were so great that the settlers "had not the means of giving much education to their children, or obtaining much information themselves from reading."[42] In a course of more than twenty years, however, these difficulties were chiefly surmounted. Towns were populated, and the physical labour of settling the province was relaxed. "Means of information, education and improvement in science," he continued, "ought now to receive that attention, which the state of the country heretofore rendered impracticable. Common schools ought to be put upon a more liberal establishment." This inhabitant called for an extensive system of education, including a network of libraries to be built where Upper Canadian families could not afford to purchase books on their own. He suggested that a voluntary tax should be collected for the school system. Schools were being built in many other places, he argued; it was a transnational phenomenon. This inhabitant feared that the "neglect necessarily introduced by the early state of this country" would operate to "retard the progress of improvement" and place Upper Canada behind other nations. He therefore called upon every "patriot and philanthropist" to take up the cause of promoting schools and libraries for the good of the colony.

Schooling for the few, or schooling for all? The debate over such a question came early in Upper Canada. The immediate push for grammar schools fuelled that debate, as certain inhabitants felt such schools were not enough. A debate among the trustees of the district school in London from 1809 to 1810 regarding where to build a new "public" school highlights the division. The trustees were divided between Woodhouse and Charlotteville, creating a standstill in which no school was built through public funds. Certain inhabitants took it upon themselves to erect a schoolhouse in Charlotteville, and in a petition to Gore on 30 January 1810, they suggested a grant be given to the school. Interestingly, they commended the teacher, Mr Mitchell, for conducting his teaching "[g]ratis to make the Legislative Grant if possible more popular."[43] In suggesting that an offer of free schooling attracted more students, the petitioners reflected not only the growing call for free schools, but also the idea that such schools should serve as many inhabitants as possible.

Calls for the expansion of the school system continued in 1811. In a more cautious tone, however, one inhabitant from the Midland District argued that the present district school system should not be altered until Upper Canada could train its own battalion of teachers to support a homegrown common system of education. As it stood, the system, he believed, was serving the community well, and while he admitted there existed a "thirst for knowledge" in the province that could not be "easily repressed," he believed that any immediate expansion of the school system "would defeat completely the designs and success of this establishment, without affording the least comparative benefit." Common schools, he argued, did indeed require support, but such support should be limited. From the district schools, the province would "be soon supplied with well educated teachers, with whose qualifications and morals we may be well acquainted. They will ultimately preclude the admission and employment of itinerant and illiterate pedagogues, who to the disgrace of our country and the injury of our youth, impose themselves, as teachers, on the community." Clearly, this writer feared that Upper Canada did not have enough teachers of its own to support a common school system, and thus any expansion would mean that foreign and dangerous teachers would have to be employed. Any change to the school legislation, he warned, "would be a paralytic stroke to the improvement of our infant country."[44]

Private schools continued to open after the passing of the District School Act, as advertisements indicate, and the movement for common schooling in this sense continued to gain momentum. With only a limited number of district schools aided by government – which themselves depended upon tuition fees that many inhabitants could not afford or were not willing to pay – the extent of government involvement in school development did not meet the demand. To what extent were the political elite prepared to expand the system of education?

On 3 September 1811, the *Kingston Gazette* reprinted the last speech Strachan delivered at the annual examination in his Cornwall school before moving to York, where he would be offered a pastoralship in 1812. In this speech, Strachan expressed what he had attempted to build in his grammar school in Cornwall and, by extension, what he believed the utility of the district schools to be. The infusion of "sound moral principles," he claimed, was the first principal of education. Strachan made no apologies for his conception of education, asserting that "the enemies of the classics are like the enemies of rank and title in society – enemies only because it is beyond their reach, or they are profoundly ignorant and the enemies of freedom." He was training British children, he believed, to take positions of leadership in a British colony. "Never forgetting that I am charged with the education of a portion of British youth, I take every reasonable opportunity to inspire them with love for their country, and loyalty to our gracious sovereign."

In closing, Strachan stressed what he hoped the seeds he had planted offered to the future of the colony: "[W]e look forward with confidence, to the time when the young men who have been educated here and at the other district schools, will give a tone to the manners and opinions of the inhabitants of this province; when their just partiality for our mother-country, their love for our gracious sovereign, and their veneration for our laws and institutions, together with the sound moral and religious principles which they have imbibed, shall spread and take deep root in the country, till the warmest patriotism, and the purest piety, adorn the banks of the impetuous St Lawrence."[45]

Continued attempts were made in the House of Assembly to limit the duration of the District School Act in the belief that the funds would be better put toward a common school system. While the Legislative Council was equally consistent in refusing to assent to the repeal of the District School Act, it sought, through a bill proposed by Richard Cartwright, to give it a wider scope.[46] The council's bill, however, was rejected by the House of Assembly.[47] The political bickering resulted in an educational deadlock in which the House of Assembly and the Legislative Council could not agree on further school legislation.

The evidence from both the print media and the legislative journals suggests that the development of the district schools was part of a central debate on elitist versus popular schooling that occurred early in the century. This debate was situated in a period of intense political strife characterized by pro-establishment and anti-establishment men seemingly unable to agree upon effective educational legislation. The different ideas in the legislature concerning to whom schooling should be made available were reflective of a print culture in which a variety of opinions about the direction of government-aided schooling in Upper Canada had surfaced. Educational discourse in the first decade of the nineteenth century was part of a complex debate about class and power and what forms of social institutions Upper Canadians would build.

Late in 1811, an ill Gore decided to return home to England to improve his health. He left the administration of Upper Canada in the hands of Isaac Brock and the Executive Council. The *Upper Canada Gazette* printed letters to Gore in which members of the legislature and inhabitants expressed their gratitude toward him and his administration. Inhabitants of the Eastern District felt that, above all, the most important contribution to the public welfare made under Gore's administration had been the "provision made for giving the youth of the Province such a liberal education as may not only qualify them for the learned professions, but establish firmly in their minds the purest moral and religious principles, principles which shall enable them to give the most salutary direction to the general manners of the Province, and revive that ardent patriotism for which their fathers have been so honorably distinguished." Executive interests and government-aided schooling went hand-in-hand according to these inhabitants, and the province was already benefiting from the School Act of 1807. "The fruits of this noble measure patronized and sanctioned by your Excellency, we begin already to enjoy; as many of the young men have left the schools crowned with literary honors, and with the fairest promise of future worth."[48] While the value of their education was still a "promise," what was certain was that many inhabitants supported a system of education and were convinced of its benefit to the general welfare of the province. For different reasons and with different ends in mind, inhabitants involved in the public discourse on education now favoured and promoted the expansion of schooling.

3

War and Schooling, 1812–1815

In 1815, one decade and a half after being called to Upper Canada to spearhead educational developments in the colony, John Strachan prepared a report for the colonial government that would leave a mark on the educational history of Upper Canada, Canada West, and Ontario. Scholars of educational history in Upper Canada have concluded that the design and content of the colony's first common school act in 1816 is largely attributed to the educational ideas found in that report.[1] Indeed, only a cursory reading of both the report and the school act will reveal that much of the content of the two are identical. Animosity felt toward the United States after the War of 1812 (which ended in 1815) and the desire to ensure that Upper Canadian children be educated within the province if they were to remain attached to the parent state and British heritage remain our best understanding of the central driving forces that led to common school legislation.[2]

While the public policy put forward in the report and school act marked a new educational era in the political arena, the evidence presented in the previous chapter suggests that the idea of centralized and regulated education in Upper Canada was in fact nothing new in the public arena. Evidence from the print media demonstrates that, for different reasons, both conservatives and political dissenters in the first decade of the nineteenth century were advocating the expansion of a system of schooling spearheaded by the colonial government. Some advocated the diffusion of common schooling to all classes in Upper Canada as a means toward expanding civic political participation and ensuring practical economic opportunities, while others argued for the need to create a common identity and obedience to the colonial government and British constitution. Such ideas, then, were promoted long before even the threat of war with the United States. To what extent, then, should we rethink the link between the Common School Act of 1816 and the War of 1812? And to what extent did the War of 1812 itself alter or perpetuate the educational development that followed?

This chapter examines these questions through an analysis of print media discourse. It revisits the era while considering recent histories that bring to light the complexity of identity and the politics of governance. The people of Upper Canada, these histories show, were much more divided on the issue of the colonial identity than we have characteristically assumed. George Sheppard convincingly contests the assumption that the War of 1812 was a determining factor in the emergence of a British identity for the colony. He effectively demonstrates that Upper Canadians were deeply divided before the war and that the war itself had many harmful effects on the development of the colony afterwards.[3] Jane Errington points out that the development of Upper Canadian political culture was much more pronounced and distinct from either British or American influence than previously contended.[4] David Mills has considered the dual nature of loyalty in Upper Canada: that of patriotism, or attachment to place; and that of loyalism, or attachment to parent. Both conservatives and reformers, according to Mills, were Loyalists who attributed different intellectual and moral qualities to loyalty, some favouring attachment to Britain, others to the colony itself.[5] Jeffrey McNairn has furthermore broadened the discourse, challenging historiographies such as those emphasizing the "conservative consensus" in Upper Canadian political culture, while arguing that Upper Canadian conservatives themselves often looked to the federalist model in the United States as a cure to the province's constitutional maladies.[6] Considering the degree to which the creation of a common school system had already been part of the public discourse among both pro- and anti-establishment Upper Canadians before 1812, we should revisit the war years to consider how, or if, they served to generate an impetus for a system of common schooling.

Between 1812 and 1815, no subject appears to have been more important than the war with the United States. On 11 July 1812,

the newspaper readers of Upper Canada learned, through a proc-
lamation by Isaac Brock, Upper Canada's top militia officer who
had become president and administrator of Upper Canada upon
Gore's departure in 1811, that the United States had declared war
on the United Kingdom and its dependencies only a few weeks earlier through a declaration by the United States Congress.[7] In his first
public address, Brock emphasized the idea of loyalty: "I do hereby
strictly enjoin and require all His Majesty's Liege Subjects to be
obedient to the Lawful Authorities to forbear all communication
with the Enemy or Persons residing within the Territory of the United
States and to manifest their Loyalty by a zealous co-operation with
His Majesty's Armed Forces in defence of the Province, and repulse
of the Enemy." Earlier that year, the House of Assembly had pledged
to work as one with the Legislative Council and Brock in any militia
measures necessary to prepare for war. Such measures would include
censorship and arbitrary incarceration.[8] Few things unite a divided
community. One of them is tragedy. Together, the conservatives and
reformers in the legislature were unified by the tragedy brought on
by war against the United States.

Were Upper Canadians as unified as their leaders? Recent writings
suggest that they were not. Many Upper Canadians wanted nothing to do with the war.[9] Certain inhabitants of Upper Canada were
clearly troubled as they faced the prospect of war with the United
States. Many of them, after all, had close ties with the United States
through family and friends and "few personal ties with the British
establishment."[10] Years of immigration from the United States only
made these ties closer. Initially, as Errington argues, "Upper Canada
was intended as a home for loyal British subjects."[11] By 1812, however, one American traveller could observe that in the western districts "the loyalist element was scarcely noticeable amongst the
diversity of people who had come to take up land or engage in
trade," and that in the Kingston area a good portion of inhabitants "had no claim to the appellation loyalists."[12] Isaac Brock himself believed that much of the population, especially in the western
districts, were disloyal. Throughout the war, it was believed that
many settlers of American origin supported or even joined the
American armies.[13] For the colonial elite, the War of 1812 was as
much a war against American invaders as it was a war against an

ideology that threatened the security of British governance within the province itself.

In the summer of 1812, Strachan addressed this problem in a sermon delivered to both branches of the legislature.[14] In "a free country like this," he warned legislators, "where differences of opinion concerning public affairs may be sincerely maintained, great danger arises, more especially in such critical times as the present, least a few designing men who are secretly hostile to the best interest of the country, take advantage of any party spirit that may exist to promote their machinations."[15] The political divisions in Upper Canada, Strachan was well aware, were represented in the Upper Canadian legislature, especially the House of Assembly, where the executive had no authority to deny reform-minded men their elected offices. Strachan thus urged the house to put opinions aside and to "carefully avoid all those questions on which we are known to differ" in order to "defend our country against the common enemy."[16]

If the executive elite believed that the war put internal harmony in danger, then the House of Assembly agreed. In September 1812, the house put forward an address to "the people" of Upper Canada in order to stress this point.[17] Sensing that the war against America was not receiving the popular support originally expected, the House of Assembly clearly directed the message at inhabitants who felt ambivalence about fighting and were uneasy about involving themselves in a war that pitted them against friends, neighbours, and not-so-distant family members. The address sympathized with these unmistakable attachments to America and thus carefully avoided blaming Americans as a people for the war. Rather, this was a war of ideas, and Americans, the address suggested, had been coerced and "bribed by the Tyrant of France." The house warned that the United States had betrayed the Anglo-Atlantic alliance through misleading negotiations with Napoleon. The war, as it was depicted for the people of Upper Canada in this address, was not so much against the United States as it was against France: "The government of this bloody Tyrant penetrates into everything – it crushes individuals as well as nations; fetters thoughts as well as motives, and delights in destroying for ever all that is fair and just in opinion and sentiment. It is evidently this Tyrant who now directs the Rulers of America, and they show themselves worthy disciples of such a master." With neighbours, friends, relatives, and parents living in America, and with many of them themselves having originated in America, the House of Assembly members who drew up the address opted to vilify France, and not America, in order to garner support for the war against the United States. What had reached Upper Canada was an Atlantic storm in which political ideologies and theories of governance were violently clashing and threatening the foundations of a nascent British colony.

On 15 February 1815, word that the war had ended was printed.[18] In the end, Upper Canada claimed victory. As a result of their own activities during the war, David Mills contends, "the Tories immediately adopted a myth that Upper Canadians had proven their loyalty. The accuracy of the myth is beside the point; the Tories believed that loyalty was earned in 1812 as it had been by the original Loyalists in 1776, except that this time it was earned by staying rather than by leaving."[19] According to Mills, the vision of Upper Canada held by many political leaders, especially the colonial elite, "was confirmed by the results of the War and, consequently, Upper Canadian conservatism was crystallized." The belief in the importance of the British connection thereafter intensified, with a particular emphasis on the need for internal unity in the province.[20] It remained clear, however, that the people of Upper Canada had come out of the war with the same divisions they had had as they had entered it.[21]

In many ways, the war served as a lesson to Upper Canadian political leaders. The security of government, and the continuation of the British constitutional heritage in Upper Canada, depended upon a loyal population. The supremacy of the established elite had been challenged in the first decade of the nineteenth century, due in large part to prominent individuals who were able, with the aid of print media, to steer the ideas of colonists in new directions. The war, for its duration, provided an obedient population while suppressing radical political factions. The task of government, now, was to perpetuate this socio-political culture. The government could do this, of course, through a common school system that inculcated loyalty. Was there a will, though, among the political elite to establish such a system? Could they act unilaterally? Who would drive forward the movement for common schooling?

With Loyalist rhetoric dominating discourse among the political elite during this period, their labours in 1815 and 1816 to arrive at a common school act could be, it is easy to see, interpreted as the result of fears concerning the loyalty of the people of Upper Canada, as well as the desire to shape a sense of identity conducive to the maintenance British imperial rule. The timing of the Common School Act of 1816 immediately after the war indeed seems to be more than simply coincidental. The war demonstrated a need for a system of schooling in which a collective identity could be shaped and formed. Still, we should not overlook that such an idea had been around for many years. Common schooling had been advocated in the colonial legislature since at least 1806, and the legislative and executive councils often served as barriers for any common school legislation that was presented to them by the house of assembly. To be sure, neither the Legislative nor the Executive Council opposed common schooling in principle. In fact, as we saw, the conservative press, namely the *Kingston Gazette*, funded in part by members of the Legislative Council such as Richard Cartwright, had supported the idea of common schooling. Opposition to proposals from the House of Assembly was the result of House of Assembly efforts at consistently attaching to its proposals for common schools measures that would eliminate or undermine the District School Act. The colonial elite, while open to the idea of common schooling, could not favour such a system over that of the district schools. The result was educational deadlock.

With this in mind, we need to rethink and retrace the process toward the making of common schooling after the War of 1812, which, clearly, was far from linear. As a result of the educational deadlock of the two houses of the legislature after 1811, a new school law was not passed prior to the War of 1812. The House of Assembly, however, did not relax its efforts to repeal the act of 1807; the Legislative Council, for its part, continued to promote the passage of a more elaborate district school act, which it saw as an essential component of any school system in the colony, even one including universally accessible common schools. With both pro-establishment and anti-establishment writers in the print media agreeing upon the utility of a common school system, it was clear that widespread support for such a system was percolating in the minds of a growing number of inhabitants.

Evidence suggests that calls in the print media for common schooling were representative of a growing movement in favour of a government-aided system of schooling. On 11 February 1812, for example, two petitions were read in the House of Assembly in which certain inhabitants complained about the inadequacy and unfairness of school funding in the province. Inhabitants of Hamilton petitioned that the grant for district schools be applied to common schools; they found the money for district schools to be "entirely useless."[22] Inhabitants of the Midland District agreed and called for the complete repeal of the District School Act. The act, they argued, "fails to provide for the educational wants of 'the middling, or poorer class of His Majesty's subjects.'"[23] In its place, they wanted provision to be made "as may be conducive to public utility." Because only one school was supported in the district, "most of the people are unable to avail themselves of the advantages contemplated by the institution. A few wealthy inhabitants, and those of the Town of Kingston, reap exclusively the benefit of it in this District." The District School Act, "instead of aiding the middling and poorer class of His Majesty's subjects," they went on, "casts money into the lap of the rich, who are sufficiently able, without public assistance, to support a school in every respect equal to the one established by law." That year, and again in 1814, the House of Assembly, both leading and responding to the movement for common schooling, unsuccessfully continued its attempts to repeal the District School Act in favour of common schools.[24]

By 1815, the drive for common schooling was clearly still alive and well, and in fact gaining momentum. Strachan's educational report of that year, then, was by no means pulled out of thin air. Public policy comes about through a process of consultation and deliberation. In terms of educational policy in Upper Canada, that process of consultation and deliberation took place both inside the legislative walls and through petitions and a print culture outside those walls that saw the calls for common schooling grow louder with each passing year. It was now time for government to respond to those calls.

In the opening words of Strachan's educational report, presented in February of 1815, he made clear that the common schools should have a utilitarian focus; they should not be preparatory schools like the district schools but should instead serve an immediate purpose. He believed his plan was "as economical as it can well be, to render it respectable and useful."[25] Unlike the district schools, the common schools were also not to be exclusive and were proposed to serve all denominations, including Catholics, and to be made available to both rich and poor. The whole population, he insisted, should be served, but this was almost an irrelevant point because the call for common schooling, he admitted, had come from "the people" themselves. "That the people have shown among themselves a most laudable zeal in this particular" was something, he stated, "which ought to be fostered & encouraged."[26] In contrast, government had theretofore failed to respond, and "nothing has been yet done to promote education among the poorer Inhabitants."[27] After resisting the currents of common school development for a decade, the ruling elite were now seemingly ready to support the cause. Had the war, in this sense, aligned their interest in common schooling with that of "the people"?

"The people's" interest in education, Strachan furthermore noted, was resulting in a number of Upper Canadian inhabitants sending their children outside of the province for education where they could not receive it at home. Dangerously, he suggested, Upper Canadian children were being educated in the United States. This was a point that Strachan believed should serve as a key reason for the executive to support a system of common schooling in Upper Canada. "[T]he necessity of sending young men out of the Province to finish their education which has hitherto existed," he insisted, "has been found both dangerous and inconvenient." In the United States, especially, Strachan feared that the children of Upper Canadian inhabitants would be imbued with foreign, republican, anti-monarchical, and anti-British – thus "dangerous" – values. Since there was no way of stopping Upper Canadian parents from sending their children to school, he thought, then the colonial government might as well get itself involved in the process.

The creation of a homegrown common school system, Strachan believed, would do much to convince Upper Canadian parents to keep their children in Upper Canada. An Upper Canadian common school system, furthermore, had to be, like all other institutions in the province, responsible to the executive. The existing district schools should not be abolished but instead, he suggested, be made "free of charge" to the scholars in an effort to expand the system and in order to "train up masters" for the common schools. Americans should not be entrusted as teachers, and in his report Strachan insisted that they be kept out of the schools: "[N]o person who is not a natural born subject of the King and fully qualified to teach these different Branches of Education shall be capable of becoming the Master of any of the District Schools."[28] Moreover, while Strachan admitted to responding to the growing appetite for common schooling, he also wanted to maintain an elitist bent to any system of schooling. The district schools were to remain intact, and at the pinnacle of Strachan's educational design was a university for the province based upon the Scottish and German models. Strachan's aim was not to extend the classics to the masses; rather, he favoured a new endeavour in a new colony, one based upon practical principles in line with the times.

A rereading of Strachan's report of 1815 requires us to reconsider who pushed for common schooling in this era and when did that push come about. Understanding the executive elite's involvement in the making of the Common School Act of 1816 must be within the context that "the people themselves" had shown "a most laudable zeal" for educational expansion. Although the creation of a loyal population in the wake of the War of 1812 has often been cited as a catalyst for the elite's involvement in common school development in Upper Canada, Strachan's acknowledgment that "the people" had been pushing for it indeed requires further attention. Common schooling, he suggested, had successfully been promoted in Upper Canada outside of government circles.

The idea that common schooling developed in Upper Canada through a deliberative process facilitated through print culture challenges the long-standing notion among historians of the British Empire generally that schooling was promoted in the colonies by imperial administrators through a centrally planned process.[29] While other parts of the empire might have been "colonized" through schooling, Upper Canada was not.[30] Of course, we cannot ignore the impact that the war had on the Upper Canadian colonial elite and especially the fears it raised of a disloyal population challenging the elite's authority and supremacy over the political life of the province.

The war might have served as a catalyst, in this sense, that compelled the executive to attempt to meet the popular demands for common schooling in a way that could also serve its own interests. Whatever their plans, however, colonial administrators in Upper Canada clearly recognized and acknowledged the will of "the people" as a central impetus for the creation of common schooling, and they provided a rather decentralized structure of common schooling controlled mainly through the locality. This happened in a much earlier period than it did in other parts of the British Empire.

The movement for common schooling in Upper Canada was, by 1815, very much alive. An administrative view of the origins of popular schooling in Upper Canada that focuses on institutional and bureaucratic developments in the mid-nineteenth century overlooks the significance of the public and political discourses in the early life of the colony for both Upper Canada and the British Empire as a whole. Upper Canadians had, by 1815, promoted a system of common schooling at a time when the British metropolis itself was not undertaking similar initiatives.

Part of the explanation for Upper Canada's populist movement for common schooling rests with its demographics. Prior to 1815, Upper Canada received the bulk of its settlers from the United States. With networks of kin and community and a permeable border that hardly separated the colony from its American neighbours, Upper Canadians were heavily influenced by developments in the United States. Specifically, the issue of schooling was a central feature of public discourse in the United States, and so, by extension, Upper Canadians borrowed from and developed that discourse within the colony. Though in a British colony, Upper Canadian settlements were "decidedly American in their peoples and practices."[31] Indeed, as literary scholar Gwendolyn Davies suggests in her assessment of the development of Loyalist literary culture, the first task of colonists in the new settlements was "to re-establish in this 'wilderness' the educational and cultural institutions left behind in America."[32]

So, what were those educational and cultural institutions left behind in America? Historians of education in the United States have suggested that popular schooling coincided with the rise of capitalism in the United States. The current consensus locates the origins of the common school reform movement sometime around

1780 and suggests that the impulse for a large-scale government-aided system can be clearly seen largely before 1820. Focusing on developments in New York State, Carl Kaestle identifies a highly local and rural school system in late eighteenth-century America with a mix of private and increasingly government-aided schools. In the cities, Kaestle finds a steady development of schools, with urban reformers increasingly paying attention to and promoting charity schooling for the urban poor. The proliferation of schools, in both town and country, and the steady increase in enrolment rates began what would eventually become a wide-scale common school reform movement in New York State, culminating in the Common School Act of 1815.[33] A new generation of scholars has more recently added to the growing body of evidence suggesting that late eighteenth-century Americans favoured and promoted the development of popular schooling. Re-examining the formation of common schooling in antebellum North Carolina through an analysis of the partisan press, Kim Tolley notes the role of newspaper editors in introducing and advocating for common schooling in the late eighteenth and early nineteenth centuries. In her analysis of education, social capital, and state formation in the northern United States, Nancy Beadie considers how patterns of school organization shaped the process of state formation itself. Beadie highlights the extent of popular support for common schools that developed prior to, and outside of, state initiative, and she then considers how the considerable social and financial capital first commanded by schools as business organizations in the early American republic came to be appropriated by the state as the nineteenth century progressed.[34]

In was from these places of early school reform that American settlers in Upper Canada came. They brought with them an appetite for schooling and a ready discourse of school advocacy transplanted from their communities of origin. Indeed, American settlers were often rebuilding the entire community they left behind. Consider the petition of Thomas Hilborn on 28 September 1805, requesting a track of land lying north of Uxbridge and east of Gwillimburg to settle himself and forty families from Pennsylvania.[35] The characteristic historical image of the independent Upper Canadian pioneer might have skewed what was often a community affair. The independent settler working to clear land and create a home was certainly commonplace, but it was often the case that groups of communities migrated together, bringing with them the familiar social and cultural institutions of their American past and re-establishing them in Upper Canada at once.

After 1815, however, Upper Canada would witness a steady stream of British and Irish migrants who would transform the colony. Would they transform the educational discourse? What were the communities they wished to (re-)establish? What type of school system would be developed in the postwar years? Who would control the schools? What curriculum would be promoted in the schools? Would the schools be places where knowledge was acquired in the prospect of utilizing it for material prosperity, as some inhabitants desired? Would they be places of indoctrination in which a common British character could be instilled, as some others desired? Could they be both? The following chapter examines these questions through an analysis of the educational discourse in the print media during the period from the passing of the Common School Act of 1816 to the passing of its second and final amendment in 1824.

4

The Rise and Fall of Common Schooling in the Postwar Era, 1816–1824

In 1816, Lieutenant Governor Gore, recently returned from his recovery in England, opened the postwar throne speech by referring to two matters of concern: first, the need to reform the militia code, so as to have regular forces should they again be required; and second, the common schools issue.[1] Addressing objectives he shared with Strachan, Gore suggested that in addition to securing further aid for the district schools and advancing higher education, legislators ought to make the matter of common schooling their first priority. "The dissemination of Letters is of the first importance to every Class; and to aid in so desirable an object, I wish to call your attention to some Provision for an Establishment of Schools in each Township, which shall afford the first Principles to the Children of the Inhabitants, and prepare such of them as may require further Instruction, to receive it in the District Schools; from them it seems desirable that there should be a resort to a Provincial Seminary, for the Youth who may be destined for the Professions, or other distinguished Walks in Life, where they might attain the Higher Branches of Education." Money and land had already been bestowed toward that end, he proclaimed. With the executive on board, there was little standing in the way of any legislation that either house might draw up.

While Gore would see through the passing of the Common School Act in 1816, he would not remain to witness its consequences. In 1818, he was replaced by Sir Peregrine Maitland, who would oversee colonial administration for the next ten years. Maitland, a former ensign in the British army who had quickly risen to the rank of lieutenant-colonel and a personal friend of Lord Bathurst, colonial secretary, was perhaps a much more strategic choice by the colonial office than previous lieutenant governors, for there was no disputing his loyalties to the British metropolis. During his administration, Maitland would oversee the repopulation of Upper Canada by waves of settlers from the British Isles, initiate public works projects such as the building of roads and canals, and see that Upper Canada moved away from "the simple pioneer society which marked the first generation of its history, and to manifest many signs of growth and progress."[2]

Central to Maitland's and the colonial office's plan for the growth and progress of the province was the development of a school system rooted in British values and traditions. But was it too late? Did the Common School Act of 1816 already grant too much power to the locality, rendering the intentions of the colonial administration useless? An analysis of the print media indicates that Strachan, Gore, and now Maitland had entered the discourse on the expansion of schooling at a much later stage than others in the province. The print culture has suggested that we should re-examine the impetus for popular schooling in Upper Canada. In doing so, we discover a widespread deliberative process toward school development in the province prior to the granting of the school act. So, did Maitland, the colonial office, and the influx of British settlers change the tone of this deliberation? It what ways did they use the common schools already established? What direction would popular schooling take in the postwar years?

There is much to suggest that the Common School Act of 1816 did little to alter the pattern and rhythm of schooling in early nineteenth-century Upper Canada. Although the new law began the process of government involvement in what had theretofore been a private matter, both the administrative intervention and financial assistance were to be minimal.[3] Despite promises of the "dissemination of letters" to all classes, government-aided schooling was still overwhelmingly restricted to a limited number of schools for children of the more privileged.[4] Many parents found it difficult or impossible to pay the fees required to supplement the government grant.[5] Moreover, efforts by educational leaders such as Strachan in nurturing the common school seem to have been limited, with greater attention after the passing of the act given to seminaries of higher learning and the establishment of a university.[6] Two amendments were made to the 1816 act in 1820 and 1824. Both amendments worked only to reduce the effectiveness of the common school system. In 1820, funds to the common schools were drastically scaled back, while the 1824 amendment required that teachers be certified by at least one member of their district board of education, thus minimizing the power of local trustees.

The evidence, then, should suggest that the act of 1816 was relatively ineffective. Scholars examining educational development in the early nineteenth century have demonstrated that the period continued to be marked by pioneer and voluntary schooling. Most of the information available about this early era, according to historian Harry Smaller, "is couched in such negative terms and images, with schools described as log shanties and teachers as 'misfits from other walks of life.'"[7] There may have been a common school act, that is, but we can hardly speak of a common school system.

But what effect did the passing of the Common School Act of 1816 have on the *idea* of common schooling in Upper Canada? To what extent did established inhabitants and new settlers discuss common schooling now that public funding for such schooling was available? Did they consider the act to be effective? To what extent were the common schools utilized or attempted to be utilized? By shifting our attention to the print media discourse, we can consider how effective Upper Canadians considered the government-aided common schools to be or not, and what they envisioned to be the next step, if any, in the development of popular schooling in Upper Canada.

Two days after Gore's throne speech of 6 February 1816, the House of Assembly created a select committee with the purpose of drawing up a school bill.[8] James Durand, member of the House of Assembly for West York, headed the committee and contributed the following points to the report, echoing, almost verbatim, Strachan's report of 1815:

Firstly: – That the education of youth is a subject worthy of the most serious attention of the Legislature.
Secondly: – That the necessity of sending young men out of the Province to finish their education, which hath heretofore existed, has been found extremely inconvenient.

Thirdly: – That sound policy dictates that our youth should be educated within the Province, or in England, if we wish them to imbibe predilections friendly to our different establishments, and attached to our Parent State.

Fourthly: – That but few of the inhabitants of this Province can support the expense of sending their children to be educated in Great Britain; and parental authority would reluctantly trust them at such an immense distance from its care, observation and control.

Fifthly: – That there is, at present, no seminary at which they can obtain a liberal and finished education.

Sixthly: – That, in order to diffuse liberal knowledge generally throughout the community, it appears expedient that a University should hereafter be established, where the arts and sciences may be taught to the youth of all denominations, in and of which establishment may be embraced the funds which are anticipated from His Majesty's munificent donation of lands for its support.

Seventhly: – That nothing has yet been done to promote education among the poorer inhabitants.

Eighthly: – That it is expedient to extend the benefits of a common education throughout the whole Province.

Ninthly: – That the people have shown among themselves a laudable zeal in this particular, which ought to be fostered and encouraged.

Tenthly: – That, with respect to the present district institutions and grammar schools, your Committee feel it their incumbent duty to state as their opinion, the advantages which were expected to be derived from this source, have fallen short of the object.

Lastly: – Your Committee, for these considerations, request that they may be permitted to submit to your Honourable House a Bill which they have framed for the establishment of common schools throughout this Province.[9]

In the midst of legislative debate for common schools, petitions were read in the House of Assembly that solidified the idea that public support for a common school bill reflected public opinion. To be sure, official petitions for schools were modest in the first twenty years of the colony's existence. Those that were submitted, however, are telling of the type and quality of discourse surrounding the want of a school system shared by all. A petition of the inhabitants from Williamstown, in the Charlottenburgh Township, demonstrating their desire for common schools, for example, was introduced into the House of Assembly on 28 February 1816, and although the colonial government no longer needed convincing, it further added to the political discourse surrounding the need for common schooling. The petitioners informed the House of Assembly that a school in Williamstown had been opened on 2 January 1815 for the "benefit of such poor children whose parents or friends have not the means of defraying the expenses attending the same." The school, having sixty children and running short of funds to pay the schoolmaster and make repairs to the schoolhouse, had to increase tuition, keeping many poor children out. The petitioners thus sought financial aid from the government.[10]

On 21 March 1816, the Common School Bill, which had been years in the making, was finally passed by the House of Assembly, and the following day it was passed by the Legislative Council without any amendment. The bill was given royal assent and enacted on 1 April 1816.[11] The act was the first significant accomplishment that marked the government's assumption of responsibility for aiding the education of the entire population. It provided a fixed annual grant of £6,000 to each of the ten districts, in which "Inhabitants of any Town, Township, Village or place" could meet together to create a common school for twenty or more children. Elected trustees were given power to make rules and regulations for the government of the schools, the selection of teachers, and the purchase of books, while school boards in each district, appointed by the lieutenant governor, would oversee matters and allocate the legislative grant among the common schools of each respective district.

To qualify for a common school grant, those requesting the grant had to meet certain conditions. These conditions were reflective of concerns emanating from Strachan and the executive in the wake of 1812. While elected trustees were given power to make rules and regulations for the government of the schools, the selection of teachers, and the purchase of books, they were ultimately responsible to the lieutenant governor–appointed board of education in each district. Moreover, the act specified that "teachers MUST be natural born subjects or have taken the oath of allegiance," and trustees were given the power to remove any teacher for any impropriety and to appoint another person.

While there was certainly a sense of oversight, the act generally afforded a great deal of local autonomy and decision-making power. What do we make of the democratic nature of the act, which placed considerable control in the hands of elected trustees at the local level? Why did colonial leaders grant such a degree of power to the locality? Was the requirement for natural-born teachers enough to address the concern of the elite that the common schools might be used as a tool to mark the colony with a loyal British character? Was the act, that is, written to appease the elite or the masses? The incomplete answer, perhaps, is that the act was designed to do both.

Without the creation of a centralized board of education, we might assume that centralization and control from above were not the key aims of those drawing up the legislation. Pursuant to Strachan's suggestions, however, the trustees were required to report on the state of schools at least once a year to their respective boards of education, which would then relay that report to the lieutenant governor and the legislature. In this way, it seems, the executive reinforced its position as head of the school system, confident that it could monitor the character of the schools. By making government funds available to all inhabitants meeting certain requirements, on the other hand, the act appeased the many members of the House of Assembly and writers in the press who had been advocating, since 1806, for a common school system that could be universally accessible. Maintaining a loyal British character, as sought out by a colonial administration concerned about the British character of the province, and providing a universal system of common schooling, then, were enough of a balance to satisfy all parties involved. Or were they?

It is generally considered an axiom among politicians that once a "public" request is bequeathed, it encourages that "public" to demand more. As the debate over education in the press was making clear in Upper Canada, the appetite for schooling had been growing stronger since the late eighteenth century. An analysis of print media in Upper Canada points to the growing number of inhabitants in favour of increased funding of common schooling and the expansion of the system itself. Print media discourse reveals a bourgeoning appetite for common schooling. Once this was granted, then, were Upper Canadians satisfied, or did they demand more?

An important statistical survey on education undertaken in 1818 begins to offer some answers to this question. Robert Fleming Gourlay travelled to Upper Canada in 1817 and quickly made his mark on the political scene with the publication of an open letter "To the Resident Land Owners of Upper-Canada," which appeared in several newspapers of the day.[12] Gourlay was a political agitator and had earlier been kicked out of his father's home for the printing of a mischievous pamphlet in Scotland. He settled in England, where he racked up a large debt on farmland and made a name for himself after publishing yet another scathing pamphlet, this time on an agricultural society in England. Eventually, he found his way to Upper Canada, where his wife had inherited land. He brought with him a flare for the dramatic but also a self-proclaimed desire to improve the living standards of the inhabitants of Upper Canada.[13]

Gourlay's 1822 pamphlet, *Statistical Account of Upper Canada*, is helpful in addressing the question of the popularity of common schooling after the passing of the 1816 act.[14] Under the premise that he sought aid for promoting emigration from England, Gourlay asked the residents of Upper Canada for answers to a series of statistical questions. Through his continued appeals in the press, Gourlay quickly raised the interest of a significant number of inhabitants, and thousands gathered in scattered communities throughout the province in an effort to galvanize the statistical data required for his account.[15] Gourlay's findings provide us with some valuable numbers for the period immediately after the passing of the Common School Act.

Gourlay's report pointed out that common schools were in abundance and that the Common School Act of 1816 provided a growing number of common schools with government aid, making the idea of sending children to school a reality for certain inhabitants. The act, "however incomplete as a system," he proposed in his account, "indicates a favourable progress of public sentiment on the subject of Education."[16] A total of 34,259 inhabitants from eight districts responded to Gourlay's statistical survey, and on the basis of that number of respondents, the report shows that by 1818 there were 193 common schools in the province and the trend was toward the establishment of an increasing number of schools every year. Gourlay's findings are supported by comparable figures that James Strachan (John Strachan's brother) offered during his visit to Upper Canada in 1819. James Strachan found that 220 students were being taught in the eight district schools and approximately 3,500 students were being instructed in the numerous common schools, and these numbers did not include "a great number of Schools of a similar description, to which the bounty of Government cannot be extended."[17]

These numbers, and the interpretation of them by contemporaries as a significant development in Upper Canadian schooling, offer pause and should force us to reconsider whether systemic schooling in Upper Canada was modest at best after the passing of the 1816 school act and prior to the developments of the mid-nineteenth century. Many of the common schools indicated in Gourlay's report were, no doubt, established prior to the passing of the Common School Act of 1816.[18] Nevertheless, Gourlay was struck by the extent to which he found the inhabitants of Upper Canada demanding schools and school improvements. Should we be as well? Gourlay's report suggests that, in the first few years of government-aided common schooling, inhabitants were utilizing the common school grants in order to increase school enrolments and furthermore that they were building more common schools.

These numbers, of course, do not measure attendance, and so we should not assume that the popularity of common schooling at this time reflected a widespread pattern of regular school attendance and participation.[19] Gourlay's report is significant, however, in that it offers the clearest data available indicating that in the years following the passing of the Common School Act of 1816, the appetite for schooling was strong and the number of schools being built was growing. Through his inquiries, Gourlay came to believe that "[a] spirit of improvement is evidently spreading. The value of education, as well as the want of it is felt."[20]

What is perhaps more significant, however, is that despite the "improvements" in education, many inhabitants were still not satisfied. The reality of government-aided schooling was far from ideal. Certain inhabitants thus also reported to Gourlay that most of the schools remained in unsatisfactory condition. Although "the liberality of the Legislature has been great in support of the District Grammar Schools," the residents of Grimsby reported, the liberality did not extend to the bulk of the people because the schools were "looked upon as seminaries exclusively instituted for the education of the children of the more wealthy classes of society, and to which the poor man's child is considered as unfit to be admitted."[21] And while common schools, these inhabitants admitted, were being erected, "the anxiety of the teacher employed, seems more alive to his stipend than the advancement of the education of those placed under his care." Thus, the common schools were not always appealing institutions for their pupils. Furthermore, certain inhabitants complained about the character of the schools and especially the unfavourable American influence in them. The executive's attempts to instil a British character into the schools, as indicated in Gourlay's report, were yet to be realized. While rules were laid down for the government of schools, inhabitants complained, they were scarcely adhered to and in many cases "in the same class you will frequently see one child with Noah Webster's spelling book in his hand, and the next with Lindley Murray's."[22] Given these complaints, Gourlay was not surprised that the province was failing to establish a homogeneous British character. And while government efforts were not necessarily berated by the inhabitants who responded to Gourlay's survey, there was a clear call for increased government involvement and a more expansive common school system.

Thus, while the grants available for the common schools were welcomed, a growing public debate over education demonstrated concerns about expanding school funding even further. On the premise that "every man should consider himself bound to contribute his mite towards the public benefit," the *Kingston Gazette* printed an "Essay on the Education of Upper Canada" in 1818.[23] To those that argued that school expansion could not be undertaken on a large scale in Upper Canada owing to its geographic and demographic makeup, the writer of this essay responded that the problems facing the construction of a school system were not unique to Upper Canada. Truancy, discipline, and the remote locations of schools were indeed troublesome to Upper Canada, but "similar miseries" afflicted the teacher "in an English, as well as in a Canadian village." "Let it then be the business of every friend to education," he argued, "to awaken more liberal sentiments with respect to both teachers and pupils. A glorious field is open to our view; and our Legislatures are aiding in its cultivation."[24] Like many of his contemporaries, this writer argued for more funds in order to expand the scope of common schooling. He suggested that an increased salary for teachers would attract more-qualified individuals to the profession and that funding for massive school expansion was well within the fiscal capabilities of government. "[A] few thousand pounds annually expended on them [teachers], would confer more time and lasting favour [to the colony], than millions wasted in destructive wars."[25] And for those in government unwilling to increase funding to the common schools, he used their own logic to refute them, insisting that only a properly funded system would secure the admiration of their educational efforts: "Dr. Strachan in the preface to his Arithmetic, very properly observes that 'he who is anxious to spare labour, ought not to be a public Teacher;' and it may be added, that, those who are anxious to withhold adequate reward, are not worthy of a good one."[26]

Despite the growing popularity of common schooling and the increased calls for greater government aid, provincial legislators made educational matters even more problematic in 1820 by amending the 1816 school act to limit funding to the schools in an effort to curb state expenditures on education. The appetite for common schooling, they reasoned, was too strong and could not be supported by provincial funds. On 21 February 1820, Lieutenant Governor Maitland opened the legislature with a speech from the throne that made this point clear. With the Common School Act of 1816 set to expire, he pleaded with legislators to consider restructuring the provisions for establishing common schools because, "on the present scale," the province could not afford to keep pace with the demand. Common schooling was important for cultivating a loyal population, Maitland agreed, and he insisted that he did not want it to be scaled back entirely. Still, he felt that government could not ignore the heavy costs, and thus he asked legislators to consider if "measures may possibly be adopted, to produce the same good at a more moderate expense."[27]

While Maitland insisted upon reduced funding to common schools, he acknowledged their importance to inhabitants. Schooling in general, he proposed, was "becoming daily more important in this Province. The population of Upper Canada is rapidly increasing; new Townships are filling with actual settlers, and the conditions of cultivation and improvement now rigidly insisted upon by His Majesty's Government, are suddenly displaying the advantage of the present system, by a lively contrast with the former." The message to legislators was to somehow maintain a common school system with reduced funds to support it.

Maitland's appeal was effective in convincing the House of Assembly that school expansion was simply not fiscally possible. The house thus responded to his request two days later, assuring the executive that "[w]e shall direct our attention to such laws as are about to expire, and give to the revision of the Common School Act that due consideration which its importance demands." It reminded Maitland, however, that the price of schooling could not be measured in fiscal terms only and that if Maitland wanted to maintain a loyal population, common school funding could not be scaled back too far.[28] The interests of government must be balanced with the interests of those whom it represented.

In the public arena, attempts to scale back common schooling were clearly not welcomed. In fact, the press continued to print articles concerning the unsatisfactory state of common schooling, such as one that compared schooling in Upper Canada to that of its neighbours.[29] While Upper Canadians could boast that their system of education was not as lamentable as that of Lower Canada, they were reminded that, on a global comparison, a lot more could be achieved. The state of New York in 1811, the article pointed out, was reported to have 5,000 common schools and more than 200,000 scholars. And for those skeptical about comparisons between the dense population of New York and the population of Upper Canada, the paper also offered figures for the year 1815: New York State reported that, not including the city and county of New York and the city of Albany, there were 2,621 common and primary schools with 140,106 scholars – and all of this was achieved with an expense of only $55,720.[30]

The House of Assembly nevertheless took measures to scale back on common schooling in 1820. Although it agreed to reduce the actual funding, it did insist upon maintaining the principle that those seeking funds would receive them. The house proposed this amendment on 4 March 1820 and two days later was informed that the Legislative Council had passed it without any changes. The Common School Act of 1820 was given royal assent on 7 March.[31] The act was printed later that month in the *Upper Canada Gazette*.[32] In the end, the act reduced substantially the amount of funding provided for schools and teachers. The legislative grant of £6,000 a year in aid of common schools was reduced to £2,500. Moreover, the board of education was instructed that any surplus in funding must be directed back to government. The provisions for residents to apply for a common school grant, however, were left unchanged. Thus, despite allowing that residents could apply for school funding, the pace of school expansion was curbed by the financial restraint of government. It was clear that common school expansion had, for the time being, reached its peak.

Although the House of Assembly acted in accordance with the wishes of the Executive and Legislative Councils in 1820, it was clear that bitterness remained among certain members of the House of Assembly. Earlier, in 1819, the House of Assembly had again made efforts to repeal the District School Act of 1807. Moreover, when legislation was first introduced for the continuance of the Common School Act of 1816 (set to expire in 1820), the Legislative Council made so many amendments on the continuance bill that it simply could not be passed by the lower house.[33] Some common ground was found, however, in the District School Amendment Bill, which was passed on 12 July 1819. This new act was considered as a sort of compromise between the District School Act of 1807 and the Common School Act of 1816. It provided for the free education in every district school of ten "promising children of the poorer inhabitants."[34] Trustees were now obligated to report annually to the lieutenant governor on "the state of the said schools, the number of scholars, the state of education, with the different branches taught in the said schools."[35] The grant to all new teachers was reduced to a maximum of £50.

While the Legislative Council was granting small concessions, the elite were also construing grander educational plans of their own. In 1819, the Executive Council met on its own to discuss options on a proposed university. The report of 1798 was dusted off, but the council found the cost estimated by the committee of 1798 to be no longer applicable. Thus, it proposed new measures in which the lieutenant governor would grant 500,000 acres of land for the purpose of establishing a university in the province; £10,000 for a library, philosophical apparatus, and botanic garden; plus £4,000 annually to pay for a principal, professors, preceptors, scholarships, librarian, gardener, and other officers. To raise the funds, it recommended the sale of land from time to time until the revenue would supply the annual expenditure. The Executive Council also recommended that a constitution be obtained for the university by royal charter.[36]

In addition, the Executive Council initiated plans to put funds toward a different type of mass educational system, one it hoped would ultimately replace the common schools. The common school in York was one of the first casualties of the reduced spending on common schooling introduced by the 1820 legislation, but the events surrounding its closing were far from simple. A close examination of the closure of the York Common School reveals one attempt by the elite to redesign the system of popular elementary education in Upper Canada.

By 1820, Strachan and the executive might have begun to question whether the common schools could effectively bring into existence a truly loyal population committed to British principles, and whether they had instead created a system that was proving to be uncontrollable. Strachan began, in that year, to seek alternatives in education that would strengthen the province's attachment to British values, as he saw them.[37] Without seeking the approval of the House of Assembly, Strachan insisted that Lieutenant Governor Maitland send to England for a Lancastrian school teacher. Joseph Spragg was selected and appointed to the York Common School, from which the common school teacher, Thomas Appleton, was fired. Appleton appealed to the lieutenant governor and the provincial board of education but was given no help.[38] The trustees, however, came to Appleton's aid via a petition to the lieutenant governor in which they stressed that Appleton enjoyed the confidence of the parents and students and that his expectations had been "increased by the great increase of Scholars and the general approval of his endeavors." They saw no need to dismiss Appleton and suggested that his call for redress was "too reasonable and just to be disappointed."[39]

Maitland replied through his secretary George Hillier, who informed the trustees that on the matter of their petition, the lieutenant governor "sees no occasion for any reference to it."[40] Appleton was, simply put, a common school teacher out of a job.

Maitland transferred control of the common school to a special board of trustees and renamed the York school the "Central School of York." While it was to remain a common school by law, it was by all means a British national school conducted on the Lancastrian system.[41] By but little stretch of the imagination, the Central School of York could be considered a state-church school. Four years after the passing of the Common School Act, this was the executive's first attempt to introduce a British school system, under the sanction of the Church of England.

Why did the Executive Council take this unilateral measure to create a British national school? Why did it not open up the idea to debate in the legislature? Did the executive fear that the House of Assembly might resist a Church of England system of instruction in the province? Did it fear that the idea did not have the popular support necessary to make it a matter of public debate? Did the efforts of the executive to introduce this system without any debate illustrate its fear that the general will of the province was not in line with the executive's conception of a British colony? And, perhaps more important to our discussion here, why did the executive not take this measure in 1816?

The "First Annual Report of the Upper Canada Central School on the British National System of Education" for the year 1820/21 sheds some additional light upon the intentions of the executive elite in establishing a British national school in Upper Canada. The success of the common schools had demonstrated to everyone in Upper Canada that there was a strong appetite for schooling. As such, "in an age when the thirst for improvement is continually increasing among all ranks," the board insisted that it must "implant with useful knowledge, good principles and notions in the rising generations." This could be achieved, of course, in the district schools. Unlike the district schools, however, the proposed British national schools would not be designed for the children of the elite only. It was the board's intention "[t]o train up, not only those who are destined for the higher departments of life, but also the rising generation in general, to proper and regular habits of application and industry combined with sound moral and religious notions." The board did not fail to mention the benefit of the system to the "general good" of the province. In Upper Canada especially, "where the population is small and where a change of many of the inhabitants is continually occurring," the necessity of shaping a common character was even more fundamental. For this purpose, "it is of essential consequence, under the frequent change of scholars that takes place, to have always a good succession of those who have, by practice, become well qualified to be teachers." Inspired by the success of the Central School in London, England, the board expressed its hope that the Central School of York would plant the seeds for a system of education that would spread "throughout the whole of this Province."[42] The board had little faith, it was clear, in planting such seeds through the common schools, which had been granted too much local autonomy. Through a centralized system that promoted attachment to Britain and to British social institutions such as the Church of England, however, the preservation of the board's conception of society and governance could be, its members believed, maintained.

The *Christian Recorder*, a periodical aligned with the Church of England and edited by Strachan between 1819 and 1821, also provides some insight into the concerns of the political elite. Central to Strachan's concerns, of course, was the issue of religion. More precisely, Strachan was concerned about the religious plurality of Upper Canada and the potential for settlers to be lured into a church other than that of the Church of England. "A wide field is open in Upper Canada for all religious denominations," he told his readers; "the majority of the people are still undecided, and of that majority, the greater part will join those Teachers who are most zealous and attentive to the discharge of their sacred duties."[43] Throughout 1819 and 1820, the *Christian Recorder* attempted to nurture a favourable sentiment among its readers toward the idea of the British national schools by printing a history of the system, along with propaganda on its advantages.[44] Such ideas, however, did not permeate other newspapers and seem to have done little to affect public discourse.

On 22 March 1821, however, the British national school at York did make the news. "*The Central School* was again visited on the

5th inst. by His Excellency the Lieutenant Governor, and Lady Sarah Maitland," the *York Weekly Post* reported, "who appeared much gratified with the growing improvement and promising aspect of the institution; which now begins to shew the excellence of the National System of instruction, on which it is established, and from which it is earnestly anticipated that the greatest good will result to the Province in general, not only from the Central School at York, but also from others, becoming established in those parts of the Province where they they [*sic*] may be needed, and their being supplied with masters duly trained in the system of our Central School."[45] The *York Weekly Post*, a pro-executive and government-funded newspaper, praised the school and promoted it as perhaps the best option for parents: "All who are sensible of the great benefits to be derived from the rising generation being well educated in good principles according to true religion will doubtless make every exertion to aid in promoting the benevolent designs most kindly introduced by our excellent Governor."

The *York Weekly Post*'s praise of the Central School of York should be taken with a grain of salt, as it does not necessarily reflect acceptance of the system on the part of the reading public or the press. As it was a government newspaper, distributed with the *Upper Canada Gazette*, any criticism of the system within its pages would have likely been sanctioned by Maitland or other members of the executive. In any event, the executive government did not have to rely on its own press for support. It was also aided by a segment of Upper Canada's print culture that had become infused with an anti-American and pro-British attitude in the wake of the War of 1812. Challenges to measures advocated by the lieutenant governor and his council were often criticized as a betrayal of the colony and a sign of disloyalty.[46] When war veterans from Hallowell, for example, complained that not enough money was being spent on public services such as compensation to soldiers and the building of schools for their children, the response in the press was that "[a] brave and generous people never boast of their courage, nor expect to be paid for defending themselves and the government they have sworn to maintain."[47]

Such pro-establishment and pro-metropolis sentiments must have provided encouragement to the executive. The remaking of the York

Common School into a British national school was an attempt by the colonial administration to bring Upper Canada in line with the character of schooling in the British metropolis. As Bruce Curtis points out, the rapid spread of elementary schooling on the monitorial model had been spurred in Britain by the necessity of educating a developing working class.[48] Whether such a system could be promoted in Upper Canada, however, is questionable in light of the historical evidence and was probably questionable by contemporaries as well. The British national schools might have been in line with the social, political, and, most importantly perhaps, religious milieu of the British metropolis, but they were out of line with the pattern of school development in British America. Even if the British migrants who came to Upper Canada after 1815 overwhelmingly supported Maitland and the colonial administration – and although they had their supporters, there is little evidence to suggest that we can speak of the support being overwhelming – they had nevertheless entered a colony where common schooling was an accomplished, legislative fact. Moreover, they had entered a colony where common schooling had been promoted by, and where legislation granted authority over the schools to, "the people." Whatever ideas Strachan, Maitland, and other colonial administrators had in regard to reshaping the schools would fly in the face of four decades' worth of school development in Upper Canada and could hardly be expected to receive a warm reception in the public sphere.

Maitland, Strachan, and their inner circle seem to have recognized this fact. A despatch from Maitland to Earl Bathurst in 1822 makes clear that it was never the intention of the Executive Council to have any debate about the establishment of a Church of England national school system in Upper Canada. "It is proposed," Maitland told Bathurst, "to establish one introductory school on the National plan in each town of a certain size."[49] Bathurst, from the colonial office, informed Maitland of royal consent to the plan in a reply in October 1822. Money to support the schools should be drawn, he directed, from the funds set aside for a university in Upper Canada through a portion of the crown reserves. These plans not only were kept from public knowledge, but were never brought before either the House of Assembly or the Legislative Council. Thus, two grand designs for elementary schools were put into operation: the first, the common schools, established and supported by the legislature; and the second, the Church of England national school, established by the authority of the Executive Council alone.[50]

With the common schools proving to be uncontrollable, then, and with the religion of the population they served proving to be unpredictable, the executive elite silently began efforts to replace the common school system with a British National one. In addition, the executive council stepped up its efforts to wrestle control of education in 1822 when it approved the appointment of a centralized general board of education, headed by Strachan, to oversee the common schools.[51]

The executive, however, still faced many challenges to its authority. Through the momentum of the petitioning movement and the growing number of newspapers in the province, public pressure continued to put the executive into check. The British government, once the proud symbol of executive authority, was, as was evident in news from Britain, now moving toward a new conception of its own in its political culture. This was a nineteenth-century Britain in which the balance of power was shifting ever more toward the representative branch of government and decreased executive authority. Could one expect it, then, to be the reliable supporter of executive supremacy in Upper Canada? Moreover, the House of Assembly in Upper Canada, which had theretofore performed its duties as the popular branch of government while still displaying a sense of deference to Upper Canada's executive, was by the 1820s itself growing tired of the small group of political heads in Upper Canada who were unwilling to relinquish any power. And with the electorate sending more and more anti-establishment men to the House of Assembly, the popular branch was daily becoming an antagonistic voice that could not easily be silenced.[52]

As a result of reduced government funding to the common schools, fewer schoolhouses were opened in the early 1820s. The house of assembly ultimately facilitated the decline of the common schools in the early 1820s. Nevertheless growing calls to rectify inadequacies in school funding forced both the house of assembly and legislative council to direct at least some of their attention toward the idea of school expansion in the colony. One such petition came from Peter Robinson and a group of Irish immigrants requesting to Maitland directly for "proper facilities, schools, school masters and religious leaders."[53] In 1823, legislators responded to certain petitions in both the eastern and western corners of the colony by establishing a grammar school in the Ottawa District and extending common school grants in the Bathurst District, while also providing financial relief to the teachers of Niagara who had been petitioning their cause for some time to both legislators and the press.[54] William Baldwin also introduced a college bill that year, but it was unsuccessful.[55] The bill was probably an attempt to reintroduce Weekes's wishes for a college into the House of Assembly.[56] More importantly, the college bill demonstrates that want of higher education was also felt by those outside the executive elite.

The Common School Act was again altered on 19 January 1824. The act incorporated the General Board of Education, which had been conceived by Maitland and the Executive Council in 1822. John Strachan was made chairman of the board, and several other members of Maitland's inside circle also served on it. The act provided for the permanency of the Common School Act, a measure that gave some assurance to ambivalent members of the House of Assembly, perhaps, that schooling for all inhabitants would continue to be an Upper Canadian value. It also gave aid in the sum of £150 annually to Sunday schools and made provision for the first time, under the authority of the legislature, for the education of Aboriginal peoples. Furthermore, it addressed executive concerns over itinerant teachers by insisting that teachers were to be tested before they were paid. The General Board of Education was granted the power to withhold teachers' salaries if it was felt that their qualifications were not up to par.[57]

Throughout the remainder of the 1820s, the zeal with which common schools were erected after 1816 was quelled by the amendments of 1820 and 1824. Yet while the building of common schools was quelled, the appetite for them was not. The idea of government-aided schooling was well planted, and although legislation was deemed necessary in the early 1820s to slow down what was clearly becoming a heavy financial strain on the Upper Canadian budget, many inhabitants continued to send their children to increasingly overcrowded common schools.

The Common School Act of 1824, the third common school act in less than a decade, fuelled the lively and interminable debate on education in Upper Canada. The executive elite were aware that there was popular interest in the common schools, and with control placed at the local level, they could not shape the character of the common school system from the top. They did, however, limit government aid to the common schools and introduced measures to establish a British national school system in Upper Canada.

In addition, the executive turned its attention to establishing a university for the privileged elite. This was a move, as will be discussed, that proved to be costly. The development of the university in Upper Canada is, like the making of the District School Act, characteristically looked at in isolation from the development of the school system in general.[58] The making of the university, however, was also part of the central debate concerning the future form of government-aided schooling in Upper Canada. The political turmoil of recent years did not sit well with the executive, leading Maitland to speculate to his Executive Council whether the goings-on in the province did not demonstrate the political necessity of establishing a university where the "principal young men might receive an education likely to impress upon them common feelings of attachment to the Crown, and of veneration for the Church of England."[59] The university, it was believed, offered the promise of shaping future leaders, both in the Legislative Council and the House of Assembly, with values conducive to a loyal and "British" colony. Maitland would remain steadfast in promoting a "British" school system anchored in the values and authority of the British metropolis.

To what extent would Upper Canadians concede to or resist the executive's conception of a British character for the province? To what extent did they concede or resist this conception in the schools? Were the British national schools successful? Ultimately, as the existing historiography already points out, we know that they were not. By 1841, there was virtually no discourse concerning these schools, and efforts toward establishing a universal public system of schooling were once again initiated. Little, however, is known about the demise of the British national schools in the 1820s. Their demise, however, was very much connected to the rise of new ideologies in Upper Canada and the beginnings of reform in the political culture of the province. The following chapters will consider the national schools question and other educational developments in light of educational discourse in Upper Canada and the ways in which government-aided schooling was shaped by emerging and competing political ideologies.

5

Education and the Rise of Radical Political Thought, 1824–1826

Several months after the War of 1812, Upper Canada's colonial administrators established a common school system that "the people themselves" had promoted; then, only a few years later, because this system did not seem to serve their purposes, they attempted to dismantle it unilaterally. The seeds of government-aided common schooling, however, had been planted, and out of those seeds would come the roots of a contentious public discourse concerning the direction that mass universal schooling should take. This educational discourse reflected the increasingly contentious debates surrounding other political matters in the province. Such a discourse was fuelled, beginning in 1824, with the establishment of two radical newspapers: the *Colonial Advocate*, founded and edited by William Lyon Mackenzie; and the *Canadian Freeman*, founded and edited by Francis Collins. Indeed, by the mid-1820s, a rapidly expanding press in Upper Canada both enlarged the scope and accelerated the speed of educational discourse throughout the province.

The educational ideas of radical reformers in the 1830s have received considerable attention from scholars of Upper Canadian education.[1] Most notably, Charles Duncombe and the reform party's 1836 report on education to the House of Assembly is seen as a crucial document outlining the educational ambitions of reformers in Upper Canada. Less, however, is written about the ideas and ambitions of reformers in the years leading up to that report. Since reformers had limited influence in the House of Assembly in the 1820s, few official records documenting reformist ideas on education are available. By turning our attention to print media, however, we can find some important sources that can contribute to our understanding of the intellectual underpinnings of universal schooling in Upper Canada from the vantage point of those who wished to reform Upper Canadian politics and society. William Lyon Mackenzie, leader of the Upper Canadian Rebellions of 1837–38 and political agitator for most of his career, launched the *Colonial Advocate* in May 1824 with the matter of education taking up a significant part of his first editorial. Indeed, throughout the 1820s, Mackenzie continued to focus on the development of education in his newspaper, as did the editors of other newspapers. In 1830, Mackenzie published a pamphlet entitled *Catechism of Education*.[2] What can we learn about reformist ideas on education from these overlooked print media sources? What can they tell us about the development of government-aided schooling in Upper Canada prior to the debates of the mid- to late 1830s? This chapter undertakes to consider these questions through an analysis of the rise of the radical press and its impact on educational discourse in Upper Canada.

There is debate among historians concerning the influence that William Lyon Mackenzie had on the inhabitants of Upper Canada. Some see him as an extreme radical who thrust peaceful Upper Canadians into unnecessary discord. Others are more sympathetic and blame the political establishment for refusing to allow Mackenzie any position of influence, despite his various election victories.[3] Still other historians depict Mackenzie as a man of ideas who was inspired by the reform movements in both Britain and the United States.[4] The province had indeed received and printed news from across the Atlantic for years. In this sense, Mackenzie offered nothing new in his newspaper, which tended to print anti-establishment and sometimes pro-republican writings gathered from both Britain and the United States. He did not, in doing this, raise the population's consciousness of new ideas. He did provide, however, an immediate medium to conduct public dialogue on certain contentious issues that other newspapers of the time were not willing to engage in. The establishment of the *Colonial Advocate* altered the tone of public discourse in 1820s Upper Canada. It was without doubt an anti-establishment newspaper intended to bolster the voices of reform. Mackenzie once again provided the province with a radical voice. In a word, he brought to Upper Canada in the 1820s what Willcocks had brought in 1807 with the *Upper Canadian Guardian*.[5]

In order to discredit Mackenzie's newspaper, the pro-executive press immediately labelled him a republican and a mischief.[6] To be sure, Mackenzie's first editorial attempted to explain his political stance.[7] However he felt about the United States, he insisted, he preferred to remain a British subject: "We like American liberty well, but greatly prefer British liberty. British subjects, born in Britain, we have sworn allegiance to a constitutional monarchy, and we will die before we will violate that oath." Mackenzie advocated a limited monarchy with representative democracy, with the House of Assembly holding the balance of power and not the executive. Such patterns of thought put him in line with advocates of nineteenth-century liberalism across the Atlantic, such as Joseph Hume and the future British prime minister Robert Peel. Mackenzie's newspaper never failed to remind Upper Canadians that they were part of an empire itself open to reform.

Mackenzie went on to highlight the importance of the dissemination of knowledge in a political democracy. He suggested "that a free and cheap exchange of newspapers between editors in this country and Great Britain would have done more for the colonies than most people are aware of." Mackenzie noted that Britain was in a new era that saw the expansion of the rights of "the people" through an increasingly empowered lower house. By contrast, Upper Canada was in the midst of an anachronistic struggle between the higher and lower branches of the legislature, or, "might against right." It was time, as he saw it, for Upper Canada to join a transnational discourse that favoured the expansion of political rights and representation to all people.

Mackenzie entered the debate on education by printing an essay concerning his personal thoughts on the direction of education in the province and the need for expanding its reach.[8] A proper education, Mackenzie thought, ought to cultivate the type and quality of character in Upper Canada that would enable the youth of the colony to serve their country. Moreover, the inhabitants of Upper Canada ought to dispel "the mist of prejudices that has so long and so injuriously operated against our own interests" and turn to the educational systems in the United States as models for that of Upper

Canada.[9] Mackenzie did not conceal his disdain for Strachan and the schools promoted by the Upper Canadian elite, but he did manage to find some common ground with his adversaries. He agreed with the need for a university, but did not believe that the university should be "an arm of our hierarchy": "[I]f students are to be tied down by tests and oaths, to support particular dogmas, as in the case in Oxford, the institution will answer here no good purpose." Upper Canada had peculiar circumstances, that, like those in Europe and America, had to be addressed. Education was tied to the needs of "the nation": "We ought to enrich the minds of our youth, by giving them such instruction and conformation of character as may able them to serve their country, by the practical application of a systematic education, and like William Pitt, to blend the wisdom of age, with the complexion of youth." Upper Canada, he believed, was in need of men with a liberal education who, "untainted by the enjoyment of power and place," would sacrifice their personal interests for the good of their country. Mackenzie advocated meritocracy over patronage and hierarchy.[10] Like certain conservatives, he spoke of the necessity of expanding common schooling and establishing a university, but he had different ideas concerning the shape and form of the school system.

Mackenzie's conception of schooling in Upper Canada entailed a popular system serving rich and poor alike. Ultimately, Mackenzie believed that the inhabitants of Upper Canada, through education, ought to produce educated leaders "to plead the cause of a poor man oppressed, rather than of a rich oppressor; who would rather *physic pomp* than pamper it – rather *despise* arrogance, clothed with a little brief authority, than cringe to and flatter it."[11] In order to achieve this in Upper Canada, he claimed, serious attention must be paid to the idea of popular schooling. "If we are, indeed, to be blessed with such pastors, counselors, and politicians – if we are to lessen our importations of the first and last classes; and if we hope to feel no inconvenience at having laid an embargo on the second, – if we really love to encourage *native talent*," Mackenzie argued, "we must encourage – *liberally encourage* – competent professors of science and literature to emigrate hither." With this, then, Mackenzie also stressed, as had Upper Canadians since the 1790s, that the school system should serve the interests of the colony before the interests of the British metropolis. It was in this way that an egalitarian society with homegrown talent could best hope to flourish.

As such, Mackenzie took aim against the existing elitist system of education, as he saw it: "The education which a boy now receives at any of the district schools is very costly. Not less, if the youth's board is included, than from seventy to ninety pounds, provincial currency, a year. – Far more – aye, *more than double* what would be required in Scotland to send a student to Edinburgh, or any other Scots university, and keep him there for the same space." Mackenzie berated Strachan and the establishment for creating what he regarded a defective school system in Upper Canada: "Knowing this, we opine that the honourable and reverend Doct. John Strachan, D. D. &c &c &c or his brother, or whoever wrote 'Strachan's Tour,' must have been half asleep, or nodding, when he or they stated that children can be instructed cheaper in Canada, and as well as at home, (Britain.) We wonder what part of Canada, and what part of Britain are meant to be spoken of?"[12] Upper Canada's system needed improvement, he insisted, and improvement meant an expansion of the system to all classes.

Perhaps above all else, Mackenzie was opposed to the connection of church and state in matters of education. Foreshadowing events that he perceived were coming, he warned against a university tied to an established church and advocated a university free from sectarian tenets, such as those found in the United States. The inhabitants of Upper Canada should not fear sending their children to the United States for education. Scottish youth, he proclaimed, were often sent to Dutch schools without them returning opposed to the British government. Any defect in the identity of the children must be from some defect in the social and political conditions of the province. And in any event, no one could deny, he thought, that the advantages in sending a child to Harvard or Yale far outweighed any dangers in halting their education at one of the district schools in the province.[13]

Francis Collins was an Irish immigrant who had worked for the *Upper Canada Gazette* as a compositor before being assigned to report on the House of Assembly debates. Although often accused of favouring the politics of reformers, Collins was not initially an agitator. When the position of printer for the *Upper Canada Gazette* opened up in 1821, however, Collins was overlooked and told that the position would only go to a "gentleman." Offended and still resentful, Collins founded his own newspaper in 1825, the *Canadian Freeman*, "and at once began attacking the administration of Lieutenant Governor Sir Peregrine Maitland and his 'reptile band' of tory advisers."[14] The *Canadian Freeman* added another radical voice to educational discourse by echoing common themes such as increased funding and school expansion. Moreover, Collins continued to decry the familiar clarion call by insisting that a revamped school system was needed in Upper Canada in order to produce homegrown talent.[15] "How could a system of Aristocracy be raised up and supported in this country? Is it under the present Common School system? No; but on the contrary, the march of the human mind must be retrograde – the dark cloud of ignorance must lower over the face of the country, and become so dense, as in a short time to exclude the rays of intelligence and knowledge from the greater part of the Colony." The newspaper called for "an entire revision of our Common School system – by the appointment of General Examinators, who would go forth throughout the Province, and sweep the drones from the hive, by making a *certain* and *suitable* provision for the active and capable labourers who are worthy of their hire – a provision so certain and so suitable, as not only to hold fast the capable persons already engaged in it, but also to induce men of learning and intelligence, to turn their thoughts to that line of life." An educated population, the newspaper insisted, secured civil liberties and guarded against arbitrary power. The good common school system promoted intelligence and "patriotism." The paper also echoed a growing theme when it pushed for funding to attract the most qualified and able instructors. With the right teachers, it believed, the right system could be established.

Whether conservative or reformer, however, virtually all participants in the print media discourse of the mid-1820s agreed upon the need for increased attention to the matter of reshaping Upper Canada's schools. Educational discourse was shifting, in this sense, from a debate on the necessity for government-aided schooling to a debate on its future scope. In a letter to the *Gleaner*, a moderate-conservative newspaper in Niagara published by local librarian and bookseller Andrew Heron, an inhabitant of Niagara criticized the government for failing to expand the system of education adequately. In particular, he addressed the lack of higher education in Upper Canada, noting the negative impact on the entire colony in that there was a failure to produce a professional class of locally born leaders.[16] "It is to be lamented that the leading men of the Province do not endeavor to have a College and an Academy established in some central part, to be provided with Presidents and Tutors sent from home." In Nova Scotia, he claimed, which was by no means "as flourishing a Province as this," there were two colleges. The result was that Nova Scotia was furnished with homegrown leaders able to promote the interests of the province.

Moreover, this inhabitant believed that education and social class were intrinsically linked: "The middle class of people are more anxious to give their children a good education than the first and you will find that the sons of the first men fill situations not at all respectable, in proportion to the situation and rank of their fathers." Without an education, men of the middle and higher ranks would not be able to fulfil their aspirations. Furthermore, education brought peace and order, as was evidenced, he believed, in Nova Scotia: "What a disgrace it is to Upper Canada, a colony inhabited by Christians, that the education of youth should be so little attended to. Gaming, and other practices prevail in a great degree, which is entirely owing in the want of education; and many other disadvantages attend the want of it."

Thus, while reform-minded individuals promoted school expansion for their own reasons, more conservative inhabitants also advocated it for their own reasons. Upon this cause, the two political extremes increasingly found common ground. Evidence suggests that even religious divisions were set aside in order to promote the cause of common schooling. Such was the case for the Catholic and Protestant inhabitants of Drummond Island, who collectively petitioned Maitland in the mid-1820s for a publicly funded school that would promote religious and moral instruction. Though "differing on some points of religious observances," they proclaimed, they were "unanimous" in their wishes to obtain a school for the Catholic and Protestant children who together would be schooled. Having insufficient funds to build a school and hire a qualified teacher, they looked to Maitland to provide the type of instruction that would "inculcate good morals" and relieve the "ignorance in which, from the above stated causes, the young are unavoidably brought up." If such a plea was not enough to get Maitland's attention, they also pointed out that "[s]everal of your Petitioners have been under the necessity, from the causes already stated, to send their children for instruction to Michillimacinack, (where there is an Institution gratuitously supported by the American Government) contrary to their inclinations; and these of your Petitioners are sorry to say they must do so, though aware their children must imbibe feelings and predilections hostile to Great Britain, but they beg to draw your Excellency's attention to the dreadful alternative which is left them, – namely, that their children must continue without moral or religious instruction or they must be placed where they will receive impressions unfavorable to their natural sovereign."[17]

Despite attachment to their religions and to the British heritage, the lure of free schooling across the border was too strong. The Upper Canadian government, they insisted, must act to provide free schools in order to provide the same at home if it wished its children to remain attached to Upper Canada. For their part, the political elite recognized that free schooling was indeed the surest means to educate the bulk of the population. They also were well aware of the impact that the Common School Act of 1816 was continuing to have on the appetite for free schooling among "the people." In the "Report of the General Board for the Superintendence of Education on Common Schools throughout the province," Strachan noted that "even the smallest allowance encourages the people and produces much greater exertions than would have been otherwise made."[18]

The popularity of common schooling transcended the characteristic divides of the early nineteenth century, be they based on religion, politics, class, or national loyalties.[19] Mackenzie himself even allowed a letter from the pro-establishment "Paget" to be printed in the Colonial Advocate. The letter suggested that Upper Canada should never allow "men who have been taught even in childhood to prefer the republican institutions of a foreign power" to teach in the province.[20] While this was a point Mackenzie clearly disagreed with, what he could agree upon with Paget, however, was that school expansion was necessary for the development of the colony. With the poorest inhabitants under "the spiritual guidance of the most ignorant and absurd enthusiasts," the only option, as Paget saw it, was for government to counter the efforts of itinerant teachers by expanding a system of education in which the poor would be sure to be taught by government-regulated teachers under a government-run curriculum. The executive, he was convinced, had been backing down from the expansion of schooling at a time when it was most needed, for ordinary inhabitants as much as for the governing elite. In order to promote "British liberty," government ought to expand education before the itinerate teachers "turn a *Province* into a *State*." Echoing many of his contemporaries, Paget called for greater government intervention in schooling, including the establishment of a university available to every inhabitant. While promoting British liberty, however, he made clear that he was no advocate of exclusivity. Sensitive to the fact that the system of education should not, as in Strachan's national school model, force an English Episcopal clergy upon the people, this inhabitant argued that the diverse population of Upper Canada "would certainly feel justly alarmed and displeased, if the British government were to support the episcopal clergy only." He thus promoted a system of education that would be available to all inhabitants and would "throw open the floodgates to the people."

Mackenzie seconded these remarks in an editorial later that spring.[21] "In a free country it ought to be the object of those in authority to enlighten the great body of the people," he insisted, "and to set a lesson of morality before them, in order that they may be fit for discharging those important duties which devolve upon them as men, as citizens, as office bearers, and as heads of families." While education was widely discussed in Upper Canada, Mackenzie believed that very little was being done to make it truly expansive. Unlike other parts of the world, and especially neighbouring New York, Upper Canada was halting educational legislation. Nothing but legislative will, he believed, was preventing the expansion of education. "To those who may complain of the inability of this province to vote much money in aid of education," Mackenzie suggested, "we could say that money so given is not lost to the province, is not paid to foreigners, but merely passes from one hand to the other, and like a refreshing shower on a dry and parched soil, causes the intellectual power of our youth to grow into maturity and will elevate the moral character of the people, and promote the best interest of the province."[22] Hand-in-glove with his conceptions for reform for the province were his conceptions for popular schooling.

Understanding the importance of the rise of a certain radical political discourse in the 1820s also requires us to understand the discourse concerning the relationship between church and state in Upper Canada. In their efforts to encourage their own conception of the British heritage in Upper Canada, the executive elite held steadfast to a determination to steer the religious and educational advancement of the province. They had made this clear in their promotion of British national schools earlier in the decade, and they maintained the trend in their plans for a university connected to the Church of England. For the executive elite, the Church of England was considered the sole established church of the colony. Such a view had for years perpetuated an acrimonious debate on the role of church and state centred upon a discourse concerning who had a right to the infamous Clergy Reserves, set aside in the late eighteenth century for the religious and educational advancement of the province. Members of the executive elite insisted that the Church of England alone could claim rights to the reserves, while the province's other denominations, together representing the majority of inhabitants, put forward claims of their own to these reserves.

Readers of the *Colonial Advocate* were clear on where the newspaper's editor stood on the question of church and state. "[W]hen we reflect that our population is not like that of Scotland, a body of people nearly unanimous regarding the fundamental points of christianity, and undivided in their manners and customs," the paper expressed, "when we consider that (we except the Catholics in the lower province) the Canadas are peopled by emigrants from many countries, and that they have been accustomed to enjoy many different religious opinions and forms of worship, or have perhaps left their respective countries that they might be enabled here peaceably to worship their maker according to their consciences." When this was reflected upon, Mackenzie argued, the inhabitants of Upper Canada must be compelled to acknowledge that the Imperial Parliament did not consult the "best interest of the people nor of Britain" by endowing the Clergy Reserves to "a militant dominant church."[23]

The Church of England, that is, could hold no claim to the reserves that could be popularly supported.

Mackenzie did not conceal his disdain for the Church of England and took special aim at Strachan, whom he held in high contempt: "We have known ministers connected with other churches, in coming into this province, change their religion and become Episcopal clergymen. Christian charity induces us to believe that their motives were disinterested, but as some of them have grown very bigotted to their adopted faith, their sphere of usefulness is diminished, many attributing the change of principles thus miraculously achieved, to far less honorable motives than either conviction or conversion."[24] Labelling him a bigot and attacking his values, Mackenzie certainly had no personal concern about making an enemy of Strachan. Every sect, Mackenzie believed, including Catholics, deserved to share in the income produced by the land that Strachan and the elite were, according to Mackenzie, hoarding.

The *Colonial Advocate* was a popular newspaper, but, it should be stressed, it was by no means the voice of the masses. Indeed, Mackenzie's brand of reformism was restricted to a small number of inhabitants with specific grievances. Mackenzie's attacks on the Church of England could certainly not sit well with the greater number of inhabitants who knew all too well how long the issue had divided the province. Still, the evidence does suggest that his willingness to speak out publicly against that church was welcomed by a small, and growing, number of inhabitants who opposed the Church of England's perceived dominance in political affairs.

Increasingly, Upper Canadian newspapers of all political leanings, in fact, were blanketed with angry and scathing letters, articles, and editorials aimed at the establishment. A letter in the *Upper Canadian Herald* from a Kingston inhabitant calling himself "Cornelius" warned of political agitation that could be stirred by establishing the supremacy of one church over another in a province as pluralistic as Upper Canada. In addition to this, he thought, declaring one church supreme would go against the trend of modernizing societies: "At this enlightened period of christianity, and in such a Province as this, containing a great majority of dissenters from the English Episcopal church, it would be as impolitic as unjust to attempt to coerce the conscience of the inhabitants by disabilities and privations, or

to establish one denomination of christians over others equally conscientious in their respective modes of worship, and equally entitled,
as good subjects, to the protection of government."[25] This inhabitant
believed that instead of strengthening the government, an established
church would divide the colony and thus lead to the government's
destruction. On the first of February of 1825, moreover, the *Upper
Canada Herald* came out in defence of Methodist rights to hold land
for religious purposes.

Such views from these newspapers should not suggest unanim-
ity among the entire population. Writing to the *Kingston Chronicle*,
"Rupert" defended Strachan and took issue with "Hampden's"
remarks in the *Upper Canada Herald*. Referring to Strachan as "the
little bigot of Little York," Hampden had suggested that Strachan
and his pupils were "parasites and sycophants" who hindered the
development of the province. Rupert argued that such slander should
never have been allowed to be printed, and he issued a challenge
to Strachan's opponents to present evidence "justifying the illiberal
remarks they have passed upon him."[26] Nevertheless, the dominance
of the Church of England was increasingly called into question in
the 1820s. In part, this was the result of the establishment of reformist newspapers. As we have seen, however, such a view found its way
into other newspapers as well. In what ways would Strachan and
the executive elite respond to challenges to their authority? Could a
system of education integrating church and state be built within this
public climate?

Strachan had been successful in influencing and shaping public
policy since his arrival in Upper Canada. He was a well-connected
individual who emerged as a prominent leader in the lieutenant
governor's Executive Council. Indeed, he might have felt an intrin-
sic sense of self-worth in knowing that successive lieutenant governors sought his advice on virtually all matters of public policy.
Furthermore, by the mid-1820s, he had the clear support of a legislative council composed of many of his former pupils. Yet, did such
overwhelming support in this political echelon cause Strachan to
improperly assess his popularity outside of elite government circles?
Or, perhaps, did he feel he did not require support outside of those
circles in order to exert his political influence? Whatever the case, in
the public arena of the 1820s, Strachan began to project a haughty

self-importance that only an unelected official could display without danger of receiving retribution from the electorate.

On 3 July 1825, Strachan delivered a sermon on the death of the late Bishop Mountain of Quebec. The importance of this sermon in Canadian history has been duly noted by successive generations of Canadian historians. Still, a brief review is in order. As his hierarchical authority, it would have been customary, if not a polite gesture, for Strachan to offer some kind words on the bishop. The sermon would have received little, if any, attention when it was printed in 1826 if it had confined itself to a reflection on the life and character of Bishop Mountain. But it did not confine itself, and it did receive considerable public attention. In the sermon, Strachan lashed out at the rising Methodist influence in the religious culture of Upper Canada. He was probably not intending to stir controversy, but he undeniably attacked the character of the Methodist population. "[W]hen it is considered that the religious teachers of the other denominations of Christians, a very few respectable Ministers of the Church of Scotland excepted," Strachan preached, "come almost universally from the Republican States of America, where they gather their knowledge and form their sentiments, it is quite evident, that if the Imperial Government does not immediately step forward with efficient help, the mass of the population will be nurtured and instructed in hostility to the Parent Church, nor will it be long till they imbibe opinions any thing but favourable to the political Institutions of England." The Methodists were spreading false teachings, the type and quality of which could destroy colonial attachment to Britain, Strachan contended, and the only way they could be counteracted would be to increase the number of Church of England ministers through massive state interjection through the means of public funds.[27]

This sharp and bitter attack on Methodists thrust the sermon into the public arena. The Methodists, Strachan argued, were "uneducated itinerate preachers" who took themselves "to preaching the Gospel from idleness, or a zeal without knowledge, by which they are induced without any preparation, to teach what they do not know, and which, from their pride, they disdain to learn."[28] These words propelled the Methodists into a larger debate over their loyalty, which was under attack from Strachan because of their connections with American conferences.[29]

Using the power of the press, a twenty-three-year-old freshly ordained minister, Egerton Ryerson, championed the Methodist response to Strachan's charges in an elaborate series of letters to Strachan that were printed in the *Colonial Advocate* and later in pamphlet form.[30] Rather than putting himself and other Methodists on the defensive, however, Ryerson counterattacked. "I am no republican," he argued, "but, I will take the liberty to observe that the United States, without the assistance of a religious establishment, can produce men, who, for piety, learning, and talents, both in the pulpit, in the closet, and in the senate, make a much more honourable display, than those who seem to despise them."[31] Ryerson claimed that Strachan's problem stemmed from the fact that the Church of England in Canada was too small and that until its pews were filled with people, "the Doctor's mournful cries of Sectarianism! Schism! Republicanism! will be screeching in our ears; and the repose of the 'Imperial Parliament' will continue to be disturbed by the desponding exclamations."[32] He argued that Strachan's aim was to mislead the imperial government in an effort to acquire more money for his own church.

Ryerson was not alone in his battle, and as the debate widened throughout the public arena, voices of discontent proliferated. "A Wesleyan" writing to the *Upper Canada Herald* claimed that loyalty was part and parcel of being a Wesleyan. This individual pointed to the example of John Wesley, George Whitefield, and the fathers of Wesleyan Methodism to denounce Strachan's charges.[33] It was a "calumny," he believed, to suggest that the Methodists were spreading disloyal teachings and that the only way to counteract them was through the fattening of the Church of England. Public opinion, "A Wesleyan" postulated, was turning against Strachan: "Clothed as he is with honorable and reverend titles, and apparently favoured by the Provincial administration, he is doing more to disaffect the people generally towards the Government, with which he is thus identified, than any or all of those, whom he has denounced as hostile to our civil and religious institutions."[34]

Mackenzie, who had granted Ryerson a public forum by printing his letters to Strachan, also printed correspondence from "Castigator." This inhabitant believed that few readers would deny Ryerson praise "for perspicuity – correctness – courteous address, fairness of explanation and quotation, and last of all, of keeping to the point." It was Strachan, Castigator believed, who should be on the defensive: "[I]f the Doctor or his friends could by any defence or explanation do away or neutralize the allegations against him, it should be done forthwith; but it must be done by a statement of facts."[35] Mackenzie himself had admitted that before he had read Ryerson's apology for dissenters, he was prejudiced against the Methodists. "We are so well pleased with it, that we mean to print 500 in a pamphlet form which will be sold at a very low price in order to facilitate their circulation."[36] To be sure, not all inhabitants supported Ryerson's views or the Methodist position in general. "Monitor," for example, was just one of the inhabitants who blasted Ryerson for slinging the Methodists into a debate in Upper Canada that was really between the Church of England and the Church of Scotland. He warned Ryerson not to speak with the authority of *public opinion* and indeed to "beware of it; for if he seeks that of the *intelligent* public, he invites his unequivocal condemnation as an arrogant, pert, and ignorant intruder."[37]

While he might not have been able to speak with the authority of public opinion, Ryerson certainly, and loudly, defended the Methodist position and directed the attention of the public to the "inaccuracies" in Strachan's charges. Ryerson's rebuttal, historian William Westfall contends, "caused a sensation; it was reprinted quickly in pamphlet form and spread like wildfire throughout the colony. The Methodist cause in Upper Canada had gained a new champion."[38] This was plain to see even for the more conservative press of the time.

Within the public arena of the print media, the result of the debate between Strachan and the "Methodist" was detrimental to Strachan. Even the conservative and pro-establishment press could do little to quell public sentiment against the executive elite. The government newspapers, of course, were expected to toe the line, and so they generally published correspondence favourable to Strachan's position.[39] The independent *Kingston Chronicle*, which had virtually always supported the executive and its members, however, could not ignore the public backlash against Strachan's charges. Although "A Church of England Man" wrote on 7 July 1826 suggesting "that in *every country* there should be a religious Establishment" and that, for Upper Canada, the Church of England should be that establishment,

"A Friend to Merit," whose letter was also printed that day, critiqued the "monopoly" of the Church of England in the Legislative Council, which worked to exclude members of other churches, such as the Church of Scotland.[40] Ryerson's letters, as they appeared in the press and as published in pamphlet form in 1828, electrified the debate in Upper Canada over the centralized powers of the executive and the extent to which individuals like Strachan, who seemingly controlled the lieutenant governor, should be allowed by the public to direct the social, political, and cultural direction of the province.

The reform press intensified its attack on Strachan early in 1826 when it was learned that Strachan had replaced John Beverley Robinson on a political mission to England. "Can the society who uphold this clergyman really approve of the active part he takes in politics?" Strachan, Mackenzie argued in the Colonial Advocate, was an opportunist who had now made his church "a mere secondary consideration." He was motivated, Mackenzie insisted, by political power, and especially wealth. Strachan earned £300 as head of education and £350 as a protestant missionary to Upper Canada. Should he abandon these posts by heading a political mission to England, then he should abandon the salary as well.[41]

While Strachan's trip initially raised suspicion, few newspapers, including the Colonial Advocate, concerned themselves with his intentions in making the trip. In 1827, however, Strachan's visit to England became the dominant theme of public discourse in Upper Canada, and thus began a series of events that would eventually lead to discourse concerning the restructuring of Upper Canada's political landscape in which education was a central theme. On 8 September, the U.E. Loyalist printed notice of the safe return of John Strachan from his trip to England. The following week, it was happier to report that "[i]t will be gratifying to the inhabitants of the Province to learn, that the object of Dr. Strachans [sic] visit to England has been most fully accomplished, and that the establishment of a University in Upper Canada, is an event, no longer to be desired, but one which will be carried into immediate execution."[42]

Although the idea of a university had been included in the print media discourse in the years leading up to the 1827 charter, its granting was a somewhat unexpected development. What was the nature of this university charter? What would the university plan look like?

Strachan and the executive elite had once again acted unilaterally in a major educational initiative for the colony, this time in securing the university charter. Yet, once the charter was brought home, it was open to scrutiny. The events surrounding the attainment of the university charter, and the print media discourse surrounding its public scrutiny, are the focus of the next chapter.

6

Ecclesiastical Exclusivity Denounced: Religious Discourse and the Politics of Education, 1826–1828

The bitter public discourse that was cultivated with the release of Strachan's sermon highlighted what some inhabitants regarded as the arrogance and sense of entitlement with which the executive elite governed the colony. Still, radical politics was no alternative for many of them. Radical ideas emerging from the reform press and certain political leaders in the middle years of the 1820s remained controversial, but for the most part, Upper Canadians made sure to express both their loyalty to the British metropolis and their opposition to the new forms of radical thought. John Huston and certain inhabitants of the Newcastle District, for example, printed a letter of support for Lieutenant Governor Maitland in early March 1826. Moreover, the controversy stoked their determination to remain "uninfluenced" by "party prejudice or feeling."[1] The times were changing, Huston and the Newcastle inhabitants wrote about their contemporary political culture, and they "perceived, with feelings of honest indignation, an attempt base, malicious, and unfounded, of rendering the Government of Your Excellency an object hostile to the best interests of the Province."

Huston and inhabitants of the Newcastle District sensed a growing polarization in Upper Canada between those who believed in the supremacy of the executive and those who believed in granting greater power to the popular branch of government. Loyalty to the British metropolis, in other words, did not necessarily equate with loyalty to the colonial administration. With the influx of news from Britain about political reform and changing conceptions of liberty, equality, and the character of the constitution generally, many individuals and groups in Upper Canada began to question why their own leaders were unwilling to open up the same discourse in the province.

Somewhere between radical and conservative thought, between black and white, emerged a grey discourse about the future of politics in Upper Canada. The period after Strachan's return from England in 1827 proved to be a watershed in both the history of politics and the history of schooling in Upper Canada. In England, Strachan had written a pamphlet with the aim of garnering support from the home government for a charter to establish a university in Upper Canada.[2] Included in that pamphlet was an appendix in which Strachan drew up an ecclesiastical chart offering a religious breakdown of the population of Upper Canada. His numbers suggested that members of the Church of England represented the population's religious majority. Strachan was immediately challenged in a public discourse on his numbers once his pamphlet arrived and was read in Upper Canada. Accused of misrepresenting Upper Canadian demographics in an effort to acquire a charter for the province's new university that would ensure its connection to the Church of England, Strachan and the executive elite suddenly found themselves on the defensive, not only against the radicals in the colony, but also against the large "grey" group in the middle of the public discourse. The debate over the proposed university prolonged the animosity begun by Strachan's 1826 sermon, and continued to pit the various religious and political sects in the province against one another. Our understanding of how that animosity affected educational development, however, is limited to histories that consider similar debates of later years. Given the degree to which the debate concerning church and state had become a major part of the print media discourse of the mid-1820s, however, an analysis of the public debate surrounding the university charter can contribute to a greater understanding of the educational developments that led to the debates of later years.

Having been aroused by the debate between Strachan and the Methodists, many inhabitants grew increasingly suspicious of executive conduct and especially of Strachan's and the Church of England's influence in politics. In his pamphlet appealing for a university charter, Strachan insisted that the defective state of education in Upper Canada was not only lamentable, but dangerous. It could not be expected, he stated, that any of the numerous students leaving the province to receive an education in the United States "on their return will give up their hearts and affections to their Parent State with the same cordiality that they would have done had they been carefully nurtured within the British Dominions."[3] Strachan insisted upon an expansion of the school system in Upper Canada capped with a university attached to and controlled by the Church of England. "In what other way," he asked, "can we ever obtain a well-instructed population by which to preserve our excellent constitution and our connexion with the British Empire[?]"[4]

The pamphlet would probably have done little, if anything, to generate concern among the majority of Upper Canadian newspaper readers had it not been for the ecclesiastical chart offered by Strachan regarding the religious breakdown of the province. In this breakdown, Strachan clearly exaggerated the number of inhabitants in Upper Canada who belonged to the Church of England, claiming that a decisive majority of the colony's population were members of the church. Such numbers, of course, helped him gain support among imperial leaders for the idea of a Church of England school establishment in the province. Although the charter, as it was then drawn up, would allow for non–Church of England members to be admitted as students, only members of the church would be professors or members of the college council. Predictably, as historian John Webster Grant argues, the prospect of a state-supported university under Church of England control stirred indignation "which was not lessened by a provision that the rector of York should ex officio be president."[5]

So, in the autumn of 1827, Strachan's university charter became one of the dominant focuses of the print media discourse in Upper Canada. While the *U.E. Loyalist* had declared Strachan's visit to England and acquisition of a university charter a success, the *Colonial Advocate* immediately pounced on Strachan's letter. "It is to be lamented," the newspaper printed, "that the Bishop and the lt. governor did not succeed in the way they wished – but as the money is open for appropriation – we trust parliament will apply for it for the purposes of education, before our 'venerable' friend and his truly loyal associates shall have entirely swallowed it up."[6] The *Colonial*

Advocate concurred with the *Canadian Freeman*'s conclusion that "the home government was deceived by the misrepresentations sent home by men in authority in the Province."[7] The consensus among the two major anti-establishment newspapers was that the established elite were consciously deceiving the home government.

In fact, neither the conservative press nor the moderate press could offer their readers a balanced view. Strachan's charter put both in an awkward position. On 29 September 1827, George Gurnett, the editor of the *Gore Gazette*, a self-proclaimed neutral newspaper (in the 1830s, Gurnett would become a major supporter of the conservatives), also turned his back on the establishment when his paper printed news about the ecclesiastical chart. While compared to the reform press he was kind to Strachan, Gurnett condemned Strachan's statistical inaccuracies. Refusing to pass any harsh judgment on Strachan himself, he did, however, agree to allow inhabitants to voice their own partisan opinions in his newspaper without censorship.[8]

Francis Collins was not so kind. Strachan's ecclesiastical chart was just the sort of thing, the *Canadian Freeman* contended, that it had been reporting for months – that is, that the Imperial Parliament had been receiving false information from a small elite group of untrustworthy leaders in Upper Canada. It was "such information as we have long contended that the home government received, from time to time, from our little *religio-political* divine, and the other advisers of the present administration – namely, a tissue of the grossest falsehoods and misrepresentations that ever appeared in public print."[9] Strachan had provided ample evidence, in the newspaper's opinion, to justify what the paper had impressed upon him and the ruling elite for years, "namely, that he was possessed of more cunning – more illiberality in politics – more bigotry and prejudice in religion – than any other man in Upper Canada." The paper expressed its hope that the Methodists would once again take immediate steps to refute Strachan's claims and to enable those in Upper Canada "to view the author in his true colours."

The *Gleaner*, although a more moderate newspaper, was equally furious with Strachan's conduct. The newspaper insisted that Strachan's ecclesiastical chart could not go unnoticed. "We have never known a document published in any of the Canadas," it claimed, "that has attracted so much attention in both Provinces." Every other denomination in the province, the newspaper argued, had to pay its clergy and build churches without the aid of government, and the newspaper expressed that it was simply fed up with the special privilege that the Church of England was receiving. Any rational person, the newspaper asserted, would find absurd Strachan's assertions that the greater part of the province would be induced to become Episcopalian. The *Gleaner* claimed that Strachan wanted to mislead the Imperial Parliament on the progress and size of the Church of England in order to subvert the other denominations. "Should the Doctor really be honest and intend (contrary to the opinion of many) to promulgate only truth," the *Gleaner* offered, "he can have complete information from every quarter; we shall therefore say little on that subject."[10]

Dissatisfaction with the executive elite was escalating. The press increasingly printed correspondence from readers in opposition Strachan, including a letter from "Philo Veritae," who opposed Strachan's actions and begged for honesty among political leaders.[11] On 25 September 1827, the *Upper Canada Herald* printed a letter from "A Member of Mr. Foote's Church" refuting the ecclesiastical chart, and on 21 September 1827, the *Gore Gazette* printed one from "A Friend to Truth," who also demanded honesty: "When the Hon. and Rev. Doctor has again occasion to draw up a Chart of a similar description, I would seriously recommend to him inquiry into the state of that Church; for, let me say, when he is reduced to the necessity of exhibiting such a statement, in order to establish the empire of Episcopacy in Upper Canada, I envy him not the glory of success."[12]

On 18 October 1827, "A Presbyterian" wrote to suggest that public discourse was galvanized by this issue. Strachan, the author believed, had made himself a public enemy. "I dare say he *little imagined* they [Strachan's statistics] would come to light in this country, where the truth is better known – but so the event has turned out, and, in the end, will do his party more harm, in the eyes of honest and good men, than all he has done besides will advantage it." The Presbyterian writer accused Strachan of lying to the Imperial Parliament so that it would favour his cause over that of his opponents: "But his dark plans have failed."[13]

"A Scot" expressed his own amazement at Strachan's actions. "O, Doctor, Doctor," he asked, "when will your misrepresentations cease?"[14] "Vindex" suggested that Strachan's charter confirmed the suspicious behaviour of the establishment and proved that Strachan had visited London "with no friendly feelings towards christians in this province, not connected with the church of England." Vindex concluded that Strachan must be held accountable and explain to the public whether he was "either *grossly ignorant* of the state of religion in this province, or that he has *willfully* misrepresented it. He is at liberty to take his choice."[15] Indeed, it was clear to most observers that Strachan had wilfully lied and ought to come clean and provide the truth. "Peter Poundtext" of Bytown wrote to the *Upper Canada Herald* attacking Strachan's ecclesiastical chart, and directing his words directly at Strachan, he exclaimed that he was "anxious that in the next edition of your observations these errors may be corrected, in order that your veracity may be cleansed from the fond aspersions, with which it is at present best measured, by divers of the heterodox."[16]

Certain inhabitants also petitioned the lieutenant governor directly for redress. Inhabitants of the Midland District believed the charter would "appear to the public at large, to [be] illiberal and unjust, and not less impolitic." While feeling a sense of gratification at the idea of higher branches of learning taking root, they could not support the idea of a university that was not adapted to the "state of the country, and meet the wishes and wants of its mixed population." They petitioned, therefore, for "a constitutional objection to the Charter of the University. It is not only degrading to a large majority of the people of the Province, but it also lays a restriction upon the free exercise of the prerogative of the Crown."[17]

Indeed, discord and discontent was widespread after the release of Strachan's pamphlet containing his ecclesiastical chart, affecting every strata of society. "A Farmer in the Home District" claimed that Strachan's true character and true motives had been "unveiled." A mounting number of inhabitants, he believed, thought Strachan had gained too much influence in civil governance and that such influence ought to be limited.[18] "A Baptist" was appalled and proposed that all denominations unite in petitioning the king that all religions be put on an equal level in the province, including equality in funding on the basis of their numbers. "This will be fair play," he believed, "and it will confirm the affections of his majesty's Canadian subjects to the British throne – whereas a contrary system will naturally tend to alienation."[19] By the end of 1827, public discontent was so widespread that one observer from the *Quebec Gazette* in Lower Canada concluded that Strachan's appeal for a university charter "has produced more newspaper discussion in both Provinces, than any other document which has ever been made public in Canada."[20]

To make matters worse for Strachan, he could not find comfort in old friends. Even the pro-establishment and ultra-sympathetic *Kingston Chronicle* could do nothing to sway public opinion on this matter. Although it did not place the blame directly on Strachan, it did suggest that all parties were to blame for the negative political climate and that both sides, including Strachan, were in the wrong.[21] Such a concession of guilt was a major departure from previous propaganda emerging from the pro-executive newspapers. The *Colonial Advocate*, reprinting the editorial, suggested that it was "[a] manly stand taken by the Kingston Chronicle."[22] Such a stand by the pro-establishment press led Mackenzie's paper to suggest that Strachan's ecclesiastical chart would "do a great deal of good in the end – its unfairness, its privacy, its want of truth and manly candour, are acknowledged by all – we learn that even the archdeacon himself blushes and is ashamed and sorry for his misconduct – so much so that in his Loyalist he is perfectly silent and allows judgment to go against him by default." The executive elite and their supporters, Mackenzie believed, could scarcely espouse propaganda that could "warp" the public mind.[23]

Mackenzie was right to draw attention to the backlash that the ecclesiastical chart had caused, but Strachan was hardly blushing and certainly did not proceed in shame. Despite a public discourse suggesting that moving forward on the university issue would not be a welcome step, the colonial administrators were intent on doing so anyway. Were they asking for retribution? Probably not, but to many Upper Canadians, it might have seemed so. While the ecclesiastical chart's inaccuracies stirred the emotions of certain inhabitants of the colony, its consequence, a university charter that gave exclusive powers of management to the Church of England, turned discontent into sheer resistance. Knowing that the charter had been granted on the basis of inaccurate demographic evidence provided to the Imperial Parliament by Strachan, an aroused public raised objections to the legitimacy of a university established under such conditions.

Both the *Colonial Advocate* and the *Canadian Freeman* were quick in condemning the proposed university. Mackenzie pointed to seven principles in the university charter that he believed should concern the people of Upper Canada: that the lieutenant governors were to be perpetual chancellors; that the archdeacons of York were to be perpetual presidents; that the professors must take sign of the thirty-nine articles;[24] that the lieutenant governor was to have the sole appointment of professors; that Strachan, Maitland, and seven professors from the Church of England were to form the college council; that the council would have sole and entire control of the university, with the scholars and graduates having no voice; and that divinity students must "swallow" all the test oaths of the Church of England creed. Should "the people," Mackenzie argued, "submit quietly and without a murmur to be priest-ridden in this fashion, if they will peaceably admit another tool of Doctor Strachan, they deserve to have the dungeons of the inquisition set up among them, priests familiars racks [*sic*] and all for the next half century." Mackenzie further emphasized that Strachan's "misrepresentations" were a glaring piece of evidence that pointed out the need for direct representation of Upper Canada in the Imperial Parliament.[25]

The *Canadian Freeman* also quickly condemned the proposed university and its utility. The values of the university, the newspaper read, were not to be based upon those of Upper Canadians generally, but "upon Dr. Strachan's own principles." The paper anticipated, when it "heard the Doctor had any thing to do with it," that the university would be "a superstructure of prejudice, erected on a base of bigotry and intolerance – and if the graduates from it be turned loose upon society, with the same character and principles that have hitherto distinguished a majority of Dr. Strachan's pupils, it will, as we before remarked, prove a curse, instead of a blessing to the country."[26]

The *Gleaner* was equally furious with Strachan's design for higher education. The newspaper insisted that the university charter acquired by Strachan in England should not go unnoticed. That the university should be established, the paper believed, was a desirable objective, "but, that an Institution of this nature should be under the exclusive controul of any one religious denomination in this Colony is in our opinion highly objectionable; particularly as our population is composed of a great variety of religious sects who so long as they conduct themselves worthy of the character of British subjects, should be equally entitled to share all privileges and enjoy all the rights which are in the [*illegible*] of the Government Trust."[27] The newspaper saw "no reasonable answer" to the question of religious exclusivity. In a direct shot at the executive elite, the paper insisted that the guiding principles of the university appeared "to be grounded in those principles of narrow minded popery which have characterized too much the proceedings of several individuals interested in administering the more important duties of our provincial Legislature."

The tone of discontent among many inhabitants crossed the line of simple criticism and entered into the realm of shear anger. "Every Body" wrote to the *Colonial Advocate* to suggest that "Strachanism," as this individual called it, was "a bane and curse" to the future development of the province. In addition to calling Strachan a bigot, this inhabitant, believing to speak for the vast majority, argued that the "inevitable consequence" of executive control over education would be "inextinguishable discord and opposition."[28] The political climate of Upper Canada was changing, he stated, and the general public would never agree to the principles of the university charter. "A friend to civil and religious rights" agreed and urged inhabitants to petition the king, who "is the most liberal of any generation," for reform. Attuned to changes in the character of politics across the Atlantic, this inhabitant blasted Strachan for deceiving the "liberal" imperial government.[29]

According to an inhabitant from Brockville, "every friend to good government & the prosperity of Canada" must lament "The Doctor's College."[30] The "exclusive disposition" that had lately been evidenced by "the high Church," he believed, had manifested itself into a university charter that had produced the most "degrading" discourse in the press that Upper Canada had perhaps ever witnessed. The editor of the *Gleaner* agreed: "Doctor Strachan's famous Chart and his Episcopalian College has attracted the public so much that a good part of a number of papers, in both *Provinces* have been filled up with strictures thereon, several of which we intend to lay before our readers from time to time which will save us much trouble in writing out our own ideas on the interesting matter contained in that famous Chart." Although Mackenzie and the *Colonial Advocate* proclaimed "PERSECUTION" and urged the "People of Upper Canada" to "rouse yourselves!,"[31] the editor of the *Gleaner* believed there was no need to persuade public opinion against the proposed university charter; it was clear, the newspaper stated, that the public backlash was heavy-handed enough.[32]

The executive elite could hardly ignore the public anger. How could they, after all, when every newspaper in the colony was printing, almost daily, something concerning the ecclesiastical chart or the proposed university charter? Beginning in the late fall of 1827, then, the executive elite increasingly used the government press to counterattack the backlash blanketing the other newspapers. When the conservative *Kingston Chronicle* printed a letter blasting what it saw as the arrogance of the ruling executive, the *U.E. Loyalist* responded by printing a communication from "A Hater of Hypocrites" that blasted the *Kingston Chronicle* itself for perpetuating the "prejudice which ignorance and Malice are endeavouring to excite against the University which, through the patriotic zeal, and perseverance of Dr. Strachan, has been established in this favored Province." "A Hater of Hypocrites" accused the *Kingston Chronicle* of betraying British feelings and not showing "a love of British Laws and Government." The university, he argued, was an establishment calculated to disseminate principles of loyalty and attachment to the king and constitution. He regretted that such principles were being endeavoured to be destroyed and called upon "calm" inhabitants to support the university.[33]

Despite the clear objections to the university charter, on 22 December 1827, the *Upper Canada Gazette*, the official government newspaper, printed a notice from the Government House, dated 17 December 1827, proclaiming the foundation of King's College. This notice marked a new beginning for a long, bitter, and acrimonious political debate concerning the future of the colony, the nature of church and state in Upper Canada, and the rights of ordinary inhabitants to influence government legislation through the elected branch. The executive elite were moving forward with their plans despite the apparent opposition in the public arena. The governing elite furthermore announced that the council of the college would be composed mainly of establishment men, including Maitland, Strachan, and other members of the Executive Council. Only one House of Assembly member, John Beverly Robinson, a well-known member of the lieutenant governor's inner circle, was appointed to the college council.[34]

When upon the opening of the legislature in January 1828 Lieutenant Governor Maitland announced the founding of King's College, a clear divide between the Legislative Council and House of Assembly was quickly made evident. While the Legislative Council thanked the lieutenant governor for the endowment, the House of Assembly's response on 21 January echoed public sentiment and warned that the university must be open to all inhabitants and made free of religious influence if it were to be accepted by the representative branch of government.[35] Almost immediately after the opening of the legislature, the House of Assembly began entertaining numerous petitions from inhabitants in all parts of the province inquiring into the principles upon which the university charter was granted.[36] On 15 February 1828, Marshall Spring Bidwell, who in the 1830s would become a major reform leader, moved for an address to the king in which the House of Assembly would formally inquire into the principles of the university charter. That session also saw the formation of a select committee, headed by Bidwell, that was authorized to inquire into the drafting of the King's College Charter. Strachan himself was called down from the Legislative Council to appear before and answer questions from the committee.

For its part, the Legislative Council called Strachan to the floor of its chambers on 6 March 1828 and gave him the opportunity to speak and defend the numbers he had claimed about the religious breakdown of the province. On 19 April 1828, the U.E. Loyalist gave Strachan a broader public platform by printing his speech of that day; later, it was also printed as a pamphlet.[37] Strachan expressed gratitude for being called to speak before the Legislative Council, as it gave him the chance to clear his "good name." He insisted that he had been harshly criticized and "exposed to much calumny and misrepresentations." Strachan also admitted that he had lost a good deal of popular support and that his damaged name needed to be restored.[38] However, he neither backed down from his assertions concerning the religious character of the province nor apologized to those offended. "We have been attacked on all sides, our exertions concealed, our success undervalued, and our actions misrepresented. – We have been charged with intolerance, selfishness, and bigotry; and we have refrained from vindicating ourselves, and preserved a silence, which some many have construed into an admission that the character and claims of our Church are indefensible."[39] Speaking as a victim rather than as a perpetrator of wrongdoing, Strachan proposed an open public inquiry into the religious character of the province. In such an inquiry, he claimed, the Church of England in Upper Canada would be vindicated.[40]

Strachan also attacked the press itself for what he deemed "slander and persecution."[41] While he admitted that he had made some errors in his famous ecclesiastical chart, especially with reference to other denominations, he nevertheless suggested that his critics "have no just reason to complain, as they have never, to my knowledge, given any authentic account of themselves, and I gave the best within my reach."[42] He regretted the public accusations of bigotry and insisted that he had always treated every denomination with the utmost respect. The unfortunate conduct of the press, he believed, had resulted in public chaos. "The torch of discord has been kindled through the whole Province, and its tranquility disturbed."[43]

On the subject of the university charter, Strachan said little, but he insisted that the university would be an open one and that "young men of every Christian denomination" were free to attend and receive the advantages of higher education. He did, however, insist that the university should not be secular. Foreshadowing his departure from political life, perhaps, Strachan spoke boldly of his accomplishments as a public figure:

I have been assiduously engaged as opportunities offered, in contributing to the formation of a system of Education for this Colony, which though still new in operation, contains the seeds of great perfection. The outline, by the Establishment of the University is now complete, but a strict superintendence will for many years be absolutely necessary. If therefore, I should not appear so often in my place, as my respect for the House would induce,

I hope my absence will meet with a kind interpretation: not that I wish to be absent when my presence is deemed necessary, or, when the interests of Religion and Education are concerned. – But in other matters I confess that I feel less interest and may be well spared, as many of my Hon. Friends are far more competent than I, to discuss and decide upon questions of policy, and the general business of the Country.[44]

Strachan's defence seems to have done little to affect public sentiment. "The march of mind will progress in spite of the most high-handed Tories & bigotted Churchmen," the *Gleaner* told its readers after reviewing Strachan's speech.[45] The winds of reform, the paper believed, were too strong and Strachan was simply not situated well enough to deal with the widespread concerns for change. "His Honor and Reverence advocates there the necessity of the connection of Church and State, as strong as was done in the Reign of our Elizabeth. The Doctor ought to take into consideration, that a great change has taken place in the minds of all the civilized world since that period – and that it is necessary (it will soon be absolutely necessary) that the laws and regulations of every country should be made to correspond with the liberal sentiments of the present enlightened age." Strachan ought to catch up to the changes sweeping the Atlantic world, the newspaper stated: "The fact is undeniable – that the population of England are becoming more dissatisfied with the despotic mandates of the Established Church; and Dissenters from that Church are becoming more and more numerous every day."

One group of reformers believed that they were left with little to do but appeal directly to the Imperial Parliament for redress. In the spring of 1828, the "Petition of Christians of all Denominations Against Doctor Strachan's University Charter, Church Monopoly, &c. &c." was drawn up and printed in virtually every newspaper throughout the colony. The petition secured roughly eight thousand signatures,[46] and it took direct aim at Strachan and the executive generally. The petitioners warned that an exclusive university would produce "alarm and jealousy" throughout the province, which would limit the benefits that might otherwise be derived from it. They proposed instead a university "adapted to the character and circumstances of the people" and which "would be the means of inestimable benefits to this province. But to be of real service, the principles upon which it is established must be in union with the general sentiments of the people."[47] Public opinion had proven, these petitioners believed, that the charter, as it stood, did not express the general will. Because they could not effect change within the balance of powers in the colony, they thought that it was up to the Imperial Parliament to rectify the injustices of an exclusive charter. The Imperial Parliament responded in petitioners' favour and immediately took up an inquiry into the ecclesiastical chart and the proposed university.

In 1828, fuel was added to the public fire with the rehashing of events surrounding the dismissal of Thomas Appleton from the York Common School in 1820.[48] Throughout the 1820s, Appleton had continued to maintain that he had been unjustly relieved of his duties as common school teacher by the elite of Church of England, who were determined to bring a church-state system of schooling to Upper Canada through the national schools. Initially, Appleton received little attention from House of Assembly members, but after years of lobbying on his part, the house finally took up the matter in 1828 and appointed a committee to report on the case.[49] The report concluded that Appleton had been fired "without any reason" and "as a matter of regret." More striking to the House of Assembly was evidence it found concerning the establishment of the "national" school. Appleton placed considerable blame for the affair on Strachan, who, he claimed, had applied to the trustees of the common school at York on behalf of the lieutenant governor to obtain the schoolhouse for the use of Spragg, the national school teacher who had been sent from Britain. Strachan did this, Appleton claimed, "without consulting your Petitioner, or obtaining his consent to remove from the Common School House." The committee found that while the York trustees supported Appleton, Strachan and Maitland went ahead with their plans anyway. When the trustees applied to the board of education to rectify the situation, they received no answer.

The committee brought forth various witnesses, including parents and trustees, to testify on the events surrounding the establishment of the national school. John Fenton testified "that it is the practice, from all he has seen and heard, that the District Board of Education gives the money to whom it pleases, and withholds it from others, as they think fit and proper." William P. Patrick, a trustee, saw no reason for Appleton being fired. David Morrison said that he did not know the cause of Appleton's dismissal, but he blamed Strachan for making an application in the name of the lieutenant governor "without his knowledge."[50] The committee of inquiry was important in that it revealed to the House of Assembly, and to Upper Canadians at large, the arbitrary and unilateral actions of the executive elite.

The House of Assembly found that the "'National School' it appears has been supported out of the revenues of the Province without the knowledge and consent of Parliament and your Committee regret, that it would have been further supported to the injury of other Common Schools, which, notwithstanding the injustice they have received, have, from their usefulness and merit, met with public support." Not only did the House of Assembly find the national school a matter of perplexing anxiety, but it also insisted that such a school represented the antithesis of the type of schooling that inhabitants of York, and Upper Canada generally, wanted. The money used to appropriate a teacher from England and then to establish and operate the national school could have been better spent, they argued, had it been used for the support of numerous common schools throughout the province. Above all, the House of Assembly found the character of the school to be most dissatisfying. "The 'National School' is founded upon the Reverend Dr. Bell's system, and is professedly adherent to the Church of England – and, therefore, ought not to be supported by the revenues of a country struggling against ecclesiastical exclusion."[51]

With the release of the committee's findings, the Appleton firing became another highly publicized event creating further debate about the conduct of Strachan and the colonial administration in recent years and the future of church and state in Upper Canada. In addition to raising religious questions, the Appleton case raised to the surface concerns about the right of the executive elite to deal with the question of education unilaterally and independently of the House of Assembly. Members of the house entertained Appleton's complaint on the grounds that the executive had overstepped the Common School Act of 1816, which did not give it unilateral decision-making powers. Moreover, another objectionable feature presented itself in this case, one against which the House of Assembly had, on more than one occasion, strongly protested; and that was the appropriation of the revenues of the province by the executive without the knowledge and consent of the House of Assembly.[52]

The House of Assembly condemned the district board of education, then under the direction of the executive, and the heavy influence that Strachan had over that board. The Appleton case provoked a strong hostile feeling between the House of Assembly and the Executive Council, one that became all the more intense as the events surrounding the granting of the university charter became known. Historian and former assistant superintendant of education for Canada West J. George Hodgins argues that the Appleton case "began a strife for supremacy between these two chief powers in the State, which was only ended, after years of conflict, in the passage of the Clergy Reserves Act of 1854, which abolished all semblance of connection between Church and State, and recognized the claims of each Church in Upper Canada to equal protection and the acknowledgment of an equal status, and of equal rights."[53]

The *Colonial Advocate* immediately made the Appleton case findings available to its readers.[54] Although the newspaper had advocated the expansion of schooling, it warned that the school system, controlled by a select elite, could potentially "become a powerful engine in the hands of a party or a faction, and be perverted to the worst and most dangerous purposes, to the destruction of civil and religious liberty, to the support of bigotry, superstition, and arbitrary power."[55] Some factions, it warned, "are too deeply impressed with a sense of its mighty power, as an engine of party," and desire to draw the system "entirely into their own hands, and to wield and exert it for their own purposes." The Appleton case, the *Colonial Advocate* argued, was an awakening to the dangerous consequences of centralized power in the executive. By 14 August 1828, the *Colonial Advocate* made the report and the evidence in the Appleton petition front-page news. It placed the blame for Appleton's firing squarely on Strachan's shoulders. The investigation into the common schools in the early 1820s had revealed inconsistencies for which the newspaper believed Strachan alone needed to answer: "[I]t appears that in 1822, only 19 schools received £10 each, and the same number in 1820. Will the Venerable

Doctor, or the Board, or the editor of the Loyalist, be pleased to favour the public with some history of the odd £30 a year, granted by the public, of which no account appears? Did the Doctor, or the board, squander that sum away in salaries to themselves or friends while Messrs. Stewart, Appleton, and others were unjustly deprived of their incomes?" Relentlessly, the *Colonial Advocate* continued its attack on Strachan's character: "While the teacher of the central school, an institution scarcely known even in this country, feasts on luxuries afforded by an income out of the public purse, amounting to nearly $2,000 a year, Mr. Appleton, Mr. Stewart, and other respectable and useful schoolmasters are denied the statuary pittance in aid of their school fees. Verily Doctor Strachan's patronage hath been something beyond an empty boast of late years. – But the day of reckoning may come."[56] The day of reckoning indeed seemed near, as Strachan's educational, political, and social influences were rapidly called into question in a heated public discourse.

The public discourse concerning Strachan's ecclesiastical chart and university charter, along with concerns about Appleton's firing, brought with it renewed calls for school reform. School expansion generally continued to be a central theme in both the legislature and the press in the late 1820s, and fuelled by the discourse concerning hegemony of power in higher education, inhabitants increasingly favoured making the school system more equitable at all levels. William Morris's resolutions in the House of Assembly in early 1827 epitomized this idea. Morris resolved, for example, that in a thinly inhabited country such as Upper Canada, "where the means of moral instruction to the poor are not easily obtained, it is the bounden duty of the Parliament to afford every assistance within its power, toward the support of education." He found the present provisions for the support of district and common schools to be inadequate to meeting "the wants of the people" and thought that the House of Assembly should respond by extending education.[57] The editor of the pro-executive *U.E. Loyalist*, however, did not agree: "The Parliament has liberally afforded 'every assistance within its power to that desirable object,' and we regret that they should consider it necessary to censure themselves (tenacious as they are when censured by others) on such a subject. In every *District* a Public School is established, and respectably supported, and an allowance made for as many *Township* Schools, as Township may be able to support."

The *Gore Gazette*, however, concurred with the message of school reformers. It believed that no subject "is more important for the legislature of the country than that of Public Education."[58] "Public intelligence," the *Gore Gazette* stated, was essential to the permanent existence of a liberal form of government and constituted the surest safeguard against the arbitrary means of power, on the one hand, and the "cajolery of the prejudiced or designing political adventure," on the other. The newspaper asserted that "[t]he Provincial Legislature, with truly laudable *intentions*, have made appropriations upon several different occasions, for the encouragement of Education within this Province; and yet, we take it to be an irrefragable fact, that there is no country in which the English language is spoken, wherein the system of Public Education is *less* efficient. We speak particularly of the Common Schools of the country, with the condition of which we have had some opportunities of making ourselves acquainted." The newspaper called for more "public attention" to schooling, which it regarded as necessary in order that the system be truly reformed.

A letter from "X. Y. Z." on 24 March 1828 indicates that some inhabitants believed "public attention" toward common schooling was in fact very widespread. "The necessity of a good education, as well as the advantages resulting from it, are so obvious, and so generally acknowledged," this inhabitant believed, "that nothing need be said on that part of the subject." X. Y. Z. argued instead that good teachers were needed and that they could only be obtained with strong support and higher wages, making the position more professional. Until "suitable encouragement is held out, and the proper compensation made, such men will never fill our schools in general." He concluded: "Such the teachers, such will be the scholars."[59] He also blamed parents for only "occasionally" sending their children to school and insisted that regular attendance was required for a successful system. Good teachers, plus proper attendance, could make the schools, he believed, meaningful social institutions. The editor of the *Gore Gazette* agreed. The newspaper begged for amendments to the existing laws on education. The editor of the *Farmers' Journal and Welland Canal Intelligencer*, a moderate newspaper intended primarily to serve agricultural and canal workers in the Niagara region, shared these sentiments, adding that education ought to be encouraged among young women as well as among young men.[60]

The pro-executive *Brockville Recorder* also believed in the need for school expansion, as did many of its readers. "Hibernicus" complained that the tuition fees in the schools served to make the schools institutions for wealthier inhabitants, to the detriment of the poor. He insisted that a fairer system be put in place, one in which extra tuition would not be charged and one in which all classes could be proud to have their children participate.[61] While not all inhabitants believed the system of schooling in Upper Canada needed to be overhauled, it was clear to most that certain changes, in both politics and education, needed to be made.

In 1828, a group of inhabitants supported these calls for change by preparing a petition for the king asking for political reform. Maitland's administration had resulted in the "practical irresponsibility of executive counsellors, and other official advisers of your Majesty's Representative, who have hitherto with impunity both disregarded the laws of the land, and despised the opinions of the public."[62] The idea of change was also reflected in the election results of 1828, which produced an even stronger majority of representatives committed to reform.

By the end of 1828, change had become a central theme in public discourse. In no small way had the controversy surrounding the ecclesiastical chart, the proposed university charter, and the Appleton case affected public sentiment. The shape and form of education in Upper Canada had aroused passions and raised voices, and the growth of the press and the increased availability of print media had allowed many more inhabitants to become a part of the political discourse surrounding the future of educational development in the province.

With a new political atmosphere came new questions. The editor of the *Gore Gazette* thought it "abundantly obvious" that "nearly the whole of the newly elected members are persons avowedly hostile to the Government." But he did not see any danger in this, as "the natural inference from this fact is, that the majority of the people entertain similar sentiments."[63] Indeed, the *Gore Gazette*'s editor believed reforms "have long been obviously necessary."[64] What's more, the evidence from the print media suggests that Upper Canadians were not merely waiting for change to arrive from the British metropolis, but rather they were actively demanding it. They were writing letters, drawing petitions, and calling for change. Still, any change in Upper Canadian politics was understood to be within the context of the colony being an extension of British cultural and social frameworks. In this regard, Upper Canadians expressed their faith in the British metropolis. "The high character of the present ministry of Great Britain forbids me to doubt even for one moment," Mackenzie himself wrote, "but that if General Maitland and his friends were removed, a government composed of men of business habits, and philanthropic patriotic characters would succeed."[65]

Change was called for, and change, it seemed, would be granted by the imperial government. In the fall of 1828, Lieutenant Governor Maitland was replaced by John Colborne. Was this move a reflection of the "high character of the present ministry of Great Britain," or was it an admission that Upper Canada could not be ruled from the metropolis? In some respects, it was the latter. Colborne was no foreigner sent from overseas. He was familiar to Upper Canadians, and this might have been a factor in the imperial government's selection process. He had served as a general in the War of 1812, and both the anti- and pro-establishment presses expressed their faith in him. Upper Canadians could thus believe that Colborne would adopt liberal and conciliatory policies in line with the interests of the Upper Canadian population generally, even at the expense of the colonial administration. These were the liberal and conciliatory policies that American settlers prior to 1815 had advocated and also the type that post-1815 migrants from the British Isles had become accustomed to in a changing nineteenth-century British culture.

Upper Canadians were at the same time informed of an imperial inquiry into the affairs of Upper Canada and specifically into the complaints of the arbitrary power of the executive. The winds of reform were sweeping Upper Canadian political life. To what extent would a change in the political scene affect the development of schooling in Upper Canada? To what extent would public discourse continue to influence those developments?

7

Renewal or Regression? Educational Discourse in a Time of Political Discord, 1828–1830

"Glorious News!" exclaimed the *Colonial Advocate* on 25 September 1828. Word that Maitland had been replaced with Colborne suggested to the newspaper "that the exalted and liberal views of the great statesmen who first offered the blessing of a free constitution upon these provinces, are not as yet forgotten at home, however our official characters here may be inclined to trample them under foot."[1] What would follow, the newspaper believed, was that Strachan's "school of intolerance" would be remodelled and established upon principles representative of broader public views in the colony.

Upper Canadian historiography has identified the replacement of Maitland with Colborne in 1828 as an important turning point in the political history of the province. With a new lieutenant governor, a number of inhabitants hoped "that Upper Canadians could now embark on the road to prosperity, united in their allegiance to the king and in their commitment to the development of a progressive North American community."[2] With the fury over Strachan's chart somewhat quelled and with a respite from denominational bitterness, Upper Canada's development is seen to have taken a turn in 1828.[3] This point of departure, Jane Errington argues, was not the hallmark of what some contemporaries believed would be an era of "good feeling," but rather "it really marked only the end of the beginning of serious political controversy in Upper Canada."[4]

To what extent did this point of departure in the province's political development reflect a point of departure in Upper Canada's educational development? Historian J.D. Purdy suggests that from

1828 until the Rebellion of 1837, reformers maintained a constant assault upon Strachan's educational design and were successful in preventing him from fully establishing his school system.[5] Still, little is known about the educational ideas of reformers in this period. The historiography is thin regarding reform views on education until 1836, when Charles Duncombe's *Report upon the Subject of Education* was published. This report has characteristically been linked to the grander ideas of radical reform in the province that led to the Rebellion of 1837 and the subsequent structural overhaul of Upper and Lower Canada, which set in motion the educational developments of the 1840s and beyond.[6] Seen in this light, Duncombe's report is considered the new point of departure in the educational development of Upper Canada. By tapping into the print media of the time, we can begin to re-examine this era and come to a clearer understanding of the educational ideas of reformers, and others, that led up to and shaped the 1836 report.

An analysis of the print media to 1828 has suggested that reformers and conservatives shared a good number of views on the subject of education, including the idea of popular schooling. Did the province's new political point of departure in 1828, then, alter the congruency of these ideas? With the rise of the reform movement and the increased involvement of anti-establishment men in official colonial politics, did conservatives become hostile to the educational aspirations of their adversaries? What can we learn about the new dynamics in the political culture of Upper Canada and their relationship to the educational discourse found in the print media? This chapter will consider these questions in an effort to link the print media discourse of the late 1820s and early 1830s to the educational developments of Upper Canada in subsequent years.

The report of the Imperial Parliament's Select Committee on the Affairs of Upper Canada was made available in Upper Canada in the fall of 1828.[7] It concluded, as the reform press had been suggesting for several years, that the disputes in Upper Canada between the Executive Council and the House of Assembly reflected the turmoil felt generally by the people of the province.[8] It especially pinpointed the events surrounding the creation of the university charter as catalysts for discord. It conceded that the charter, which "might have been drawn up hastily, and perhaps ill-advised," should be remodelled. In a province where only a minority adhered to the dictates of the Church of England, the committee reported, "a suspicion and jealousy of religious interference would necessarily be created" with an ecclesiastical exclusive charter. The committee thus recommended rewriting the university charter. It furthermore suggested that two permanent theological professorships be established, one of the Church of England and one of the Church of Scotland, but that the president, other professors, and all others connected with the college, should have no religious requirement. Nevertheless, the report stipulated that professors should agree that when religion was taught, the "Christian faith" ought to guide the lessons.

The immediate reaction to the imperial report and to the anticipated political changes in Upper Canada – from the reform and conservative presses and the broader public – was optimistic. Both the radical *Colonial Advocate* and pro-establishment *Kingston Chronicle* believed that the imperial report was "evidently drawn up with every wish to meet the wishes and conciliate the prejudices of the people generally."[9] Gerald Craig suggests that the report "was interpreted as a great blow to the oligarchy in each province, and as an 'extraordinary document' that promised much hope for the future."[10] The reaction from some inhabitants seems to support this analysis. "Cincinnatus" wrote to the *Canadian Freeman* expressing his hope that with a new attitude taken by the Imperial Parliament, a new house of assembly, and a new lieutenant governor, it was only a matter of time before a new executive council would be formed as well. "Sir John [Colborne] I trust, will ponder well on these things upon his arrival amongst us, before he involves himself with a council which might better be exchanged for another free from Clerical influence, and sympathizing more with the feelings of the people over whom he is appointed to preside."[11] An inhabitant from Brockville also held faith that Colborne would "adopt the most liberal and conciliating line of policy to the country over which he is destined to preside – instructions, which we are informed, fully comport with his Excellency's own feelings and principles."[12] Even the pro-establishment *Kingston Chronicle* remarked, "We hope the reign of theory and declamation is near its close."[13]

Among reformers, there was certainly reason to believe that reforms in Britain would soon be transplanted to Upper Canada.

By the late 1820s, the British government was well enmeshed in a debate concerning the social, political, and economic future of the country. When the Tory government of Arthur Wellesley, traditionally opposed to reform, proposed the Catholic Relief Act, repealing laws that prevented Catholics from becoming members of Parliament, the gates were open to further parliamentary reform.[14] With anti-reformers now conceding to changes, it had become clear both to politicians and to the public in general that change was imminent.[15] News from George Ryerson, Egerton's brother and an agent in London for certain petitioners to the Imperial Parliament, suggested that such changes would spread to Upper Canada. In a letter addressed to Dr Morrison, the secretary of the reformist York Central Committee, that was reprinted in the *Colonial Advocate*, George Ryerson suggested that the British government wanted to promote the "true interests" of the colony as suggested in its public discourse.[16] He found "Liberal" and "conciliatory" feelings in the British House of Commons. Reforms were sweeping Britain, Ryerson optimistically observed, and so there was reason to believe that these reforms would permeate Upper Canada as well. Having been born in British North America to Loyalist parents who emigrated from the United States, George Ryerson had never been to the British metropolis. His early impression of British politics would have come from only the handful of colonial administrators who presided over Upper Canada and were aligned with Strachan and the conservative elite. Once in Britain, however, he found a political culture "above the mercenary selfishness, the illiberal and contracted views and crooked ways that we have been too much accustomed to see in some other countries. There is every thing in the Parliament and Government of Great Britain, that should inspire in us respect and confidence." The *Kingston Chronicle* agreed: "[L]et it [the Upper Canadian legislature] meet the beneficent views of the British Government towards this country but half way," the newspaper read, "and it will deserve the gratitude of the present and the admiration of succeeding generations."[17]

The initial optimism surrounding Colborne's arrival was marked with great hopes for a new era of educational development in Upper Canada. Public discourse surrounding the common schools had revealed that the schools were in a lamentable condition.

Colborne's arrival seemed to suggest that the system of education in Upper Canada was going to receive the needed overhaul that had been advocated in the public arena throughout the 1820s. Indeed, in Colborne's first speech from the throne in 1829, he announced major changes. "The Public Schools [by which he meant the district schools] are generally increasing," he noted, "but their present organ- ization appears susceptible of improvement." He promised meas- ures to reform the York District School, which he would rename the Royal Grammar School and incorporate with the recently endowed university. In this sense, it would serve as a preparatory college along the lines of the grammar schools of England. Reflecting opin- ions formed in the public arena in the late 1820s concerning the teaching profession, Colborne also expressed his determination that "[u]nceasing exertion should be made to attract able Masters to this Country, where the population bears no proportion to the number of Offices and employments, that must necessarily be held by men of education and acquirements, for the support of the Laws, and of your free Institutions."[18]

The tone in which each respective house responded to Colborne's speech was significant. The House of Assembly was excited to "dir- ect our anxious attention to the state of the Public Schools, and con- sider what improvements, in the present imperfect and unsatisfactory system, are best calculated to open to the youth of this Province the means of receiving a liberal and extensive course of instruction." The House of Assembly was happy that the lieutenant governor con- curred in the view that the present state of education was in need of repair. The Legislative Council, however, was not so sure that the present state of education, which it had largely been the architect of, was lamentable. Nevertheless, and "[n]otwithstanding that Your Excellency considers the organization of the Public Schools suscept- ible of improvement," it too agreed to give the issue of education serious attention in that session.[19] It is perhaps also an interesting commentary on the dichotomy of the legislature, as well as a sign of the times, that the members of the House of Assembly addressed themselves as the "Canadian people," while the legislative council preferred to use the term "Canadian subjects."

Colborne's first speech, then, reflected the optimism, as evidenced in the print media, that the matter of education would finally be dealt with in accordance with general public sentiments. It also renewed educational discourse throughout the province concerning the common schools. For too long, it seems, educational discourse had been confined to a debate concerning Strachan and the elite's university plans. Colborne's grand vision for schooling in the province offered an opportunity to revisit the unsettled common school debates of previous decades.

The *Gore Gazette* of 17 January 1829 printed an elaborate article on education that reflected the renewal of discourse. Certainly, the newspaper remarked, "the common schools of the country – upon which a vast majority of the rising generation are solely dependant for their education – we know to be miserably defective." The reasons for such a defective system, it argued, were numerous: unqualified and underpaid teachers, incompetent trustees superintending the schools, and an overall ill-advised foundational structure. Nevertheless, the problems with the system, the paper stated, could be remedied.[20] The *Gore Gazette* suggested that the quality of common school teachers was the primary cause of schooling's maladies. In Upper Canada, where the value of labour was high, the newspaper asserted, it was difficult to attract respectable teachers, as the remuneration provided in the schools did not meet that provided in manual-labour occupations.

To remedy the situation, the newspaper presented three solutions. The first was "a direct tax upon the people, the proceeds of which should be applied to a school fund, and to no other purpose." Neighbouring New York had a successful tax, the newspaper remarked, so why not Upper Canada? The second solution entailed "the organization of a *competent* Board of Education in each District." And third was that "in lieu of the present common school trustees, superintendents should be appointed – say two for each township – whose duty it should be, to visit the schools in their respective townships, say once a month, to examine the teachers and the scholars, and to report thereon to the Board of Education, which board should be empowered, on the certificate of the superintendents, to pay the teachers' salaries, and to remove such as are unfit to discharge their duties."[21] With these recommendations, the newspaper offered the framework for a centralized, government-inspected, universal system of education. With Colborne in power, the newspaper believed, the time had come to consider enlarging and expanding the system.

For others, school expansion and centralization raised some concerns. The *Gleaner* questioned the province's ability to pay for teachers, but suggested that whatever money was put into education, it ought to go to "those township schoolmasters who both more need and deserve it" and not be consumed by "salaries" to a board of education.[22] Pointing out that Strachan was receiving a wasteful salary as head of the board of education, the newspaper suggested that inhabitants should be weary of the cost of centralization. Upon the issue of funding, however, the *Gleaner* generally agreed with views put forward in the *Gore Gazette*. It firmly insisted that there was a clear "advantage of a public over a private education."[23] The plan as it stood, allowing for a certain sum for each district, was no longer conducive to the educational needs of Upper Canadian inhabitants. Some districts, with numerous schools, had to spread the money out thinly, while the less populated districts could afford to better equip the schools. The newspaper called upon parents to contribute funds through some form of taxation. "Much is said in every Parliament, respecting the education of our youth," the *Gleaner* continued, but "[a]ll that can be done will be of no avail unless parents are more interested in the education of their offspring."

The members of the House of Assembly responded to the growing public sentiment in favour of "publicly" funded schools. Early in 1829, Mackenzie, who was one of the new members of this reform-dominated house, immediately brought up the topic of schooling. Within days of the opening of the legislature, he gave notice of a move for a standing committee on education. A host of others took up the cause alongside Mackenzie, and the House of Assembly made clear its intention to take into consideration the state of education in the province.[24]

Among the educational issues occupying the attention of the House of Assembly was that of money, and especially the interminable debate concerning the proceeds of the Clergy Reserves. The majority of the House of Assembly agreed that such funds should be put toward the advancement of education in the province. After presenting the lieutenant governor with such an idea, Colborne advised the house members that he concurred.[25] The Select Committee on

Education of the House of Assembly in 1829 continued its inquiries into education in the province throughout the session. Along with petitions from various inhabitants, such as those in support of the incorporation of the Grantham Academy in Niagara and public funding for its teachers, the committee requested documents and reports from across the province so that its review might be as extensive as possible.

Not to be outdone by the House of Assembly in its meticulous review of education, the Executive Council undertook its own review of education, which culminated in John Strachan's 1829 *Report from the President of the General Board of Education of Upper Canada*.[26] Strachan visited district and common schools throughout the province, examining both teaching and management in the schools. In several of the schools he found the attendance "thin and discouraging," but he also noted that in many parts of the province "the business of instruction was well conducted and the system [was] such as to merit his approbation." Strachan admitted that he could not provide concrete numbers on attendance, as many families sent their children to schools in rotation. He estimated that between 40,000 and 50,000 should be going to the schools, but that public money only provided for 10,000. As a result, Strachan admitted that increased funding, as many inhabitants had been demanding, was necessary. This was especially the case in the more populated districts, where "the salaries allowed to the Schoolmasters of the Common Schools are exceedingly small." The "natural consequence," he wrote, was a decrease in the quality of instruction. The system was well constructed, he concluded; all that was needed was greater financial support. Moreover, as both a matter of charity and duty, government had "obligations" to provide this support.

Despite agreement among the upper and lower branches of government that the schools required an infusion of support, the two continued to have difficulty working out legislation together. Two months after the opening of what many considered a promising session for educational matters, Colborne prorogued what was becoming an unworkable house. With neither the House of Assembly nor the Legislative Council compromising in order to make the legislature work, Colborne expressed regret that the session would close without deliberations on "two subjects of primary importance –

improvement of Public Schools, and the measures that should be adopted to ensure good Roads and safe Bridges throughout the Province."[27] Still, while issues of schooling and regional infrastructure would be delayed because of what seemed to be increasingly irreparable party politics, the public discourse concerning the revamping of the school system had cemented itself as a central political discourse.

The establishment of a new government paved the way for a new era in the social, economic, and political life of the province, but the optimism that marked Colborne's appointment quickly dwindled as it became apparent to some reformers that the new lieutenant governor was not as enthusiastic about overhauling constitutional politics in Upper Canada as they had first supposed. Owed to this viewpoint was the fact that Colborne clearly positioned himself within the established elite who had been dominating the superstructure of politics in Upper Canada for years. Moreover, the Executive Council itself was not altered when he took office; the members remained the same as those who had served under the "expelled" Maitland.

The shift from hope to fear after Colborne became lieutenant governor was made apparent in the decision to establish Upper Canada College in 1829. While Upper Canadians could support the establishment of an institution of higher learning, the college as it was designed was intended to provide a classical curriculum in line with the elitist preparatory schools of England, such as Eton. In many ways, the establishment of Upper Canada College represented both Colborne's desire to further the interests of education in the province and his refusal to break ranks with the conservative establishment.

The college did not receive popular support. The House of Assembly expressed its suspicion of Colborne's intentions in its response to the throne speech of January 1830.[28] While the house was glad to see the lieutenant governor's involvement in and enthusiasm for education, and while it did not question the need for such an institution in Upper Canada, it did express concern that before Colborne begin his educational undertakings he address the concerns raised by the House of Assembly in the previous session – namely, the expansion of common schooling and the religious questions surrounding the university charter. Above and beyond all else, the house wanted to ensure that educational institutions in Upper Canada be founded upon "equal rights and liberal principles," and this meant, especially, that Upper Canada must abolish its exclusive and elitist model of schooling and implement a system of schooling "for the general extension of the means of education among the people in every Township."

Certain inhabitants picked up on the legislative debate over Upper Canada College and expressed their own views about the need for a preparatory college in Upper Canada. Of particular importance to a number of inhabitants was the curriculum. "A Father" wrote to the *Brockville Gazette* suggesting that "[i]n this transit age to reform," inhabitants of Upper Canada should question the classical system of education offered by the college. Education, he thought, ought instead to reflect the "intellectual and political change" of the times.[29] The *Canadian Freeman* added that while grateful to Colborne for his promotion of higher education, it felt he was "badly advised" by an elite few who were out of touch with the particular needs of most Upper Canadians. The newspaper believed it "right, under such circumstances, that the wishes of the people should be met."[30] "One of the People" certainly agreed. Supporting the editor's views, he suggested that the York District School be re-established for those parents wishing a more practical education for their children, "so as to make a School far more efficient than Upper Canada College, and prevent us from being any longer cursed with Masters who are under no responsibility – who substitute beating for teaching – and who being paid whether they have Scholars or not, laugh at us in the sleeves, and say the fewer Scholars the better."[31] This individual asked Colborne if he thought "that the inhabitants of the District are blind to the grievances they are suffering through your miserable cowardice." He urged the lieutenant governor to relieve their grievances and represent the interests of the majority rather than work to appease his own advisors, who had themselves lost popular support. Indeed, the establishment of an elite preparatory college in Upper Canada might have seemed peculiar to a good number of inhabitants at a time when they were increasingly advocating for an expansive system of free common schools to replace the old elitist model. Why should Upper Canada have an elaborate system of grammar schools, they were asking, when the majority of inhabitants could get no use from it? Why should it establish a college on the model of England's Eton when there was no Cambridge or Oxford in Upper Canada to which students could graduate?[32]

Ultimately, Colborne's new plans could not prevent reformers from using the power of print media to continue to affect public discourse on the subject of schooling in the colony. In the autumn of 1829, Mackenzie made that clear when he put education at the forefront of public discourse in his newspaper. On 17 September 1829, he devoted an extensive section of the *Colonial Advocate* to the subject, pointing to the progress of education in both the United States and Germany. The *Colonial Advocate* reprinted statistics from the *New York Observer* showing that there was, "on an average, one student in college for every 2,000 inhabitants." In the middle states, there was one for every 4,000, and in the states south and west of Pennsylvania, one for every 6,000. Information reprinted from the *Boston Courier* showed that in Germany "the lower orders of the German population are among the most favored in the world. It is said that the system employed throughout Austria for spreading instruction among the lower orders is attended with great success." In each village, the paper told its readers, there were schools in which, unlike Upper Canada, the masters were paid in full by the government.[33]

The *Advocate's* readers, responding to Mackenzie's provocative numbers, expressed great hope for possibilities in Upper Canadian schooling should they follow the American model. On 1 October 1829, "Tyro" praised the development of education as reported in the United States. "Some of the American papers literally overflow with notices of the approaching sessions of Schools, Colleges, Universities, Academies, and other literary institutions throughout the Union," he noted.[34] Speaking in particular of one affordable college in Ohio, Tyro implored other Upper Canadians to "compare this cheap and valuable institution on the banks of the Ohio, to which any farmer or mechanic may easily send a son without inconvenience to his means of living, with the gorgeous and costly education of an English University, unapproachable by the youth of Great Britain, unless the favoured few who riot in islets of wealth and grandeur in the midst of an ocean of national misery." The American offered a model for education in Upper Canada, but such a model,

Tyro declared, could not be implemented in Upper Canada so long as Strachan remained at the helm of education. Colborne, he thought, "may allow himself to be flattered by executive councillors, judges, and senators," but these were men "in whom this country has ceased to have confidence." Too many inhabitants were, and would remain, he believed, opposed to Strachan and what he stood for. "[P]ublic opinion on this continent has declared itself opposed to clerical bigotry and courtly extravagance, and a *parental* government would best prove its character by taking heed to the signs of the times, for they are such as those who run may read." It was time, Tyro wrote, to bring Upper Canadian political culture in line with the times. Should this be done, a proper school system could be forged.

The newly established and conservative newspaper in Kingston, the *Patriot and Farmer's Monitor*, agreed with its reform counterparts and also argued that it was time to revamp Upper Canada's school system to reflect developments around the world. The newspaper suggested, in its first issue, that the province needed a system of "national education in which the poor will be equal participators with the rich."[35] The editor of the *Patriot*, Thomas Dalton, a brewer, banker, and supporter of reform politics, promised to promote the expansion of education in his newspaper. The importance given to education by the popular press was reflected in his opening editorial. Addressing himself "To the Canadian Public," Dalton suggested that "[e]ducation is a matter of such high importance, such deep and intense interest to a free people that no pains or expense shall be spared to enrich these columns with every kind of information that can give light to the subject."[36] In the United States, he stated, educational discourse had been all-engrossing and, as a result, a universal system of education was created in which "the better instructed of the working classes" could meet in organized assemblies, to propound, discuss, and resolve issues of the day. Education enabled the lower ranks to participate in the political process. Such a system, he believed, ought to be fostered in Upper Canada. "A grand system of national education, in which the poor will be equal participators with the rich, is professed to be the object, and sanguinely expected to be the fruit, of this universal agitation." It was his duty, as he saw it, to lay before his readers any piece of writing promoting this objective.

Writing to the *Colonial Advocate*, "A Canadian Farmer" applauded the editor of the conservative *Patriot* for promoting common schooling. "Had it not been for the blessings of Education and the advantages derived from Common Schools," he wrote, "in how miserable a state would this continent have been at the present day!"[37] Education, however, was not useful unless it was spread to all inhabitants. Education was dangerous, in fact, "where it is in possession of a few, while [the] community is deprived of its choicest blessings. Such is the case at this day in some of the British Colonies." Education, as established by Strachan, he sarcastically pointed out, was carried out "on a plan so very liberal that nine-tenths of the people will derive no advantage from it." It was time, he thus thought, to spread schooling to the masses.

This newspaper reader clearly did not have faith in the establishment, but neither had he any faith in the members of the House of Assembly. The house, he cautioned his readers, should not be counted upon to promote measures reflective of public sentiment. The House of Assembly, he believed, was composed of self-interested men, and "their war losses, and their peace losses, weigh heavier than their patriotism or love of country." Were education more widely diffused throughout the province, however, "more faithful stewards & sentinels would be found, and more active and intelligent watchmen and aide-camps would be at hand to cheer them in the good work." In a direct public cry for reform, "A Canadian Farmer" asked his "dear fellow countrymen, is it not high time that something should be done in this province, in order that our offspring may be capable of vindicating their rights, maintaining their civil and religious privileges, and holding civil offices of trust, instead of being passive like wax in the hands of Doctor Strachan and other ambitious men of education from other countries, and whose wishers are not, as I and my neighbours think, after the good of society, but merely that a few may be taught to inherit the labours and industry of the youth of the colony as if we were so many slaves living in the West Indies." It was time for Upper Canadians to take control of education, he exhorted, in order for them to take control of their destiny: "Parents, I address myself to you." Popular schooling, he was convinced, would rescue Upper Canada from its elitist confinement.

"A Friend to Education" supported the idea of extending education to all inhabitants and insisted that education, industry, and religious studies must be united in a system promoting the needs of the
colony, within the colony. Even the best education attained abroad
would not benefit the youth of the province "[i]f they must return
and spend their days in searching or preaching in the new settlements of Canada."[38] Upper Canada, he believed, was in need of a
practical, well-funded system of education adapted to the particular
needs of the province. "A Friend to Union" concurred. He suggested
that the "mechanics and the labouring class in Kingston unite in a
school, on the plan adopted in Quebec, Montreal, and many other
places" so that inhabitants might receive the benefit of education at
a moderate cost.[39]

"Balaam's Ass" added to the discourse concerning a homegrown
system when he lamented the absence of colleges in Upper Canada.
He was convinced that too many Upper Canadian students still travelled to the United States for an education and that nothing was
being done to reverse the trend. Balaam's Ass, moreover, did not
believe that schooling should be reserved for a privileged few. In
remarks that were "intended as much for the government, as for
the public," he called Strachan and the established elite "[m]iserable
drivellers!" in their endeavours for school reform. "Little can they
appreciate the spirit of freemen, when they tell us we *shall* have neither colleges nor schools, but which they approve of; and that our
ministers and elders *shall* continue to wear the badge of inferior-
ity, notwithstanding every effort of our houses of assembly on their
behalf."[40] While he could agree with men like Strachan on the necessity for a distinctly Upper Canadian system of schooling, he did not
share in the elitist conception of schooling. Schools were needed, he
firmly believed, for the masses.

"A Trustee of a District School" wrote to the *Kingston Chronicle*
in the fall of 1829 to add his thoughts to the public discourse. Believing that the general population favoured popular school expansion,
"A Trustee" insisted that he "shall waste no time in expatiating upon
the advantages of Education, or upon the necessity of some public provision for rendering those advantages generally accessible;
because from the one there is no dissentient voice, and the other
seems to be sufficiently recognized in the present direction of the

public anxiety to the subject."[41] The time was ripe, he wrote, to advance schooling, as "public men" were "more alive" than ever to the consideration of education. It only remained that improvements "keep steadily in view the benefit of all classes of the community." Education, he believed, ought to be made free and universal. The current system saw far too many of the lower classes using an over-burdened common school system, while the more wealthy could afford to send their children to private schools. He furthermore identified low teachers' salaries in the common schools as the primary cause for the inadequacy of common schools, and argued that better teachers were needed in order for better schools to be created. In sum, more money was needed, and it was only through an injection of public funds that this money could be made available to the schools.

Indeed, in the late 1820s the Office of the Civil Secretary was inundated with petitions for such funding. Robert Addison of Niagara wrote: "To crowd seventy children (the number belonging to our School) into a small room, is neither healthy nor convenient." Money, ultimately, was the problem, and he thus petitioned for increased funding for teachers so that the lower classes could also reap the benefits of an education provided by the best teachers: "If respectable Men are expected to preside over these Institutions, their Salaries ought to be doubled."[42] William Casgrave kept an old debate alive and petitioned for the repeal of the District School Act, suggesting that that money be divided among the common schools instead. He asked that, at the very least, common school teachers' salaries be restored to pre-1820 levels.[43] Other petitions included familiar requests for money to build schools[44] but also for the public funding of privately run schools.[45]

"A Trustee," moreover, reiterated concerns raised by the more conservative elements in the province about sending children abroad for education. He argued that more district schools were needed so that everyone, including mechanics and farmers, could afford to send their children to school without the expense of boarding them.[46] He did not, however, see a "national" danger in sending children to the United States. For him, building more district schools in Upper Canada was a matter of extending equality, not identity. "If we are to remain a British colony, and God forbid that we should," he stated, then surely sending children to the United States would not encourage the British identity. More importantly, Upper Canada ought to establish its own identity, and this would require a solid school system in which to foster a local identity. "It is probably the habit of *all* young countries," he wrote, "to make their national and political topics a more common and popular theme than is want to be the case in older governments." The United States was successful in this, and he did not blame them for it. "They are right to train up *their* youth sedulously in the principles of their own peculiar polity." It was up to the inhabitants of Upper Canada to now stake their own claim to national education. He thus advocated an elaborate system of education, with common and district schools made free and universal and capped with a university. Universities were important, he believed, because they "contribute to the glory, the safety, the happiness of a nation."[47] The universities, he contended, promoted national unity and paved the way for an independent identity.

Certainly, then, there was a renewal of discourse concerning the building of a school system in Upper Canada. The established elite, for their part, would not remain silent on the issue. In a pamphlet on the management of the district schools, Strachan admitted that the schools had been inadequate in accomplishing what they had set out to do, especially in providing an adequate quality of instruction.[48] Strachan lay out five principles upon which the schools should be revamped, principles that echoed the public discourse of both conservatives and reformers in the late 1820s. First, the system should be uniform throughout the province. Second, the schools should be preparatory for the university. Third, better teachers were needed. Fourth, trustees needed to be better instructed in the inspection of schools. Fifth, the district schools should qualify students to "finish their education at an English University."[49] Strachan also provided, in a pamphlet, a new curricular framework that heavily emphasized the classics and had only two hours of mathematics per week. Nevertheless, he also stressed the need for the schools to qualify students for the different professions in Upper Canada.[50] Strachan was no doubt determined to maintain a modicum of elitism in his model of schooling, but we can see that he was influenced by the public discourse that called for widespread regulations and better teachers. "The management of every well regulated School," he concluded, "resolves itself into two great departments of Government and Instruction."[51]

The extent to which Strachan could maintain an elitist hold on the school system, however, was, by the end of the 1820s, seriously called into question. The renewal of the discourse on the subject of common schooling allowed space for new participants to present their ideas. One of these participants was Strachan's religious rival, Egerton Ryerson, who in 1829 became the first editor of the Methodist newspaper the *Christian Guardian*. With this newspaper, Ryerson, who had proved a successful writer and powerful voice in the public forum, quickly usurped Mackenzie as the most outspoken critic of the establishment in Upper Canadian print culture. In an editorial on civil authority and education, Ryerson argued that Upper Canada was at the inauguration of its national existence and thus needed to abandon old conceptions of religious division: "The present is a most eventful period to the religious and civil interests of this interesting and important portion of the British Empire. The nature of our depending relations – the principles of our foreign intercourse – the complexion of our internal regulations – and the aspect of our literary and religious institutions, are about taking the hue of a permanent character."[52] According to Ryerson, the foundation of civil governance in Upper Canada should be the principles of Christian morality. This was a non-sectarian Christian morality, however, from which Ryerson believed every member of society was protected equally. It was the duty of government to provide a good and just form of governance, and in turn it would receive "obedience to the properly constituted authorities."

Governance and education went hand in hand, Ryerson insisted, and education must be considered as being of the highest importance to the comforts of life, the suppression of evil, "and the stability of Good Government."[53] In this light, it was essential that education be available to "the poor as well as the rich," and Ryerson was convinced that the present government must remain committed to educational expansion. Making education available to all classes also meant freeing it from sectarian divisions, he believed. Ryerson was certain that a common, non-sectarian system of education would abolish religious indifference. The Clergy Reserves should be sold, "and a fund formed from their proceeds to support a general system of education free from all religious tests and disabilities; that Colleges, open to all denominations, may be endowed on the same principles."[54] Should the government adopt such a policy, Ryerson was sure, "it would bring blessings incalculable to the cottage of every poor man in the community – it would banish religious feuds and animosities, and in their place excite a praise worthy and holy emulation between Christians of different opinions."

As Upper Canada entered the 1830s, a new era in its political and cultural existence was dawning. Reformers and conservatives were divided, but in the print media, they both supported the idea of school expansion and the need to extend education to the masses. For many Upper Canadian inhabitants, the educational ideas of Strachan and the establishment came to represent a past from which the colony was breaking. The ideas surrounding a fully funded school system were emerging as subjects of a congruent discourse in the print media. That money might be contributed by all inhabitants and set aside for the purpose of education was an idea increasingly promoted by conservatives and reformers alike. Although the two groups were divided politically on the question of education, the public discourse in Upper Canada suggested that government should take a more active role and that education should be made universally accessible to every child.

In this sense, the divide between reformers and conservatives in the political arena was not reflected in the print media discourse on educational development in the province. Still, reformers and conservatives were finding it difficult to work together in the legislature, and thus drawing up new and effective educational legislation reflecting the ideas found in the print media posed a real challenge. As Upper Canada entered the 1830s, could this imbalance be rectified?

8

Toward Mass Universal Schooling: Societal Reorganization in the Age of Movable Type, 1830–1832

By the 1830s, Upper Canada's political culture had been transformed, even if its political system had not. On issues of public policy, the province was more divided in opinion than it had ever been. Yet, despite the divisions, considerable optimism about Upper Canada's future was still expressed daily in the popular press. Much of this optimism stemmed from the widespread discourse concerning the social institutions, including universally accessible schools, that provided a unifying force in the colony. Nevertheless, Upper Canada's political scene was unstable. A divided legislature, a radical faction in the House of Assembly, and certain elected representatives seemingly bent upon opposing the Legislative and Executive Councils, on principle, challenged the authority of a ruling elite who for decades had been untouchable.

John Colborne tried to stabilize the political climate when he dissolved the legislature and called for new elections in 1830. The election results indicated that the electorate was not in favour of radical change, as that year the voters reversed the trend toward radicalism by sending more conservatives to the House of Assembly than they had done in either of the previous two elections. Yet, as the discourse on schooling in the press made clear, conservatives in Upper Canada had to adopt a more moderate and reconciliatory tone, as well as demonstrate that they were indeed open to the ideas of reformers. Educational discourse suggested that conservatives and reformers could find common ground on a number of ideological principles that would otherwise pit them against each other.

The 1830s ultimately came to represent a decade of turbulent political discord between reformers and conservatives, one that was only stabilized after the threat of widespread revolution ceased in 1839. But the trends were clear earlier than that. Upper Canada had been moving in the direction of political reform by at least the late 1820s. As Upper Canada entered the 1830s, it was evident that the divide in politics was very deep, and thanks to the print media, the bruises were very much exposed. The evidence we have seen from the print media also suggests, however, that the divide in the political arena was not necessarily reflective of a divide in popular opinion concerning schooling. On the issue of popular schooling, in fact, the ideas of conservatives and reformers of all stripes generally converged. This is especially true among the most moderate of the two groups.

This chapter will consider some of the major ideas about popular schooling that were being promoted in the public arena in the early 1830s by leading conservatives and reformers. One key document on education in this period is William Lyon Mackenzie's 1830 pamphlet *Catechism of Education*. This pamphlet sheds a considerable amount of light on the ideas of certain reformers, leading up to Duncombe's 1836 report on education. Considering the extent to which Mackenzie was a central figure in the societal reorganization of the Canadas in the 1830s, this document, and the light it sheds on the educational ideas of reformers, should be examined closely.

This chapter will also examine the educational writings of Egerton Ryerson as put forth in the editorials of the *Christian Guardian* in the early 1830s. Ryerson is the most central figure in the development of the school system in the mid-nineteenth century, and thus his early writings on education broaden our understanding of the roots of a universal school system in Upper Canada.[1] How were these ideas received by both leading conservatives and the general public? Were they, in fact, new ideas or simply the culmination of four decades of discourse concerning the making of popular schooling in Upper Canada? To what extent did the ideas of educational reformers like Mackenzie and Ryerson converge?

On 24 December 1829, Mackenzie began to publish in the *Colonial Advocate* extracts of writings on education entitled *Catechism of Education.* The complete volume of these writings was published in pamphlet form in 1830.[2] This pamphlet is a watershed document in the history of education in Upper Canada. In it, Mackenzie published the first detailed model of education based upon reformist ideas. The pamphlet itself reflected the late-1820s public discourse concerning the expansion of schooling, the need for free schooling, and the idea that schooling itself could be instrumental in creating an equal society. Mackenzie, among others of course, had already been espousing such notions in the press from his newspaper's first issue in 1824. With the *Catechism*, however, Mackenzie attempted not only to express his ideas for schooling but also, more generally, to link these fundamental principles to bigger political ideas concerning the foundations of a new society.

The *Catechism* itself was based on Joseph Hume's "Essay on Education," which had earlier appeared in Britain.[3] The *Catechism* opened with a very abstract and vague philosophical discourse concerning the nature of education. Quoting heavily from Adam Smith, John Locke, William Paley, and John Stuart Mill, it reeked of the ideas of Enlightenment thinkers that had permeated British culture since the seventeenth century. Borrowing ideas from these thinkers, the "individual," Mackenzie expressed, was to be made an instrument of happiness through education.[4] Mackenzie also emphasized the connection between a highly educated populace and the success of the nation.[5] For him, efforts in education were efforts in nation building. In a system of education for the colony, Mackenzie found the potential to shape a new generation with the values and morals conducive to consolidating a national character for Upper Canada.

Mackenzie's pamphlet did not remain vague and philosophical, but in fact laid out some concrete applications for the transformation of schooling in Upper Canada. Mackenzie's paramount idea was that schooling should be free and universal. Although he conceded that only a certain "class of society" would "have wealth and time for the acquisition of the highest measure of intelligence," he advocated the extension of schooling to apprentices, mechanics, labourers, and others who were not able, through their own means, to acquire an education.[6] This would mean rethinking the very foundation of the school system as it stood. Fashioning Upper Canada's schools after "old and opulent establishments for Education in Europe" was "far less useful" than following the more accessible American model and would serve only to instil subordination to whoever held political power.[7] Borrowing from the discussion on "national free schools" that was taking place in the United States Congress, Mackenzie argued that the expansion of free schooling in Upper Canada would see representative power extended.[8] "Until lately," he wrote, "it was denied, that *intelligence* was a desirable quality in the great body of the people."[9] But make no mistake, he insisted, it was desirable: "[I]f Education be to communicate the art of happiness; and if Intelligence consist of knowledge and sagacity; the question whether the people should be Educated, is the same with the question whether they should be happy or miserable."[10]

Mackenzie thus called for "a judicious system of *National Free Schools*" in which both government and "the people" would be served. The "beneficial effects" attending such a system, he insisted, were incalculable: "Additional stability would be given to free institutions; the sum of public and private happiness would be greatly increased; the power of the people extended; crime diminished; an inviolable respect for the laws maintained; and a constitutional vigilance more increasingly exercised, against all encroachments upon national or individual rights."[11] The consequences of keeping an elite model of education in the hands of the establishment, Mackenzie thought, would be too devastating for the population unable to afford schooling: "They are trained generally to habits of servility and toleration of arbitrary power, in as far as precept and example can influence their minds."[12] If education were expanded, however, and greater numbers allowed to "obtain those keys of useful knowledge, the faculties of reading and writing," then "they are prevented from becoming instruments of evil, and enabled to form a just and correct estimate of their own situation, and of the conduct and character of the government under which they live."[13] Education, he believed, was the best means by which to counter the arbitrary power of executive rulers in Upper Canada. In this sense, Mackenzie's pamphlet stressed schooling's potential to liberate those ruled from the constraints of Upper Canada's social-class structure.

Mackenzie's pamphlet was well received in the public arena. "W.C." believed that the infrastructure for schooling was indeed the root from which all other social infrastructure could be developed. "We may go on improving in canals and roads; form bible societies and Sunday schools; our clergy may increase yearly," he noted, "but unless we have a firm basis laid of intelligence, morality, and virtue, we build but upon a sandy foundation."[14] The expansion of government-aided schooling, he believed, should be made the priority in order that the foundations might be laid for a stable and progressive social and economic structure.

The editor of the moderate-conservative *Gleaner* believed that Mackenzie's *Catechism* was one of the best articulations of the province's educational needs in recent years. Although a long time critic of Mackenzie and his political views, the *Gleaner* hoped that the pamphlet be met with a "favourable reception" among the political elite, but feared that it would not. Although optimistic about the direction of government-aided schooling, the newspaper was still pessimistic about the press's ability to effect change in the present political climate.[15]

A "Gentleman in the Eastern District" responded to Mackenzie's *Catechism* in a letter entitled "The Importance of Education to the Farmers and Mechanics of Upper Canada" and printed in the *Colonial Advocate* on 9 August 1832. The "Gentleman" was happy that Mackenzie was against making "a monopoly of knowledge," and outlined the benefits of Mackenzie's ideas, especially those concerning the education of the poor. He concurred that education in Upper Canada could be improved through certain measures, including the regulation of the teaching profession through annual examinations of teachers and compulsory education. He expressed his faith that education could uplift inhabitants from ignorance and poverty, which he saw as two sides of the same coin, and, by extension, from oppression. He called upon government to act quickly in developing a more favourable school bill. He believed that the inhabitants of Upper Canada were waiting for such a system. "Some are (very unjustly) censuring the illiterate for not having an appetite for education," he wrote, "but how can such have a relish for a thing they never tasted[?]" Education, he insisted, "is a successful weapon in the hands of others"; it was time for education to move beyond the realm of the elite into an expanded system of schooling for a broader population.[16]

Mackenzie was not, of course, the only voice of reform in Upper Canada. What's more, he was not the only reformer in possession of a printing press with which to spread educational ideas. Egerton Ryerson, editor of the Methodist *Christian Guardian*, believed that no topic was more important for the executive government to address than that of education. From its onset, the *Christian Guardian* was used as a vehicle to express the educational ideas of Methodists in general but its editor in particular. And Ryerson was never one to mince words. As he saw it, education was an especially important topic of public interest in Upper Canada because the colony's existing system was ideologically driven by intolerance and elitism. "Those literary and ecclesiastical fabrics that were reared in the days of superstition and selfishness, still bear the unseemly marks of their bigoted origin."[17] Maintaining such a hierarchical system of education in Upper Canada, he thought, placed the colony at the stub of the world. "If the *foundation* be not based upon the 'chief corner stone' of public *expedience* and *utility*," Ryerson insisted, "expenditure lavished upon the superstructure is worse than *useless*, if not *criminal*, prodigality. We go not to the infancy of modern kingdoms to learn the wisest maxims of state policy – we go not to the infant ages of modern literature to become acquainted with the sciences – nor should we go to literary institutions established in ages of bigotry and exclusion, for exemplars of those that may be established in this Province." In a word, Ryerson called for a complete overhaul of schooling in Upper Canada.

Upper Canada's system of schooling, Ryerson advanced, needed to be remade to reflect the province's unique circumstance as a new colony in a new political age. The existing system was not favourable to the peculiar economic and social conditions of the province. Upper Canada, although a colony within the British Empire, was on the verge of laying the foundations of a new society: "What may suit one age and one country, may not suit another age and another country. What may be adapted to the circumstances of the parent, may not be adapted to the circumstances of the child. What may be very suitable to an older and more wealthy branch of a family, may be very unsuitable to a younger and poorer branch of the same family. Hence then as the literary events of this Province arise from the local circumstances of its inhabitants, it must be by a reference to those local circumstances, that a suitable and adequate relief can be imparted."[18] His remarks, he made clear, "lay the foundation for the principal position we [the Methodists] would assume in reference to a judicious system of education in this Province." Two things in particular, he argued, were necessary: "1. It should be popular; 2. It should not countenance any sectarian exclusion or supremacy." Schools "must," he insisted, "receive the approbation of public sentiment or they will not receive the support of public patronage. They should therefore be popular. In order to this, they should be free from all *sectarian supremacy and exclusion*." Most importantly, he insisted that the system be a "public" one. By "public," Ryerson made clear that he meant popular schools available to, and supported by, all. He further argued that sectarian discord had brought about a type of interminable turmoil in the parent country from which the schools of Upper Canada should be freed.

The separation of church and state was a pivotal part of Ryerson's plans. It was on this point, in fact, that his ideal system hinged. No value was closer to the hearts of the inhabitants of Upper Canada, he believed, and certainly the turmoil over the university charter had proven as much. Moreover, the winds of change sweeping the Atlantic world, he argued, demanded a clear separation of church and state. "Hence then while the Government of Great Britain is steadily and firmly advancing towards recognizing the principles of general emancipation: and while we are informed on good authority, that His *Majesty* King George the Fourth is the *primum mobile* of these improving changes; we are also assured by His Excellency from the Throne, that it is the earnest desire of his Majesty – to *guard* this colony against evils that have to be remedied in the Mother Country – 'that this portion of his dominions should reap the full benefit of good Laws and FREE INSTITUTIONS.'" The inhabitants of Upper Canada, Ryerson suggested, had made clear their will for reform. "In this his Majesty and his faithful subjects have the inhabitants of Canada so fully and so warmly expressed their opinion and wishes, both at the fireside, at the Hustings, in petitions to the Provincial and Imperial Legislatures, in and out of Parliament, as they have on the subjects of *Education and Religion*: and on every occasion the united cry has been, let us 'enjoy the FULL benefit of FREE Institutions.' If therefore, they do not enjoy it, the fault cannot, according to his

Excellency's statement, lie with his Majesty – nor can it lie with the people of this country; the blame must lie elsewhere – it must lie at the door of those who have gotten up a University Charter, that his Excellency gives us to understand, ought to be '*revised*.'"[19] In sum, public discourse had made clear the educational aspirations of Upper Canadian inhabitants. It was now time for the school laws to reflect those aspirations.

Ryerson's conception of education centred on the idea that the system be designed, legislated, and controlled by "the people" within the colony itself. Who, Ryerson asked, were the most proper persons to plan and establish these "free institutions?" To determine this, he insisted, "no candid person can scarcely be at a loss. It should be constitutionally the people themselves." On this point, he insisted that Upper Canada design and legislate for itself a school system. "It may be said, that our Legislators are not so wise, and learned as those of the Mother Country. This is granted, but can a learned philosopher, or a profound statesman, the other side of the Atlantic, be as well acquainted with the local wants, local circumstances, local wishes of the inhabitants of this country, as even a common Canadian farmer, who knows them from *individual* experience and *personal* observation?" Ryerson thought not. For too long Upper Canada had been at the mercy of the parent state through the authority of an unjustly ruling colonial administration; Ryerson offered a clean break. "A contrary course of proceeding would, in our opinion, blast the brightening prospects of one of the fairest portions of the globe." Like Mackenzie's, then, Ryerson's conception of education was clearly imagined in response to the ideas put forward by Strachan and the executive elite. It was also one that put the interests of the colony before those of the metropolis.

Ryerson adamantly lamented the hierarchical nature of education in Upper Canada, which favoured the Church of England in all matters. "This failure," he made clear, "is attributed to the appointment of trustees, for the public schools, from one communion only, thereby depriving other denominations of that benefit, which they had a right to expect would have arisen from them."[20] The executive, he believed, was acting unfairly by excluding other denominations from school governance. "And this strong *political* bias," Ryerson insisted, had hindered the development of a universal system of education. He placed the blame, as did many other educational thinkers, squarely on Strachan. "[B]eing originally created by an *ecclesiastical* dominancy, and a Dignitary of a certain communion, not remarkable for his liberality of sentiment or feeling, being *ex-officio* President of these Boards of Trustees, the public schools, intended by the Legislature to be *national*, both in their character and benefits, become comparatively circumscribed in their advantages, and engines of an influence not the most favorable to the moral and civil interests of the country." The solution, as he saw it, was to eliminate the boards of education, including the overarching General Board of Education, and to let the schools "be altogether controlled by the representatives of the people." Such a sentiment, he believed, was widespread and had been advocated from all corners of the colony for years.

Ryerson's proposals to reverse Church of England exclusivity, however, ironically foreshadowed the seeds of a religious controversy that would plague the province thereafter. "[T]o meet the views and circumstances of those who wish to educate their children in their own religious communion, let other provisions be made." Upper Canada could have a non-sectarian system of education, he wrote, that could also provide for dissentient schools. "This can be done in perfect consistency with, and in subserviency to, other literary regulations which have been asked for, and which are now contemplated by our Provincial Legislature. Equal rights and privileges are the acknowledged maxims of sound policy in matters of religion; so let them be in literary affairs."

Although the Methodists themselves were committed to non-sectarian schooling, other denominations, such as the Catholics and Presbyterians, it was clear to Ryerson, were not. Thus, "[i]n acceding to their wishes, we hope our House of Assembly will pass a general bill authorizing (by giving power to form corporations) each religious community, under certain restrictions, to erect at least one literary institution." Such institutions should be funded by government. This, he hoped, would help encourage a homegrown system of education. "Many persons who now look on with cool indifference, or send their children to a foreign country to be educated, would devote a liberal portion of their property and their utmost influence, in promoting the means of education in our own country; and very many parents who now, through ignorance, mistaken views or limited means, leave their children to grow up with scarcely learning enough to read and write, would then be prevailed upon and enabled to impart to them the inestimable blessings of a liberal education." Ryerson tolerated separate religious schools on the condition that the superstructure of education remain funded by government and universally accessible; no one denomination alone should "receive a slice from the golden loaf." He clearly favoured a system in which Upper Canadian children were educated in the province – even if this meant in different schools – rather than in different countries or by foreign teachers.

In 1831, the Methodist community initiated its own design of education in response to Upper Canada College by building its own preparatory school, Upper Canada Academy. In an editorial on 23 April 1831, Ryerson reflected upon the intellectual foundation of Upper Canada Academy, making his second major apology on education in Upper Canada. Upper Canada needed, Ryerson continued to insist, a universally free system of schooling: "On the importance of education generally; we may remark, it is as necessary as the light – it should be as common as water, and as free as air." Schooling was as necessary to the individual, he thought, as it was to the community: "Education among the people is the best security of a good government and constitutional liberty; it yields a steady unbending support to the former, and effectually protects the latter. An educated people are always a loyal people to good government – and the first object of a wise government should be the education of the people." But Ryerson did not advocate subservience. Rather, he believed that education empowered the individual, not to obey, but to serve: "An educated people are always enterprising in all kinds of general and local improvements. An ignorant population are equally fit and liable to be the slaves of despots, and the dupes of demagogues; sometimes, like the unsettled ocean, they can be thrown in incontrollable agitation by every wind that blows; at other times, like the stupid ass, they tamely submit to the most unreasonable burdens." In a word, "[e]ducation, like seeing, is one of the most fruitful sources of public, social, and individual happiness."[21] In this sense, Ryerson advocated a complex ideological design for a system in which children would receive an education that would make them easily governed by, and yet liberated from, their rulers.

The blueprints for education put forward by Mackenzie and Ryerson were, of course, part of a widespread public discourse on the development of popular schooling. And the idea of popular schooling within that public discourse generally supported their blueprints. The ideas of universal and free schooling for all inhabitants increasingly dominated the public discourse on education. Writing to the conservative *Brockville Recorder* on 4 May 1830, "Presbuteros" argued that, on the issue of free schools, "[n]o money if judiciously laid out is better spent by any government."[22] Pointing to what he believed to be happening in Britain, he noted that systems of government around the world were promoting the causes of education and that a free government such as Upper Canada's should not "be alarmed from an increase of light and knowledge among all classes of the people." "Universal education," Presbuteros argued, was a fundamental Upper Canadian value. Both the District School Act of 1807 and the Common School Act of 1816 were based on this idea, which was held by both "the members of the House of Assembly" and also "the inhabitants generally" – namely, that "they should be *Free Schools*, that is, that there should be no charge for education, and they understood this to be the meaning of the term *Public Schools* and in some instances the Trustees and Teachers acted on this principle and made no charge for tuition." The inhabitants of Upper Canada wanted free schools, he insisted, and he pointed to the overwhelming number of students attending the less expensive common schools rather than the district schools as proof of his assertion. Moreover, he supported the idea that free schooling should come under the regulation of all inhabitants and should not fall under the authority of an elite body. Presbyterians, Methodists, and Baptists, although comprising the majority of the population, he thought, must have had a "painful feeling" in being required to support schools they could not regulate, as the appointed trustees and members of the boards of education were always members of the Church of England.[23] The elitist system of education had seen its course, he was certain, and it lacked "public confidence" because its superintendence had been denied public representation.

"An Observer" agreed with Presbuteros. "The School system," he told the *Brockville Recorder*, "must be reformed. Complaints against its defects and abuses are coming from every part of this Province."[24] It was the duty of the assembly, he cried, to reform the system and to stop bringing down the various common school bills being introduced, such as that of William Buell Jr, a reform member for Leeds County, in the last session, aimed at increasing common school funding.[25]

In a letter to the *Colonial Advocate*, an inhabitant under the pseudonym "Clio" expressed her belief that a more effective form of school funding might be developed, and she urged her readers to consider ways in which to raise the revenue needed. "Poverty, and a thin population," she observed, "might, in some parts, render considerable aid necessary; while, in others, little or none would be required. It is the poor that require assistance – not the rich."[26] "A Canadian" echoed this sentiment and insisted that better education for all classes required an increase in the salaries of teachers in order to attract the best people.[27] Both favoured the expansion of schooling.

The *Upper Canada Herald* expressed its own views on the financing of public education. "It is mortifying to see so much money already wasted," the newspaper read, and without some sort of alteration in the system, more money would be improperly wasted.[28] At the centre of the inadequacy of the system, the newspaper noted, was the injustice of the funding, whereby the district schools received the lion's share; instead, the paper argued, these funds should go to "the children of those in poor and moderate circumstances." The schools, the newspaper held, ought to be accountable to "the public." "No person can have any objection to another spending his money in educating his children in Latin and Greek, and other useless languages. But the public have a great objection to their property being taken away from them, and applied in that disguised way for such purposes." The time had come, the newspaper insisted, for schooling to benefit the masses.

Not everyone enthusiastically supported the idea of school expansion. The influence of reformers on the Upper Canadian public discourse and public opinion on this and other issues of political importance could hardly be overlooked. John Carey, editor of the pro-establishment *York Observer*, was especially concerned with the growing influence of Ryerson and the *Christian Guardian*. "During the late session your influence in the assembly was all-powerful," he wrote to Ryerson through an editorial appearing in the *York Observer* in 1830. "The base majority obeyed your nod with as much alacrity as a slave does the orders of a West India planter!"[29] "A Traveller" agreed, and as "a British Subject," he wrote to the *Canadian Freeman*, he felt compelled to speak up against Ryerson and the impact of the *Christian Guardian*, blaming the newspaper for initiating political disruptions that the province was attempting to be done with.[30] "Stentor" addressed himself to "the Friends of Loyalty in Upper Canada" and suggested that the "two radical and venal organs, the 'Advocate' and 'Guardian,'" were misrepresenting the motives of and ridiculing the principles of the executive while promoting their own selfish interests.[31]

Nevertheless, it was clear that on the issue of popular schooling, the idea of educational expansion was clearly favoured over that of maintaining the status quo. And thus public policy on education had to reflect this idea. The debates on education continued at the first sitting of the legislature in 1831. Two attempts at forming a new common school bill were made in a second sitting of the legislature in the fall of that year. One, by William Buell Jr, promoted a moderate view of universal education and focused on increased funding so that schooling could be made available to a greater number of inhabitants. The other was made by Mahlon Burwell, a conservative member for Middlesex County.[32] In the spring of 1831, Burwell had earlier moved for a standing committee on education with a focus on settling the question of how much of the Clergy Reserves were initially intended for the purposes of education.[33] The committee, headed by William Morris, a conservative member for Lanark County, reported its findings on 22 February 1831. It found that the report of 1797 clearly expressed the desire of the executive to work with the House of Assembly to establish grammar schools, colleges, or a university. The original allotment of 500,000 acres should be respected, the committee believed, and should be put toward school expansion. It pointed out that efforts were made in 1819 to utilize the land, but that the lieutenant governor at the time, Peregrine Maitland, had scoffed at the idea. In thirty years, the committee reported, "no apparent benefit has resulted to the inhabitants of the country from the school reservation," despite efforts to utilize the land. Although the district schools had been established in 1807, the committee found that the spirit of school expansion that had inspired the 1797 plans had somehow "been lost sight of" and it was this spirit that it wished to rekindle.[34]

Rekindling this spirit was not a difficult task. Public discourse demonstrated a desire for school expansion, and there were few in the House of Assembly who would reject a plea for such a goal. What was more difficult, however, was presenting a conservative agenda of education in an era in which reformist ideas were leading the discourse in Upper Canada. The committee recommended setting aside the money from land sales for the support of eleven additional "respectable Seminaries" that would provide a liberal education to local children, who would otherwise be sent away. It called for the district schools to be made free, as per the original intentions, and for expanded funding for additional common schools and raises in common school teacher salaries. Once this plan was in place, the committee believed, the House of Assembly's energy could be put toward erecting King's College.

Finally, and of crucial importance to our understanding the change of tone in the development of schooling in Upper Canada among conservatives by the 1830s, Burwell's committee recommended that control of the money arising from the sale of the school lands should be put into the hands of the receiver general, and not the executive, allowing for "the general superintendence and organization of the whole system of management [to] thus be open to public inspection and approval." Conservatives were clearly reflecting the same views as reformers concerning the "public" nature of schooling in Upper Canada. That "public" was a much broader one than was served in the opening decade of the century with the establishment of the District School Act.

The report had an immediate impact on the executive. The next year, Colborne called for a full explanation as to why the district schools had yet to be made free. He further concluded that the original intentions were to make the schools free and that the executive and his advisors had thus failed in this regard. Conservatives had adopted reformist policies in education, and schooling in Upper Canada had entered a new stage of development.

The convergence of ideas among conservatives and reformers on the need for educational reform in these years translated into real developments in education. Late in 1831, Duncombe, seconded by the radical Absolom Shade, made a motion to address the lieutenant governor in order to make clear "that there is in this province a very general want of Education, that the insufficiency of the common school fund to support competent, respectable and well educated Teachers, has degraded common school teaching from a regular business to mere a matter of convenience to transient persons or common idlers."[35] The quality of schooling had to improve, he insisted, and this required a mobilized effort on a scale theretofore not seen. Duncombe argued that if better teaching were available, the teaching in common schools would soon become a regular and respectable calling. Respectable, well-educated teachers could be attracted, and the scholars would benefit. The province would benefit as well. With a well-functioning school system, Duncombe argued, "Upper Canada would then form a national character that would command respect abroad and ensure peace, prosperity and happiness at home; perpetuate attachment to British principles and British institutions, and enable posterity to value, as they ought, the inestimable blessings of our glorious Constitution." Duncombe's speech was adopted as a resolution on 26 December 1831 by both conservatives and reformers in the House of Assembly.

Public discourse concerning the need for universal schooling had set a new tone for educational discourse in Upper Canada, and a new wave of educational leaders was emerging in Upper Canada that reflected that tone. Buell's and Burwell's educational efforts continued in the House of Assembly in late 1831 and into 1832. Buell promoted the idea of school expansion while granting superintendence of the schools to the localities, but his proposed bill failed to pass and was dropped by the assembly on 5 January 1832.[36] Burwell sought to make education more generally accessible as well, but his efforts focused on the importance of the district schools and on maintaining the character of a classical British curriculum. Nevertheless, the tone, whether reform or conservative, continued to favour school expansion. The idea of change had permeated public and political discourse. In a deed that foreshadowed the changes to come in the system of schooling in Upper Canada, the colonial administration ordered the dissolution of the General Board of Education, headed by John Strachan, in 1832. The popular appetite for universal schooling had been clearly demonstrated in the print culture discourse, and both conservatives and reformers reflected that appetite in the legislature.

Conclusion

Ideas, according to twenty-first-century popular thinker Malcolm Gladwell, have tipping points at which moment they cross a threshold and, like an epidemic, begin to spread like wildfire.[1] It is difficult to say precisely when the idea of popular schooling reached its tipping point in Upper Canada, but by the 1830s the fire was raging. Despite varying opinions on the means and ends of popular schooling, there was widespread agreement about its need. The debate was no longer about whether a system of popular schooling was desirable, but rather about what specific kinds of schools should be established.

Understanding the origins of the school system in Ontario requires us to appreciate the importance of late eighteenth- and early nineteenth-century education as the focus of a central public discourse. Inhabitants of early Upper Canada participated in an intellectual exchange with much broader significance in the process toward mass universal schooling than we have previously assumed. Upper Canadians had begun writing about, conceptualizing, and forging a system of schooling from the time of Upper Canada's first Loyalist settlers. Developments and debates leading to the District School Act of 1807, the Common School Act of 1816, and the educational reforms of the 1820s and 1830s were more than small steps in the progression toward mass universal schooling. They clearly demonstrated a complex and contested history surrounding the origins of schooling in Upper Canada, one involving a greater number of participants than we have given credit to. In revisiting the statue of Egerton Ryerson on the grounds of Ryerson University in

Toronto, commemorating the nineteenth-century school advocate as the "Founder of the School System of Ontario," we might be right to ask: should such credit (or blame) be given to one person alone? The evidence from the print media suggests not. Upper Canadian political leaders did not unilaterally create a system of popular schooling. The people of Upper Canada were not passive recipients of a school system imposed from above, but rather they were active participants in the making of that system.

The idea of popular schooling came early to Upper Canada. Even before the colony itself was founded, settlers on the western banks of the St Lawrence River were petitioning for a system of schooling that would be funded through government expenses. And though government funds were not made available for education in those early years, the idea remained. The establishment of district schools in 1807 provided educational opportunities for some inhabitants, but this was not enough to quell the calls for something more universal and the district schools were condemned by many as elitist. Through popular writing in the press, petitions to the legislature, and the help of political dissenters bent upon subverting what they considered an arbitrary colonial government, Upper Canadians successfully promoted a common school system available to all inhabitants, and a bill to that effect was enacted in 1816.

The 1816 Common School Act was a major development in the movement toward mass universal schooling. It had a lasting influence and a direct impact on the legislation drawn up in the mid-nineteenth century and beyond. Post-rebellion, mid-nineteenth-century Canada was a contentious society, one that stimulated greater interest on the part of the British metropolis in colonial public policy than ever before. That Canada was also a Canada heavily influenced by the influx of migrants from the British Isles. As a result, the school system developed in those years through the ideas and policies carried over, and borrowed, from the British Isles. Both the colonial administrators, whose roots were British and who aimed to instil the values of the metropolis in the colony, and the growing population, who brought with them metropolitan conceptions of social and cultural institutions, continued to design and shape a system of education that was to a great extent culturally transferred from the British Isles. Ryerson's rise to power after defending Metcalfe during the constitutional crisis of 1844, his educational tours of Europe, and the importation of textbooks from the British Isles, most notably the Irish National Readers, offer clear examples of the colonial administration's plan to institute a system of centrally planned schooling whose cultural and intellectual roots lay across the Atlantic.[2] Print media in early Upper Canada, however, challenges us to qualify our understanding of the developments in that later period by situating those developments within the context of what came earlier. In particular, when considering educational influences from across the Atlantic, we must assess them within the context of the number of educational developments that we see occurring before the first major wave of migrants from the British Isles in 1815.

The settlers who came to Upper Canada from the British Isles after 1815 entered a colony in which government-aided common schooling was already a foregone conclusion. Moreover, the school system was democratic and gave considerable power to the locality. The idea that common schools should be run by "the people" was developed and turned into legislation before the influx of transatlantic settlers. In years when the British metropolis was itself experimenting with the idea of a potentially centrally controlled Dr Bell's National Schools system, Upper Canadians, who were at the time more American in their sentiments and replicated in the colony the educational and cultural institutions they had left behind, had already established the superstructure for popular schooling that would see educational decisions made at the local level. Indeed, the attempt to introduce Dr Bell's system in Upper Canada in the 1820s was doomed to fail. This was not because the idea was necessarily foreign to Upper Canadians – it was anything but foreign to the post-1815 settlers from the British Isles. The idea of British national schools failed, however, as did the idea of a university linked to the Church of England, because it ignored the context of educational discourse as it had already been cultivated in the colony. The Common School Act of 1816 had created an educational context in which "the people" were central architects in the development of government-aided popular schooling. This was the context that post-1815 settlers entered into. To understand the origins of popular schooling in Upper Canada, we must understand the power of this context in shaping the ideas, attitudes, and discourse surrounding schooling for the years to come thereafter.

Given the efforts on the part of the colonial elite to reduce funding to the common schools in 1820, little else was done in the political arena to develop a system of popular schooling after the passing of the 1816 act. Indeed, the 1820s were a contentious period of politics in Upper Canada, and the legislature was often divided on what course to take in the educational sphere. The colonial administration, for its part, began to push for an ecclesiastically linked system of education that would, especially in the realm of higher education, favour the Church of England in the development and management of both the educational structure and the curriculum. The rise of the radical press in that decade, however, ensured that the idea of popular schooling under the control of all Upper Canadians remained a central feature of public discourse. It was neither radicals nor reformers alone, however, who expressed ideas about universal schooling. The idea of free, universal schooling was also commonly expressed in moderate and conservative newspapers, and Upper Canadians increasingly used the press both to condemn the plans of the colonial administration and to promote their own ideas about the future of schooling in Upper Canada. Neither the radical nor the pro-establishment press supported any plan by the colonial elite to subvert the idea of popular schooling. By the 1830s, both radicals and conservatives, and all the political shades of grey in-between, were discussing the shape and form of free, universal schooling in a public discourse that permeated political lines.

Schooling was still a predominately private affair in the 1830s. Most children continued to receive their education at home through a private tutor or family member or in some other type of informal community setting. But we should not confuse the unavailability of a popular system of schooling with indifference to the idea. The people of Upper Canada were not sheep waiting for their educational shepherd. From the beginning, they debated ways in which they could collectively school their children. By the 1830s, the debate had shifted from one of lament for schools to one of opportunities for school expansion. Government was more than ever expected to play a central role in establishing schools to which all inhabitants could send their children. Despite differences of opinion concerning the kind of education children would receive, the need for massive government intervention was agreed upon as a prerequisite for a successful system of schooling in Upper Canada.

While ideas converged on the need for a system of government-aided schooling, there was hardly consensus among Upper Canadians about the form, character, and content of such schooling. The following decades would pit school advocates against one another, even while they remained unified on the need for government involvement. Thus there was divergence in ideas and ideals, but schooling held a promise for everyone.

By the 1830s, two general models of education had presented themselves to the inhabitants of Upper Canada. These two models reflected two general political groupings struggling for hegemony in the colony. John Strachan and the executive elite proposed that common school education in Upper Canada be rooted in the faith of, and led by the leaders of, the Church of England. Although aided by a number of inhabitants who supported their ideas, the elite were not able to appeal to the majority of inhabitants in the public sphere, including many of their own conservative supporters; and with the emergence of the reform press in the 1820s, the voice of opposition placed their educational plans in check. Indeed, once Strachan's religious "falsehoods" and "misrepresentations" had been exposed in print, the reform cause grew considerably more credible.

William Lyon Mackenzie's *Catechism of Education* illustrates the anti-establishment educational ideas of the more radical element of reformers – or the second general model of education that had presented itself to Upper Canadians. Mackenzie and other reformers advocated the extension of schooling to apprentices, mechanics, labourers, and others who were not able by their own means to acquire it. Central to reformist concerns were the models upon which Upper Canada's schools were based. Fashioning the schools after elitist institutions found in Europe was less appealing than following the more accessible American model, which would put in check "the habits of servility and toleration of arbitrary power."[3] Mackenzie argued that through schooling "the power of the people" could be extended.[4]

These two models, what we might consider the elitist and the popular, represented the general political dichotomy in the province.

Upper Canada was in the midst of a political battle that would eventually bring into question in the 1830s the future of governance in Upper Canada. Education was a central theme in that battle. The two models of schooling, however, only offer a general framework within which to make sense of educational discourse. As with the future of politics in the province, the future of schooling was further complicated by the various opinions in public discourse that crossed party lines. Conservatives and reformers had educational ideas that overlapped, making the discourse on education much more complex and uneven than any generalization can explain. The discourse often pitted allies against each other and made the future of schooling a contentious issue for anyone involved.

The province was at a crossroads in the 1830s. "One of the People," writing to the *Kingston Chronicle*, made this idea the focus of a series of letters to the editor that appeared in 1831 concerning the divide between reformers and conservatives in Upper Canada. "These are fearful times" throughout the world, he commented. "The people are struggling for supremacy, unlimited and uncontrolled as the winds of heaven." He pointed to both the French and British examples as evidence of the winds of change. Upper Canada, he warned, did not "escape the general infection." Change was imminent, he suggested to his readers. Disloyal and dangerous reformers such as Mackenzie and Ryerson, he feared, were taking control of Upper Canadian politics.[5]

Considering the important influence that Ryerson would have in the development of popular schooling in Canada West and Ontario, that he was linked with radicals like William Lyon Mackenzie is striking and should suggest a need to reassess what we know about the ideas of the person who would spearhead the school system during the mid-nineteenth century. In contrast to "One of the People," educational historians tend to depict Ryerson as a social conservative aligned with the executive and bent upon creating a stable and controllable society. There is good reason for this characterization. In 1844, it was Ryerson himself who came to the defence of the conservative governor general, Charles Metcalfe, who was struggling with Robert Baldwin, Louis-Hippolyte La Fontaine, and a reformist ministry determined to introduce "responsible government" in Canada. Any link with Mackenzie was clearly broken by the 1840s.

Something seems to be missing, then, in our historical understanding of Ryerson's ideas. How and why did Ryerson, a perceived radical reformer by his contemporaries – a reformer who made his name lashing out against the establishment in the 1820s – ultimately come to be remembered by posterity more for his role as a conservative in defence of the established order? And what can his apparent metamorphosis, or what seems to be a significant transformation in character, tell us about his role as superintendent of education thereafter?

Such questions illustrate the complexity of Ryerson's ideas in the context of Upper Canada's educational history and the complex and uneven educational ideas in which they were enmeshed. Consider Ryerson's letter in 1844 to Governor General Charles Metcalfe in which he stated the following regarding the opposition Metcalfe was facing from reformers: "In the present crisis, the Government must of course first be placed upon a strong foundation, and then must the youthful mind of Canada be instructed and molded in the way I have had the honor of stating to your Excellency if this country is long to remain an appendage to the British Crown."[6] While these words make clear Ryerson's intentions to undermine the reform cause, the deeper meaning of this statement is still not clear. This statement has been interpreted in a variety of ways by different scholars. Chad Gaffield suggests it reveals that a dominant theme in Ryerson's promotion of education was the importance of the British "heritage."[7] Bruce Curtis uses the same statement to suggest that a dominant theme in Ryerson's school promotion was indoctrination for political stability.[8] In order to acquire a deeper understanding of the statement, we must come to understand what was meant by "British." As Gaffield points out, this is difficult to determine and there is no consensus among historians on Ryerson's use of the term. Nor, as an analysis of the Upper Canadian print media in this study suggests, was there a general consensus on that term among the inhabitants of Upper Canada.

Some evidence in print culture, such as the writings of "One of the People" cited above, shows that Ryerson was believed by a number of his contemporaries in the late 1820s and early 1830s to be anti-British, disloyal, and clearly aligned with the more radical elements of reform. The *Brockville Gazette* believed that Ryerson was in fact too radical and that he used the *Christian Guardian* to propagate radical ideas.[9] Francis Collins of the *Canadian Freeman* warned that "the Ryersonians" had "assumed the control of public opinion, bearded the government, and put all others at defiance."[10]

As a reaction to the perceived danger, many conservative inhabitants condemned Ryerson and the radical reformers. "An Anglo-Canadian" attended the "splendid meeting of the *really Loyal Inhabitants*" of the Eastern District for the purpose of "expressing our abhorrence of the seditious principles of Mackenzie, Ryerson, & Co." whom he believed were both disloyal and in opposition to the crown.[11] "Canadianus" found anti-British radicals to be an abomination. "Thank heaven," he wrote, "I *now* know that I am living under the British flag, among a people devoted to their king, their country, and their glorious constitution."[12] "Hibernicus" agreed and urged Upper Canadians to read the radical newspapers and their "Republican principles" with caution.[13] Numerous letters poured into the *Kingston Chronicle* in the spring of 1832 suggesting that the reform movement was treacherous. "An Anglo-Canadian" identified Mackenzie and Ryerson as "false patriots" with "plans of rebellion."[14] Their real intent was to overthrow British institutions in the province. "Upper Canadian" claimed that the province was at a crossroads between two factions whom most inhabitants knew little about.[15] "A British Subject" agreed but implied that the province was in the midst of civil discord, divided between Strachan's "oligarch faction" and the "*Ryersonian*" faction. Neither party, he believed, could be trusted.[16]

Ryerson himself distanced his ideas from those of radical reformers and instead proclaimed his loyalty and attachment to Britain. He certainly saw himself as a reformer in the early 1830s but attempted to clarify questions concerning the principles of reformers in Upper Canada in a balanced way that would disassociate him from political radicals. In an elaborate article printed on 10 May 1832 in the *Christian Guardian*, Ryerson specifically addressed what his being a "reformer" meant. To be a reformer, he thought, did not make one a radical. "This question has been differently answered by persons differently interested," he admitted, but there were clear trends. Reformers were not, as their opponents had attempted to portray, "advocating principles Anti-British, Revolutionary, and Republican in their nature and tendency." Indeed, he suggested, reformers had never lied about what they stood for and had always been clear and honest, something he believed that the established political elite could not claim. Reformers did not stand for the elimination of the British constitution, but rather their principles had consistently been in favour "of reform as far as it relates to the enjoyment of equal religious and civil privileges by the several christian denominations in this Province – the removal of all Clergymen from the Legislature – a system of common and classical school education adapted in the wishes and the wants of the people." The three pillars of reform then, as Ryerson saw them, were religious tolerance, the separation of church and state, and free schooling. "On other points," he said, "we leave every reader to judge for himself."[17] John Cameron shared this viewpoint and suggested that the establishment was spreading rumours, the chief among them that "the methodists are going to overturn the Government."[18] "Canadians," he argued, were being "divided" and "kept in the dark" in an era when reform was sweeping the world.

Religious freedom was crucial to Ryerson's conception of reform. In this sense, he was anti-British in as far as "British" suggested the legitimacy of an established church. Ryerson did not believe that it did. In 1832, the *Brockville Recorder* reprinted for its readers a letter from Ryerson to John Colborne concerning the lieutenant governor's demographic plans. Colborne had previously suggested that within a few years Upper Canada would be populated "by millions of our own countrymen," and implied that such inhabitants would be naturally predisposed to favour conservatives and, by extension, would support the supremacy of the Church of England.[19] "His Excellency seems to anticipate a great change in public opinion in the Province," Ryerson speculated, "on the subject of a Church Establishment by the influx of emigration."[20] Colborne did not appear to be aware, he went on, that "nine tenths of the European population are decidedly favourable to the principles of civil and religious liberty." There was little reason to believe, then, that the incoming migrants would think any differently. Ryerson believed that Britain itself was in the midst of change and that Britons themselves would bring that spirit of change to the colony. Given the debate on Catholic emancipation, religious tolerance, and the nature of reform across the Atlantic, he had good reason to think so. Attachment to Britain, then, did not necessarily mean attachment to British institutions such as the Church of England. The politico-religious developments across the Atlantic proved to Ryerson, in fact, that a member of a religious minority like him could find great solace in advocating British values.

But what did being British mean to Ryerson in an age of bourgeoning colonial identity? To what extent can we situate his ideas among those of others in the colony? Print media analysis allows us to examine the multiple answers to these questions in a way that a focus on government documents and correspondence among the elite does not. It is especially Ryerson's initial years in public life that allow us to understand the social and political ideas that shaped him in the 1820s and brought him into public prominence in the 1830s. It is his growth and maturity in these years and his understanding of Upper Canada's growth and maturity that might allow us to understand his seemingly contradictory transition from an anti-establishment radical in 1826 to a staunch supporter of the conservative governor general in 1844.

Future studies of the origins of schooling in the nineteenth century will need to focus more closely on the print culture discourse in order to determine how educational advocates like Ryerson arrived at their positions and the extent to which they were either initiating or reacting to public discourse. Such studies will allow us to rethink what we know about the policy debates surrounding educational development in Canada West and Ontario. A preliminary look at the print media in the mid- to late 1830s already reveals some trends and themes. Most striking to educational historians should be a set of letters written to the London *Times* by Ryerson in 1836, on the eve of the Upper and Lower Canadian Rebellions. Ryerson wrote these letters in response to efforts by Duncombe, who had travelled to London in 1836 to present a petition to the Imperial Parliament for political reform in Upper Canada. In these letters, Ryerson offered a remarkable view of the culture and heritage of the colony, one that sheds light on his subsequent educational ideas in the 1840s and provides the contextualization that allows us to situate Ryerson's political leanings. "I am, what I assume to be," he proclaimed in the British press, "A Canadian."[21] Arguing that the clash between conservatives such as John Strachan and radical reformers such as William Lyon Mackenzie and Charles Duncombe had brought the colony to the brink of political disaster, Ryerson offered a third option for governance of the colony, one from a distinctly "Canadian" perspective. This option involved an attachment to Britain and the maintenance of the constitution, which put him in opposition to radicals; but it also insisted upon colonial self-government and rejection of certain British institutions such as a Church of England establishment, which put him in opposition to a number of conservatives.

Sensing the growth of republican ideology in Lower Canada as well and the potential loss of Lower Canada to the United States or to a republic of its own making, Ryerson even urged British parliamentarians to consider uniting Upper and Lower Canada and establishing a "national" system of education.[22] Voluntary participation in the British Empire was waning, and such a system was needed in order to promote and maintain the British link, not only in Lower Canada but throughout all of British North America. If nationalism were on the rise, then Ryerson thought it better to promote that nationalism within the framework of the British Empire. The threat, he warned, was an otherwise independent and republican Lower Canada to the east, a hostile republic to the south, and the inevitable influx of republican thought and propaganda into an already unstable Upper Canada. Ryerson emphasized adamant support of the tripartite constitution and explained that he feared the growth of republicanism in North America. For this reason, he advocated a British constitutional link.

Maintaining the constitution seems to have legitimized the British heritage in Upper Canada and its sister colonies for Ryerson. It was that constitution, after all, that protected the rights of Methodist minorities and allowed him to take on John Strachan and the Church of England establishment. What the British heritage meant to Ryerson, then, as seen in this preliminary reading of the print media, was constitutional legitimacy. That he was a "Canadian" advocating the British heritage was, perhaps, an articulation of a burgeoning local identity that sought a to achieve balance between the need for self-rule and the need for political stability through a shared constitutional heritage.

It must have also meant more. It was no small statement for a colonist to proclaim himself anything but "British." Being "Canadian" meant something to Ryerson, and he wanted the British public and the imperial government to know it.[23] It is probably impossible to empathize with Ryerson's "Canadianness" or to ever fully understand what he meant by "Canadian." But it was clearly a message. "Canadians," whatever that meant, were different. They constituted a distinct part of the empire. As the debate on education in Upper Canada suggests, the social and political infrastructure of Upper Canada would not be directed through plans emanating from the British Isles. Ryerson was aware of this fact. It was he, after all, who emerged as a leader against the dictates of Strachan's and the imperial government's plans for a university in the 1820s. Canadians were a different kind of Briton, and they required different kinds of solutions to their social and political problems.

To what extent, however, was Ryerson's Canadian identity reflective of a broader public sentiment? Newspapers in both Upper and Lower Canada suggest that others indeed shared his feelings. The *Patriot*, a conservative newspaper in Toronto, attacked Duncombe's petition as an attempt "to poison the minds of the people of England against his Excellency Sir Francis Head,"[24] and it deemed Ryerson's letters a "fervid and vigorous" defence of what is right. It labelled Duncombe's petition incompatible with the interests of ordinary Canadians and begged its subscribers to peruse it: "Read that petition our subscribers; read it every man, woman, and child in the land; read it reformers and non-reformers, constitutionalists and revolutionists, monarchists and pure democracy men, and find us, if it be possible, a single human being with effrontery enough to speak of it approvingly."[25] The editors at the *Montreal Gazette* concurred with the *Patriot* and attacked Duncombe for the inconsistency of his political opinions. The newspaper praised Ryerson's letters in England and claimed that those who supported the constitution in the Canadas "owe much to the activity and perseverance of the author of these letters; for the able *exposé* of Canadian affairs he has volunteered for the information of the British public."[26] The *Kingston Chronicle* praised Ryerson for "opening the eyes of [British] ministers to the *real* state of our affairs."[27] Ryerson, who only a few years earlier was attacked in the print media as an anti-

British radical by newspaper readers such as "An Anglo-Canadian" and "Canadianus," was now accepted, it seemed, as the advocate for British constitutional rule in the Canadas as such rule should reflect "Canadian" affairs.

In this sense, Ryerson might have offered a third model of schooling when he came to office in 1844. This model embraced neither the elitist vision of conservatives hoping to maintain social-class divisions within the colony nor the radical vision of reformers hoping to subvert the political order and charter a republican course for Upper Canada. The schools, he thought, should promote a morality favourable to the constitutional link with Britain while allowing space for new ideas of identity and self-government within the colony. Ryerson was what he believed to be a "Canadian," seeking to build, not a school system based upon the "circumstances of the parent," but rather one firmly centred upon the "circumstances of the child."[28] It was a much more complex model than the history typically conveys. It was a system, as Garth Lambert has demonstrated, that saw Ryerson partner with Strachan in the promotion of "unmixed" classical grammar schools for boys, while remaining his bitter rival through the promotion of non-denominational common schools.[29]

Such conclusions reflect the value of an analysis of Ryerson's involvement in Upper Canada's print culture. Ryerson was a public figure who emphasized the need to take into account the views of "the public." We must therefore situate his ideas within the print culture discourse in which he took part.[30] Understanding the print culture context that guided his behaviour and that of all other political leaders and ordinary Canadians, is central to acquiring a deeper understanding of the origins of popular schooling. The evidence from the educational discourse in the early nineteenth century reveals that it was not "great men" and colonial administrators alone who were involved in the development of schooling in Upper Canada. These individuals were involved in, and influenced by, a debate on education that had affected the social and political development of the colony from its inception. The discourse in early Upper Canada suggests that, unlike other parts of the empire, colonial administrators in mid-nineteenth century Canada were not building a school system aimed at "making colonial subjects,"[31] but rather they were the heirs and partners of colonial subjects in the making of the school system. To understand the development of schooling in the mid-nineteenth century, we must understand the educational discourse that preceded it.

An analysis of print culture and public discourse highlights the importance of the intellectual discourse surrounding the origins of schooling and, more importantly perhaps, broadens our understanding of the ways in which ideas about schooling were exchanged in the colony. The example of early Upper Canada suggests that ordinary inhabitants participated in the making of educational legislation in an unofficial capacity that had a direct influence on the official making of the school system. The making of a popular school system in Upper Canada was a deliberative process in which many inhabitants, both inside and outside of government, participated. It was this deliberative process, rooted in the late eighteenth and early nineteenth centuries, that framed the policy debates of the mid-nineteenth century and the idea of popular schooling for years to come.

Notes

INTRODUCTION

1 See A.N. Bethune, *Memoir of the Right Reverend John Strachan, First Bishop of Toronto* (Toronto: Henry Rowsell, 1870); Nathanael Burwash, *Egerton Ryerson* (Toronto: G.N. Morang, 1903); J. Harold Putnam, *Egerton Ryerson and Education in Upper Canada* (Toronto: William Briggs, 1912); C.B. Sissons, *Egerton Ryerson: His Life and Letters*, 2 vols (Toronto: Clarke, Irwin, and Company, 1937–47); George W. Spragge, "John Strachan's Contribution to Education, 1800–1823," *Canadian Historical Review* 22 (1941): 147–58; C.E. Phillips, *The Development of Education in Canada* (Toronto: W.J. Gage, 1957); Silvia Boorman, *John Toronto: A Biography of Bishop Strachan* (Toronto: Clarke, Irwin, 1969); J.L.H. Henderson, *John Strachan, 1778–1867* (Toronto: University of Toronto Press, 1969); David Flint, *John Strachan, Pastor and Politician* (Toronto: Oxford University Press, 1971).

2 See J. Donald Wilson, Robert M. Stamp, and Louis-Philippe Audet, eds, *Canadian Education: A History* (Toronto: Prentice-Hall, 1970); Susan Houston, "Politics, Schools, and Social Change in Upper Canada," *Canadian Historical Review* 53 (1972); Michael B. Katz and Paul H. Mattingly, eds, *Education and Social Change: Themes from Ontario's Past* (New York: New York University Press, 1975); Alison Prentice, *The School Promoters: Education and Social Class in Mid-Nineteenth Century Upper Canada* (Toronto: McClelland and Stewart, 1977); Neil McDonald and Alf Chaiton, eds, *Egerton Ryerson and His Times* (Toronto: Macmillan of Canada, 1978).

3   See Bruce Curtis, "The Political Economy of Elementary Educational
    Development: Comparative Perspectives on State Schooling in Upper
    Canada" (PhD, University of Toronto, 1980); Susan Houston and Alison
    Prentice, *Schooling and Scholars in Nineteenth-Century Ontario* (Toronto:
    University of Toronto Press, 1988); Bruce Curtis, *Building the Educational
    State: Canada West, 1836–1871* (London: Althouse Press, 1988); Bruce
    Curtis, *True Government by Choice Men? Inspection, Education, and
    State Formation in Canada West* (Toronto: University of Toronto Press,
    1992).

4   Two major exceptions in the historiography are J.D. Purdy's 1962 doctoral
    dissertation, "John Strachan and Education in Canada, 1800–1851"
    (University of Toronto, 1962); and J. Donald Wilson's 1971 doctoral dis-
    sertation, "Foreign and Local Influences on Popular Education in Upper
    Canada, 1815–1844" (University of Western Ontario, 1971). See also J.D.
    Purdy's article "John Strachan's Educational Policies, 1815–1841,"
    Ontario History 64 (1972): 45–64; and J. Donald Wilson's chapter "Edu-
    cation in Upper Canada: Sixty Years of Change," in J. Donald Wilson,
    Robert M. Stamp, and Louis-Philippe Audet, eds., *Canadian Education: A
    History* (Toronto: Prentice-Hall, 1970). These scholars, however, while
    giving more attention to decisions made at the level of the locality,
    overwhelmingly concentrate on educational decisions made at the level of
    the political elite. A more nuanced approach to the major school promot-
    ers can also be found within Purdy's and Wilson's work, as well in G.M.
    Craig's biography of John Strachan and R.D. Gidney's biography of
    Egerton Ryerson in the *Dictionary of Canadian Biography* (Toronto:
    University of Toronto Press, 1965–).

5   See R.D. Gidney, "Centralization and Education: The Origins of an
    Ontario Tradition," *Journal of Canadian Studies* 7, no. 4 (1972): 33–48;
    R.D. Gidney, "Elementary Education in Upper Canada: A Reassessment,"
    Ontario History 65, no. 3 (1973): 169–85; R.D. Gidney and D.A. Lawr,
    "Egerton Ryerson and the Origins of the Ontario Secondary School,"
    Canadian Historical Review 60, no. 4 (1979): 442–65; R.D. Gidney and
    D.A. Lawr, "Bureaucracy vs. Community? The Origins of Bureaucratic
    Procedure in the Upper Canadian School System," *Journal of Social His-
    tory* 13, no. 3 (1980): 438–57; D.A. Lawr and R.D. Gidney, "Who Ran the
    Schools? Local Influence on Education Policy in Nineteenth-Century
    Ontario," *Ontario History* 72, no. 3 (1980): 131–43; R.D. Gidney, "Mak-
    ing Nineteenth-Century School Systems: The Upper Canadian Experience

and Its Relevance to English Historiography," *History of Education* 9, no. 2 (1980): 101–16; R.D. Gidney and W.P.J. Millar, "From Voluntarism to State Schooling: The Creation of the Public School System in Ontario," *Canadian Historical Review* 66, no. 4 (1985): 443–73; R.D. Gidney and W.P.J. Miller, *Inventing Secondary Education: The Rise of the High School in Nineteenth-Century Ontario* (Montreal and Kingston: McGill-Queen's University Press, 1990); Harry Smaller, "Teachers and Schools in Early Ontario," *Ontario History* 85, no. 4 (1993): 291–308; Michael F. Murphy, "The Common School Amendment Acts of the 1830s and the Re-shaping of Schooling in London, Upper Canada," *Historical Studies in Education* 8, no. 2 (1996): 147–66.

6 Gidney and Millar, *Inventing Secondary Education*, 82.

7 The two major studies on educational development in this period are J.D. Purdy, "John Strachan and Education in Canada, 1800–1851" (PhD, University of Toronto, 1962); and J. Donald Wilson, "Foreign and Local Influences on Popular Education in Upper Canada, 1815–1844" (PhD diss., University of Western Ontario, 1971).

8 Jeffrey L. McNairn, *The Capacity to Judge: Public Opinion and Deliberative Democracy in Upper Canada, 1791–1854* (Toronto: University of Toronto Press, 2000).

9 Carol Wilton, *Popular Politics and Political Culture in Upper Canada, 1800–1850* (Montreal and Kingston: McGill-Queen's University Press, 2000).

10 These findings are also in line with recent historical sociological studies examining the rise of social movements and contentious politics. In his analysis of the British press between 1758 to 1834, for example, Charles Tilly finds over 8,000 "contentious gatherings" described. He suggests that "ordinary British people" abandoned traditional forms of protest in favour of petition drives, public meetings, and other forms of popular politics. The result was a movement toward "mass participation in national politics." See Charles Tilly, *Popular Contention in Great Britain, 1758–1834* (Cambridge, MA: Harvard University Press, 1998).

11 Research into the growth of a deliberative democracy in Upper Canada is further supported by a growing international body of work examining the importance of the press in shaping and disseminating public opinion. See Jonathan Paul Thomas, *The Sense of the People: Politics, Culture, and Imperialism in England, 1715–1785* (Cambridge, UK: Cambridge University Press, 1995); Jeremy Black, *The English Press, 1621–1861* (Stroud,

UK: Sutton Publishing, 2001); and Hannah Barker and Simon Burrows, eds, *Press, Politics and the Public Sphere in Europe and North America, 1760–1820* (Cambridge, UK: Cambridge University Press, 2002). For a discussion on the importance of the press to and within the imperial context, see Julie F. Codell, ed., *Imperial Co-histories: National Identities and the British Colonial Press* (Madison, NJ: Fairleigh Dickinson University Press, 2003).

12 Chad Gaffield, "Children, Schooling, and Family Reproduction in Nineteenth-Century Ontario," *Canadian Historical Review* 72, no. 2 (1991): 157–91.

13 Elizabeth Jane Errington, *Wives and Mothers, Schoolmistresses and Scullery Maids: Working Women in Upper Canada, 1790–1840* (Montreal and Kingston: McGill-Queen's University Press, 1995); and "Ladies and Schoolmistresses: Educating Women in Early Nineteenth-Century Upper Canada," *Historical Studies in Education* 6, no. 1 (1994): 71–96.

14 Errington, *Wives and Mothers*, 77.

15 Paul Axelrod, *The Promise of Schooling: Education in Canada, 1800–1914* (Toronto: University of Toronto Press, 1997). See especially chapter 2, "Building the Educational State."

16 Some recent international literature has made the case for a synthesis of the research examining both popular and official discourse in the making of public policy. See Jeremy Black, "The Press and Politics in the Eighteenth Century," *Media History* 8, no. 2 (2002): 175–82. A special issue of *Parliamentary History* in 2006 was devoted to the idea of public opinion and the shaping of politics in Britain; see especially the introduction to that issue, Kark W. Schweizer, "Parliament and the Press: A Case for Synergy," *Parliamentary History* 25, no. 1 (2006): 1–8.

17 Marshall McLuhan, *The Gutenberg Galaxy: The Making of Typographic Man* (Toronto: University of Toronto Press, 1962).

18 Marshall McLuhan, *Understanding Media: The Extensions of Man* (Cambridge, MA: MIT Press, 1994), 204.

19 McLuhan, *The Gutenberg Galaxy*, 130–3.

20 McLuhan's communication theories were built upon those of historian Harold Innis. Especially important was Innis's conception of time-bending media, such as speech, and space-bending media, such as writing. Time-bending media transmit knowledge and allow communication to move forward in time into subsequent generations. Space-bending media, such as newspapers, carry knowledge across distances and allow mass transient

communication. The balance between both of these media was central, Innis believes, to the development and sustainability of societies and empires. See Innis's *Empire and Communications* (reprint, Toronto: Dundurn Press, 1950, 2007) and *The Bias of Communication* (Toronto: University of Toronto Press, 1951).

21 Jurgen Habermas, *The Structural Transformation of the Public Sphere: An Inquiry into a Category of Bourgeois Society* (Cambridge, MA: MIT Press, 1991).

22 Benedict Anderson, *Imagined Communities: Reflections on the Origins and Spread of Nationalism* (New York: Verso, 2006).

23 McLuhan, *The Gutenberg Galaxy*, 199.

24 Christopher A. Bayly, *Imperial Meridian: The British Empire and the World, 1780–1830* (New York: Longman, 1989); Linda Colley, *Britons: Forging the Nation, 1707–1837* (New Haven: Yale University Press, 1992); David Armitage, *The Ideological Origins of the British Empire* (Cambridge, UK: Cambridge University Press, 2000); Kathleen Wilson, *The Sense of the People: Politics, Culture, and Imperialism in England, 1715–1785* (Berkeley: University of California Press, 2002); J.G.A. Pocock, *The Discovery of Islands* (Cambridge, UK: Cambridge University Press, 2005); Phillip Buckner, ed., *Canada and the British Empire* (Toronto: Oxford University Press, 2008); Nancy Christie, ed., *Transatlantic Subjects: Ideas, Institutions, and Social Experience in Post-Revolutionary British North America* (Montreal and Kingston: McGill-Queen's University Press, 2008).

25 Bernard Bailyn and Philip D. Morgan, eds, *Strangers within the Realm: Cultural Margins of the First British Empire* (Chapel Hill, NC: University of North Carolina Press, 1991); J.M. Bumsted, "The Consolidation of British North America, 1783–1860," in Buckner, *Canada and the British Empire*; J.M.S. Careless, "Frontierism, Metropolitanism, and Canadian History," *Canadian Historical Review* 35 (1954): 1–21.

26 Beginning in the 1830s, several grant schemes aimed at extending schooling to the poor and middle classes were put forward in Britain. The Elementary Education Act of 1870 provided for the first popular system of schooling in Britain. For thorough overviews of the development of schooling in Britain, see Gary McCullock, ed., *The RoutledgeFalmer Reader in History of Education* (New York: Routledge, 2005); and Roy Lowe, ed., *History of Education: Major Themes* (New York: Routledge, 2000).

27 This idea will be discussed in further detail in chapters 2 and 3. The plan
    drawn up in 1815 for common schooling that I have referred to was in
    John Strachan's educational report of that year, which would influence the
    Common School Act of 1816. As will be seen, however, it was by no
    means the only influence on that act, as a lively public discourse had set
    the wheels of common schooling in motion decades earlier.

28 I am indebted to Carl Kaestle, who read and commented on a version
    of this chapter in conference paper form, for helping me develop this
    idea.

29 William Lyon Mackenzie, *Sketches of Canada and the United States*
    (London: Effingham Wilson, 1833), 133; McNairn, *The Capacity to
    Judge*, 131.

30 Prentice and Houston, *Schooling and Scholars*, 85.

31 For a discussion on the significant role played by women in the overall
    economy of Upper Canada, see Errington, *Wives and Mothers*.

32 McNairn, *The Capacity to Judge*, 133. Through an analysis of school
    notices in the colonial press, Errington has revealed a considerable degree
    of female participation in the educational development of the colony; see
    Wives and Mothers.

33 McNairn, *The Capacity to Judge*, 133.

34 Harvey Graff, *The Literacy Myth: Cultural Integration and Social
    Structure in the Nineteenth Century* (Vancouver: University of British
    Columbia Press, 1991).

35 For Graff's other work that specifically looks at literacy in the Canadian
    context, see "Literacy and Social Structure in the Nineteenth-Century
    City" (PhD diss., University of Toronto, 1975); "Toward a Meaning of
    Literacy: Literacy and Social Structure in Hamilton, Ontario, 1861,"
    History of Education Quarterly 13, no. 3 (1972); "Literacy and Social
    Structure in Elgin County, Canada West: 1861," *Histoire Social/Social
    History* 6, no. 11 (1973); and "The Reality behind the Rhetoric: The
    Social and Economic Meanings of Literacy in the Mid-Nineteenth
    Century: The Example of Literacy and Criminality," in Neil McDonald
    and Alf Chaiton, eds, *Egerton Ryerson and His Times* (Toronto:
    Macmillan of Canada, 1978), 187–220. For another discussion on the
    prevalence of literacy in Upper Canada, see Smaller, "Teachers and Schools
    in Early Ontario," 291–308.

36 Carl Benn, "The Upper Canadian Press, 1793–1815," *Ontario History* 70
    (1978): 100.

37   Douglas McCalla, *Planting the Province: The Economic History of Upper Canada, 1784–1870* (Toronto: University of Toronto Press, 1993), 114–15; McNairn, *The Capacity to Judge*, 130.

38   McNairn, *The Capacity to Judge*, 131.

39   Benn, "The Upper Canadian Press," 100.

40   Thomas S. Maitland to William Lyon Mackenzie, 8 March 1825, quoted in McNairn, *The Capacity to Judge*, 132.

41   McNairn, *The Capacity to Judge*, 132. For a discussion on boarding patterns in Upper Canada, see Michael B. Katz, *The People of Hamilton, Canada West: Family and Class in a Mid-Nineteenth-Century City* (Cambridge, MA: Harvard University Press, 1975).

42   Habermas, *The Transformation of the Public Sphere*, esp. 30–6.

43   John Howison, *Sketches of Upper Canada, Domestic, Local, and Characteristic: to which are added, Practical Details for the Information of Emigrants of every class; and some recollections of the United States of America* (East Ardsley, UK: R.R. Publishers, 1821; Toronto: Johnson Reprint Corp., 1965), 207–8.

44   Julia Roberts, *In Mixed Company: Taverns and Public Life in Upper Canada* (Vancouver: University of British Columbia Press, 2009).

45   As Julia Roberts suggests in her analysis of the participation of Aboriginals and blacks in the public life of taverns in Upper Canada, inequitable access to land and occupation, segregated schools, churches, and voluntary associations, and the like meant that an overall "constrained freedom" for Upper Canadian minorities was a fact of life. See Julia Roberts, "'A Mixed Assemblage of Persons': Race and Tavern Space in Upper Canada," *Canadian Historical Review* 83, no. 1 (2002): 1–28.

46   McNairn, *The Capacity to Judge*, 134.

47   Nancy Christie and Michael Gauvreau, "Modalities of Social Authority: Suggesting an Interface for Religious and Social History," *Histoire Sociale/Social History* 36, no. 71 (2003): 1–30; Michael Gauvreau, "Covenanter Democracy: Scottish Popular Religion, Ethnicity, and the Varieties of Politico-religious Dissent in Upper Canada, 1815–1841," *Histoire Sociale/Social History* 36, no. 71 (2003): 55–83; Nancy Christie, "'On the threshold of manhood': Working-Class Religion and Domesticity in Victorian Britain and Canada," *Histoire Sociale/Social History* 36, no. 71 (2003): 145–75; Donald H. Akenson, *The Irish in Ontario: A Study in Rural History* (Montreal and Kingston: McGill-Queen's University Press, 1988); Brian P. Clarke, *Piety and Nationalism: Lay Voluntary Associations and*

the Creation of an Irish-Catholic Community in Toronto, 1850–1895 (Montreal and Kingston: McGill-Queen's University Press, 1993); Mark McGowan, *The Waning of the Green: Catholics, the Irish, and Identity in Toronto, 1887–1922* (Montreal and Kingston: McGill-Queen's University Press, 1999); Todd Webb, "How the Canadian Methodists Became British: Unity, Schism, and Transatlantic Identity, 1827–54," in Nancy Christie, ed., *Transatlantic Subjects: Ideas, Institutions, and Social Experience in Post-Revolution British North America* (Montreal and Kingston: McGill-Queen's University Press, 2008), 159–98.

48 Roberts, *In Mixed Company*, 6.

49 Some issues have been lost or destroyed, but most of them have survived and have been micro-reproduced. The Early Canadiana/Canadian Institute of Historical Microreproduction (hereafter CIHM) collection of Upper Canadian newspapers was primarily utilized. Some newspapers and issues not found in the CIHM collection were also examined at the Thomas Fisher Rare Book Library of the University of Toronto and at the special collections reading room of Library and Archives Canada. In addition to commentary, editorials, letters to the editor, advertisements, and official and non-official proclamations and announcements, the newspapers also served as valuable resources for the reportage of public gatherings and the printing of petitions.

50 A number of pamphlets not examined here might be useful to an examination of Upper Canada's intellectual development but were not directly relevant to this study. These pamphlets typically include literature, short stories, poetry, and other forms of fiction, as well as almanacs, self-help books, and other forms of what contemporaries often called "useful information." The CIHM collection of pamphlets was utilized. Some other pamphlets that were not micro-reproduced were also examined at Library and Archives Canada. Additionally, a number of pamphlets that cannot be found in any of our archival collections were printed in series within the newspapers of the day and were drawn out from a reading of those newspapers.

51 RG 5-A1, the Civil Secretary's Correspondence, otherwise known as the "Upper Canada Sundries," at Library and Archives Canada (hereafter LAC), consists of the central papers in which petitions to the civil and provincial secretaries can be found. Owing to its sheer volume and vast array of content (over 144,000 pages on every aspect of public administration in the colony), the Sundries were segregated into various sub-

groups of records. For the purposes of this study, RG 5-B3, petitions and addresses to the civil secretary, and RG 5-B11, records relating to education, were also examined.

52 J. George Hodgins (compiler), *Documentary History of Education in Upper Canada, from the Passing of the Constitutional Act of 1791 to the Close of the Reverend Doctor Ryerson's Administration of the Education Department in 1876*, 28 vols (Toronto: L.K. Cameron, 1894–1910).

CHAPTER ONE

1 The standard introductory text remains Gerald M. Craig, *Upper Canada: The Formative Years, 1784–1841* (Toronto: McClelland and Stewart, 1963).

2 Axelrod, *The Promise of Schooling*, 3.

3 "Petition of the Western Loyalists," 15 April 1787, in Arthur G. Doughty and Adam Shortt, eds, *Documents Relating to the Constitutional History of Canada, 1759–1791* (Ottawa: J. de L. Taché, 1918), 2:949–51.

4 There was only one newspaper for most of the 1790s, the government-sponsored *Upper Canada Gazette*, which began publication in the city of York (later Toronto) in 1793. While the newspaper was government sponsored, its editors did not always see eye-to-eye with the colonial government. Its first editor, Louis Roy, was criticized for being "indifferent about his work" and was dismissed after only one year, while the newspaper's second editor, Gideon Tiffany, "aroused official displeasure" for failing to toe the official line and was eventually dismissed as well. Two additional newspapers began publication at the turn of the century, the short-lived *Canada Constellation* in 1799 and the only slightly longer-lived *Niagara Herald* in 1800. Both newspapers, published by Gideon and Silvester Tiffany, were independent and can be considered moderate newspapers in that they neither toed nor defied government lines. For a more detailed discussion on Upper Canadian newspapers in this period, see Carl Benn, "The Upper Canadian Press, 1793–1815," *Ontario History* 70 (1978): 93–102.

5 E.A. Cruikshank, ed., *The Correspondence of Lieut. Governor John Graves Simcoe, with allied documents relating to his administration of the government of Upper Canada* (Toronto, 1923–31), quoted in Craig, *The Formative Years*, 25.

6 "Petition of the Western Loyalists," 15 April 1787, in Doughty and Shortt, *Documents Relating to the Constitutional History of Canada*, 2:949–951.

7   L.F.S. Upton, "William Smith," in George W. Brown and Marcel Trudel, eds, *Dictionary of Canadian Biography* (Toronto: University of Toronto Press, 1965–).

8   On the other hand, the report has received relative amount of attention in Quebec educational history. See, for example: Louis-Philippe Audet, *Histoire de l'enseignement au Québec, 1608–1971*, 2 vols (Montreal: Holt, Rinehart, and Winston, 1971); Andrée Dufour, *Histoire de l'éducation au Québec* (Montreal: Boréal, 1997); and Roger Magnuson, *The Two Worlds of Quebec Education during the Traditional Era, 1760–1940* (London, ON: Althouse Press, 2005).

9   *Report of a Committee of the Council on the Subject of Promoting the Means of Education/Rapport du commité du conseil, sur l'objet d'augmenter les moiens d'éducation.* Quebec: Samuel Neilson, 1789.

10 Ibid., 2.

11 Ibid., 3.

12 Louis-Philippe Audet, "Attempts to Develop a School System for Lower Canada: 1760–1840," in *Canadian Education: A History*, 150; Roger Magnuson, *The Two Worlds of Quebec Education during the Traditional Era, 1760–1940* (London, ON: Althouse Press, 2005), 11.

13 Ibid., 6.

14 Ibid.

15 Ibid., 7.

16 Ibid., 11.

17 Ibid.

18 Ibid., 11–12.

19 Ibid., 20.

20 Ibid.

21 Ibid., 20–1.

22 Ibid., 21.

23 Ibid., 24–5.

24 Ibid., 21.

25 Ibid., 23–4.

26 Ibid., 24.

27 Anonymous, *A Tour Through Upper and Lower Canada. By a Citizen of the United States. Containing, A View of the present State of Religion, Learning, Commerce, Agriculture, Colonization, Customs and Manners, among the English, French, and Indian Settlements* (Litchfield, 1799), 11.

28 Ibid., 25–6.

29 Ibid., 55.

30 Ibid.

31 Ibid., 57–8.

32 *Upper Canada Gazette*, 18 April 1793, 26 October 1796.

33 *Upper Canada Gazette*, 2 November 1796. A similar announcement was made a year later in the 25 November 1797 issue.

34 See especially *Upper Canada Gazette* 3, nos 6–12.

35 McNairn, *The Capacity to Judge*, 118.

36 *Upper Canada Gazette*, 30 November 1796.

37 Ibid., 21 December 1796.

38 Carl Benn, "The Upper Canadian Press, 1793–1815," *Ontario History* 70 (1978): 91–114.

39 *Upper Canada Gazette*, 20 November 1796. That some previous issues of the *Upper Canada Gazette* are missing makes it impossible to say with certainty that this was the first school advertisement in the history of the province.

40 Ibid., 8 March 1797.

41 Ibid.

42 Ibid., 10 March 1798.

43 Ibid., 11 August 1798.

44 Ibid., 16 March 1797.

45 Patricia Lockhart Fleming, Gilles Gallichan, and Yvan Lamonde, "Editors' Introduction," in Patricia Lockhart Fleming, Gilles Gallichan, and Yvan Lamonde, eds, *History of the Book in Canada* (Toronto: University of Toronto Press, 2004), 5.

46 *Upper Canada Gazette*, 28 June 1797.

47 "Address from the Upper Canada Legislature to the King's Most Excellent Majesty," in J. George Hodgins, compiler, *Documentary History of Education in Upper Canada, from the Passing of the Constitutional Act of 1791 to the Close of the Reverend Doctor Ryerson's Administration of the Education Department in 1876* (Toronto: L.K. Cameron, 1894–1910), 1:16. Hereafter cited as *DHE*.

48 *DHE*, 1:17.

49 *Journal of the House of Assembly of Upper Canada*, 15 June 1799, 104.

50 *Journal of the Legislative Council of Upper Canada*, 29 June 1799, 96.

51 *Upper Canada Gazette*, 6 July 1799.

52 Holding certification, however, was not an enforced requirement, and the lack of records dealing with this issue leads me to conclude that it was

purely symbolic. Nevertheless, the idea that government could play a role in what was generally considered a private matter was alive.

53 *Upper Canada Gazette*, 13 July 1799.

54 John Strachan, autobiography, reprinted in DHE, 1:9.

CHAPTER TWO

1 For a discussion of their relationship with colonial officials, see Carl Benn, "The Upper Canadian Press, 1793–1815," *Ontario History* 70 (1978): 91–114.

2 *Canada Constellation*, 4 January 1800.

3 McCalla, *Planting the Province*, appendix B, statistical table 1.1.

4 *Niagara Herald*, 16 May 1801. The *Niagara Herald* was published by the Tiffany brothers, Gideon and Silvester. Gideon had been the editor of the *Upper Canada Gazette* in the 1790s before being fired for failing to toe the official line.

5 The act provided a total of £800 for eight grammar schools that were to be centrally located in each of the colony's eight districts. Five trustees in each district, appointed by the lieutenant governor, were given powers to appropriate funds and appoint teachers. Teachers were to be natural-born subjects and could be unilaterally dismissed from their positions by the lieutenant governor. See DHE, 1:60–1.

6 Houston and Prentice, *Schooling and Scholars*, 25.

7 *Upper Canada Gazette*, 10 January 1801.

8 *Niagara Herald*, 21 February 1801, 28 February 1801, 7 March 1801.

9 *Upper Canada Gazette*, 24 July 1802.

10 This author's ideas support historian Christopher Bayly's argument that one effect of the French Revolutionary Wars was to promote religion as an integral component of British imperial rule. In this sense, religion was Christian but not necessarily linked to the Church of England. Some form of tolerance for other Christian sects was necessary in order for the empire to be defended against atheistic France. Such tolerance and Christian indoctrination, according to the author in the *Upper Canada Gazette*, could be supported by government through the aiding and funding of schools. See Christopher Bayly, *Imperial Meridian: The British Empire and the World, 1780–1830* (London: Longman, 1989).

11 *Upper Canada Gazette*, 21 August 1802.

12 Alison L. Prentice and Susan E. Houston, *Family, School, and Society in Nineteenth-Century Canada* (Toronto: Oxford University Press, 1975), 6.

13 *Journal of the House of Assembly of Upper Canada*, 16 February 1804, 429–30; see also *DHE*, 1:48–9.

14 *Journal of the House of Assembly of Upper Canada*, 1804, 16, 17, 20 February 1804, 430–2, 435, 438; and 19, 25, 27 February 1805, 34, 43, 46.

15 *Journal of the House of Assembly of Upper Canada*, 22–28 February 1806, 85–101; *Journal of the Legislative Council of Upper Canada*, 28 February to 1 March 1806, 267–9.

16 See D'arcy Boulton, *Sketch of His Majesty's Province of Upper Canada* (London, UK: C. Rickaby, 1805).

17 Jane Errington, *The Lion, the Eagle, and Upper Canada,*" 49.

18 For a more elaborate discussion on radical politics in this period, see Wilton, *Popular Politics and Political Culture.*

19 *Upper Canada Gazette*, 30 August 1806.

20 For example, see *Upper Canada Gazette*, 4 October 1806, 11 October 1806.

21 For more elaborate discussions on political culture and ideology in Upper Canada, see Mills, *The Idea of Loyalty*, and Errington, *The Lion, the Eagle, and Upper Canada.*

22 Wilton, *Popular Politics and Political Culture*, 24.

23 Ibid., 26.

24 Carl Benn, "The Upper Canadian Press, 1793–1815," *Ontario History* 70 (1978): 100.

25 Anonymous, *To the Right Honourable Lord Castlereagh one of His Majesty's Principle Secretaries of State* (Quebec, 1809), 3. Historians generally agree that the author of this pamphlet was Richard Cartwright, member of the Legislative Council.

26 John Mills Jackson, *A View of the Political Situation of the Province of Upper Canada, in North America in which her physical capacity is stated; the means of diminishing her burden, encreasing her value, and securing her connection to Great Britain are fully considered, with notes and appendix* (London, UK: W. Earle, 1809), 18.

27 *York Gazette*, 25 April 1807.

28 Ibid., 11 November 1807.

29 John Strachan, *The Christian Religion, Recommended in a Letter to his Pupils* (Montreal: Nahum Mower, 1807).

30 Ibid., 7.

31 Ibid., 15–20.

32 See chapter 1 and Christopher Bayly, *Imperial Meridian: The British Empire and the World, 1780–1830* (London, UK: Longman, 1989). For a contrast to Bayly's emphasis on the struggle for British imperial hegemony, see Eliga Gould "A Virtual Nation: Greater Britain and the Imperial Legacy of the American Revolution," *American Historical Review* 87, no. 2 (1999): 476–89; and "America's Independence and Britain's Counter-Revolution," *Past and Present* 154 (1997): 107–41. Gould suggests that imperialist rulers gradually accepted a new multicultural empire that helped redefine Britishness in the nineteenth century.

33 *York Gazette*, 20 January 1808; *Journal of the House of Assembly of Upper Canada*, 20 January 1808, 191–2; *Journal of the Legislative Council of Upper Canada*, 20 January 1808, 297–8.

34 *Journal of the House of Assembly of Upper Canada*, 2 February 1810, 284–5.

35 Anonymous, *To the Right Honourable Lord Castlereagh*, 7.

36 Ibid., 8.

37 *Journal of the House of Assembly of Upper Canada*, 3 February 1810, 286–287. The bill was dropped after second reading.

38 Aaron David Whelchel suggests that the same assumption was later made in 1816, when a common school bill was finally passed. Aaron David Whelchel, "'The Schoolmaster Is Abroad': The Diffusion of Educational Innovations in the Nineteenth Century British Empire" (PhD diss., Washington State University, 2011).

39 *Kingston Gazette*, 25 September 1810. The newspaper's editor, Stephen Miles, although a supporter of the official government line, was a Methodist and not a member of the Church of England clique that dominated executive politics. While the *Kingston Gazette* was certainly a pro-establishment publication, this did not mean that it was closed to ideas that were not supported by the colonial government. It often printed contributions from conservatives themselves that diverged significantly from the interests of the colonial government.

40 Ibid.

41 Ibid., 30 October 1810.

42 Ibid., 13 November 1810.

43 Library and Archives Canada (hereafter LAC), RG-5 A1, pp. 4565–8, "Petition of the Trustees of the Public Schools, London District," 30 January 1810.

44 *Kingston Gazette*, 12 February 1811.

45 Ibid., 3 September 1811.

46 *Journal of the Legislative Council of Upper Canada*, 23 and 25 February 1811, 377–9.

47 *Journal of the House of Assembly of Upper Canada*, 26 February 1811, 432–3.

48 *York Gazette*, 11 December 1811.

CHAPTER THREE

1 George W. Spragge, "John Strachan's Contribution to Education, 1800–1823," *Canadian Historical Review* 22 (1941): 147–58; Alison Smith, "John Strachan and Early Upper Canada, 1799–1814," *Ontario History* 52 (1960): 159–73; J.D. Purdy, "John Strachan and Education in Canada, 1800–1851" (PhD diss., University of Toronto, 1962), and Purdy, "John Strachan's Educational Policies, 1815–1841"; Silvia Boorman, *John Toronto: A Biography of Bishop Strachan* (Toronto: Clarke, Irwin, 1969); J.L.H. Henderson, *John Strachan, 1778–1867* (Toronto: University of Toronto Press, 1969); J. Donald Wilson, "Foreign and Local Influences on Popular Education in Upper Canada, 1815–1844" (PhD diss., University of Western Ontario, 1971), and "Education in Upper Canada: Sixty Years of Change," in J. Donald Wilson, Robert M. Stamp, and Louis-Philippe Audet, eds., *Canadian Education: A History* (Toronto: Prentice-Hall, 1970), 190–213; David Flint, *John Strachan, Pastor and Politician* (Toronto: Oxford University Press, 1971).

2 Houston and Prentice draw a connection between the impact of the war on people like John Strachan and the rise of anti-Americanism and the making of the Common School Act of 1816 and the desire to forge a British legacy in the common schools. See Houston and Prentice, *Schooling and Scholars*, 27–9.

3 George Sheppard, *Plunder, Profit, and Paroles: A Social History of the War of 1812 in Upper Canada* (Montreal and Kingston: McGill-Queen's University Press, 1994).

4 Jane Errington, *The Lion, the Eagle, and Upper Canada: A Developing Colonial Ideology* (Montreal and Kingston: McGill-Queen's University Press, 1987).

5 David Mills, *The Idea of Loyalty in Upper Canada, 1784–1850* (Montreal and Kingston: McGill-Queen's University Press, 1988).

6 Jeffrey McNairn, "Publius of the North: Tory Republicanism and the American Constitution in Upper Canada, 1848–54," *Canadian Historical Review* 77, no. 4 (1996): 504–37; "Towards Deliberative Democracy: Parliamentary Intelligence and the Public Sphere in Upper Canada, 1791–1840," *Journal of Canadian Studies* 33, no. 1 (1998): 39–60; and *The Capacity to Judge.*

7 *York Gazette*, 11 July 1812.

8 Ibid., 12 February 1812

9 Sheppard, *Plunder, Profit, and Paroles.*

10 Errington, *The Lion, the Eagle, and Upper Canada*, 18.

11 Ibid., 36.

12 Michael Smith, *A Geographical View of the Province of Upper Canada* (Philadelphia: Thomas and Robert Desliver, 1813), 82, quoted in Errington, *The Lion, the Eagle, and Upper Canada*, 36.

13 Mills, *The Idea of Loyalty in Upper Canada*, 26.

14 John Strachan, *A Sermon Preached at York before the Legislative Council and House of Assembly, August 2nd, 1812* (York: John Cameron, 1812).

15 Ibid., 17.

16 Ibid.

17 House of Assembly of Upper Canada, "Address of the House of Assembly to the People of Upper Canada," *Kingston Gazette*, 5 September 1812, 12 September 1812, 19 September 1812, and 26 September 1812.

18 *York Gazette*, 15 February 1815.

19 Mills, *The Idea of Loyalty in Upper Canada*, 26.

20 Ibid., 27.

21 Sheppard, *Plunder, Profit, and Paroles.*

22 *Journal of the House of Assembly of Upper Canada*, 11 February 1812, 15–16.

23 Petition of the inhabitants of the Midland District, *Journal of the House of Assembly of Upper Canada*, 11 February 1812, 16–17.

24 *Journal of the House of Assembly of Upper Canada*, 26 February 1812, 54; *Journal of the Legislative Council of Upper Canada*, 3 March 1812, 427; *Journal of the House of Assembly of Upper Canada*, 4 March 1814,

132–3; *Journal of the Legislative Council of Upper Canada*, 4 March 1814, 446–7.

25 LAC, MG24-J1, John Strachan Fonds, Letterbooks and Miscellaneous Papers, "Report on Education," 1815.

26 Ibid.

27 Ibid.

28 Ibid.

29 Patrick Walsh, "Education and the 'Universalist' Idiom of Empire: Irish National School Books in Ireland and Ontario," *History of Education* 37, no. 5 (2008): 645–60.

30 Catherine Hall, "Making Colonial Subjects: Education in the Age of Empire," *History of Education* 37, no. 6 (2008): 773–87; J.A. Mangan, ed., *"Benefits Bestowed"? Education and British Imperialism* (Manchester: Manchester University Press, 1988).

31 Elizabeth Jane Errington, "British Migration and British America, 1783–1867," in Buckner, *Canada and the British Empire*, 140–1.

32 Gwendolyn Davies, "Consolation to Distress: Loyalist Literary Activity in the Maritimes," *Acadiensis* 16, no. 2 (1987): 56, quoted in Jonathan Vance, *A History of Canadian Culture* (Toronto: Oxford University Press, 2009), 60.

33 Carl Kaestle, *Pillars of the Republic: Common Schools and American Society, 1780–1860* (Toronto: HarperCollins Canada, 2001). Kaestle's emphasis was on the urban schools. In a 1980 correction to both his and other revisionist educational histories of the 1960s and 1970s, most notably Michael Katz's *Irony of Early School Reform*, Kaestle and Maris Vinovskis suggest that rural areas often led the way in the common school reform movement. Carl Kaestle and Maris Vinovskis, *Education and Social Change in Massachusetts* (Cambridge: Cambridge University Press, 1980).

34 Kim Tolley and Nancy Beadie, "Socioeconomic Incentives to Teach in New York and North Carolina: Toward a More Complex Model of Teacher Labor Markets, 1800–1850," *History of Education Quarterly* 46, no. 1 (2006): 36–72; Nancy Beadie, "Tuition Funding for Common Schools: Education Markets and Market Regulation in Rural New York, 1815–1850," *Social Science History* 32, no. 1 (2008): 107–33; Nancy Beadie, "Toward a History of Education Markets in the United States: An Introduction," *Social Science History* 32, no. 1 (2008): 47–73; Nancy Beadie, "Education and the Creation of Capital: Or What I have Learned from Following the Money," *History of Education Quarterly* 48, no. 1

(2008): 1–29; Nancy Beadie, "Education, Social Capital and State Formation in Comparative Historical Perspective: Preliminary Investigations,"
Paedagogica Historica 46, nos 1–2 (2010): 15–32; Nancy Beadie, *Education and the Creation of Capital in the Early American Republic* (New
York: Cambridge University Press, 2010).

35 LAC, RG5 A1, pp. 1436–8, "Petition of Thomas Hilborn to Alexander
Grant," York, 28 September 1805. This is one example of hundreds of
letters sent to the civil secretary's office by groups of settlers looking to
establish complete communities.

CHAPTER FOUR

1 *Journal of the House of Assembly of Upper Canada,* 6 February 1816,
167–70.

2 Craig, *Upper Canada: The Formative Years,* 106.

3 Houston and Prentice, *Schooling and Scholars,* 27–30.

4 Smaller, "Teachers and Schools in Early Ontario," 291.

5 Wilson, "Education in Upper Canada: Sixty Years of Change," 200.

6 Purdy, "John Strachan's Educational Policies," 51.

7 Smaller, "Teachers and Schools in Early Ontario," 292.

8 *Journal of the House of Assembly of Upper Canada,* 7 and 8 February
1816, 170–3.

9 Ibid., 27 February 1816, 207–8.

10 Ibid., 28 February 1816, 209–11.

11 "An Act Granting to His Majesty a Sum of Money, to be Applied to the
use of Common Schools Throughout this Province, and to Provide for the
Regulations of Said Common Schools," in *DHE,* 1:102.

12 *Upper Canada Gazette,* 10 October 1817; *Kingston Gazette,* 18 November 1818; *Spectator,* 9 April 1818.

13 For more on Robert Gourlay and his effect upon Upper Canadian political
culture, see Lois Darroch Milani, *Robert Gourlay, Gadfly: The Biography
of Robert Fleming Gourlay, 1778–1863, Forerunner of the Rebellion in
Upper Canada, 1837* (Thornhill, ON: Ampersand Press, 1971); Wilton,
Popular Politics and Political Culture in Upper Canada; Mills, *Idea of
Loyalty in Upper Canada;* Errington, *The Lion, the Eagle, and Upper
Canada;* Craig, *The Formative Years.*

14 Robert Gourlay, *Statistical Account of Upper Canada,* 2 vols (London:
Simpkin and Marshall, 1822; reprint, Toronto, 1966).

15 A plethora of town meeting notices can be found in all the newspapers in response to Gourlay's address, and roughly one-third of the colony responded to his survey.

16 Gourlay, *Statistical Account of Upper Canada*, 258–9.

17 James Strachan, *A Visit to the Province of Upper Canada, in 1819* (Aberdeen: D. Chalmers & Co., 1820), 132.

18 R.D. Gidney, "Education and Society in Upper Canada, 1791–1850" (MPhil thesis, University of London, 1969).

19 For valuable discussions on school attendance in nineteenth-century Upper Canada, see Michael Katz, "Who Went to School?," *History of Education Quarterly* 12, no. 3 (1972): 432–54; Ian Davey, "The Rhythm of Work and the Rhythm of School," in Neil McDonald and Alf Chaiton, eds, *Egerton Ryerson and His Times* (Toronto: Macmillan of Canada, 1978), 221–53; Ian Davey, "Educational Reform and the Working Class: School Attendance in Hamilton, Ontario, 1851–1891," PhD diss., University of Toronto, 1975; Ian Davey "School Reform and School Attendance: The Hamilton Central School, 1853–1861" (MA thesis, University of Toronto, 1972).

20 Gourlay, *Statistical Account*, 247.

21 Ibid., 225.

22 Ibid., 226.

23 *Kingston Gazette*, 9 June 1818.

24 Ibid.

25 Ibid.

26 Ibid. Author's quotation taken from John Strachan, *A Concise Introduction to Practical Arithmetic; For the use of Schools* (Montreal: Nahum Mower, 1809), vi.

27 *Journal of the House of Assembly of Upper Canada*, 21 February 1820, 205–8.

28 Ibid., 23 February 1820, 211–12.

29 *Upper Canada Gazette*, 13 January 1820.

30 Ibid.

31 *Journal of the House of Assembly of Upper Canada*, 4, 6, and 7 March 1820, 247, 253–4, 261–2.

32 *Upper Canada Gazette*, 31 March 1820.

33 *Journal of the House of Assembly of Upper Canada*, 15, 16, 17, 23, 24, and 30 June 1819, 114–115, 118, 120–121, 133–134, 136, and 157–158; *Journal of the Legislative Council of Upper Canada*, 21, 22, and 28 June 1819, 469–470, 471–472, and 477.

34 "An Act to Repeal Part of, and to Amend, the Laws Now in Force for Establishing Public (Grammar) Schools in the Several Districts of this Province, and to Extend the Provisions of the Same," clause 6, in DHE, 1:148–50.

35 Ibid., clause 5.

36 "Report of the Executive Committee of 1819," DHE, 1:150–2.

37 J. George Hodgins, DHE, 1:175.

38 The assembly took up the matter eight years later, in 1828, and it became, as historian J. George Hodgins calls it, a *cause célèbre*, evoking a great deal of feeling, as well as a politico-religious discussion, both acrimonious and bitter, throughout the province. It developed into a prolonged struggle against the alleged attempt to introduce a quasi state-church system into Upper Canada, pitting the public in direct opposition to the Family Compact. The events surrounding the 1828 public backlash will be discussed in chapter 6.

39 LAC, RG5 B11, document 33, "Petition of the Shareholders of York Common School House, that the present teacher be allowed to continue to teach." See also "York Trustees to Lieutenant Governor Maitland," 28 August 1820, DHE, 1:175.

40 "George Hillier to the Trustees of the Common School of the Township of York," 31 August 1820, DHE, 1:176.

41 DHE, 1:175. The Lancastrian system was a form of monitorial schooling adapted by the British educational reformer Joseph Lancaster in the early nineteenth century. More advanced students would aid the teacher by tutoring students not yet at their level. As the idea of popular schooling grew, so too did this method, as it allowed for larger class sizes per teacher.

42 "First Annual Report of the Upper Canada Central School on the British National System of Education," DHE, 1:177–8.

43 *Christian Recorder*, March 1819.

44 See in particular May 1819 and September 1820.

45 *York Weekly Post*, 22 March 1821. From 1821 to 1828, the *Upper Canada Gazette* was published in two parts. The first part – the official part – continued to be named the *Upper Canada Gazette*, while the second part – the news part – was called the *York Weekly Post* from 1821 to 1822, the *Weekly Register* from 1822 to 1826, and the *U.E. Loyalist* from 1826 to 1828.

46 See Mills, *The Idea of Loyalty in Upper Canada*.

47 *Upper Canada Gazette,* 21 January 1819.

48 Bruce Curtis, "Monitorial Schooling, 'Common Christianity,' and Politics: A Transatlantic Controversy," in Christie, ed., *Transatlantic Subjects,* 251–79.

49 "Maitland to Bathurst," 1822, in *DHE,* 1:179.

50 *DHE,* 1:179.

51 Purdy, "John Strachan's Educational Policies, 1815–1841."

52 Craig, *Upper Canada: The Formative Years,* 118. For a general discussion on the parliaments of Upper Canada and their relationships with the executive, see J.K. Johnson, *Becoming Prominent: Regional Leadership in Upper Canada, 1791–1841* (Montreal and Kingston: McGill-Queen's University Press, 1989).

53 LAC, RG5 B3, pp. 216–17, "Petition of Peter Robinson's Irish Immigrants," Peterborough, circa 1823. A similar request was also made by seventeen Catholic petitioners in the Niagara District. That petition is undated, however, and so it is difficult to say whether it would have been made at the same time or at another point in Maitland's tenure (which lasted to 1828); LAC, RG5 B3, p. 351, "Petition of James W. Campion, Catholic Missionary for Niagara and St Catharines, and the Catholic Inhabitants, to Sir Peregrine Maitland," undated.

54 *Journal of the House of Assembly of Upper Canada,* 19 March 1823; *Gleaner, and Niagara Newspaper,* 4 January 1823.

55 *Journal of the House of Assembly of Upper Canada,* 4 March 1823, 372.

56 William Weekes had left provisions in his will for part of his estate to be used toward the creation of a college in Upper Canada. The legislature could not decide on what form the college should take and thus could not agree upon how to use Weekes's estate for that end.

57 Common School Act of 1824, *DHE,* 1:198–9.

58 It is usually, in fact, the focus of entire studies of its own. See, for example, A.B. McKillop, *Matters of Mind: The University in Ontario, 1791–1951* (Toronto: University of Toronto Press, 1994).

59 Craig, *The Formative Years,* 119.

CHAPTER FIVE

1 See especially Curtis, *Building the Educational State,* 22–96.

2 William Lyon Mackenzie, *Catechism of Education. Part First* (York: Colonial Advocate Press, 1830).

3   J.M. Dent, *The Story of the Upper Canadian Rebellion*, 2 vols (Toronto: C. Blacknett Robinson, 1885); Colin Read, *The Rebellion of 1837 in Upper Canada* (Ottawa: Canadian Historical Association, 1988).

4   S.F. Wise, *God's Peculiar Peoples: Essays on Political Culture in Nineteenth-Century Canada*, edited by A.B. McKillop and Paul Romney (Ottawa: Carleton University Press, 1988).

5   See chapter 2.

6   For one of the most scathing attacks on Mackenzie's character, see *Weekly Register*, 27 May 1824. Other, more moderate newspapers also got into the mix; see, for example, the *Gleaner, and Niagara Newspaper*, 28 August 1824.

7   *Colonial Advocate*, 18 May 1824.

8   Ibid. The lengthy essay was continued in the following issue of 27 May 1824.

9   *Colonial Advocate*, 27 May 1824.

10 Ibid., 18 May 1824.

11 Ibid.

12 Note that Mackenzie felt compelled to clarify to his Upper Canadian readers that "home" was a reference to Britain.

13 *Colonial Advocate*, 27 May 1824.

14 H.P. Gundy, "Francis Collins," in George W. Brown and Marcel Trudel, eds., *Dictionary of Canadian Biography* (Toronto: University of Toronto Press, 1965–).

15 *Canadian Freeman*, 1 December 1825.

16 *Gleaner, and Niagara Newspaper*, 9 July 1825.

17 LAC, RG5 B3, pp. 138–41, "The Petition of the Protestant & Catholic Inhabitants of Drummond Island," circa 1825. A second petition was sent in 1827. LAC, RG5 B11, document 133, "Petition of John Munroe on behalf of the inhabitants of Drummond Island," 8 August 1827.

18 LAC, RG5 B11, document 73, "Report of the General Board for the Superintendence of Education on Common Schools throughout the province."

19 Of course, support of mixed religious schooling was by no means unanimous. Consider the petition of Samuel Armour, a recently emigrated and appointed school teacher in Peterborough. Writing to the lieutenant governor in 1826, he insisted that Catholic and Protestant children could hardly be expected to read scripture or pray together and that secular schooling might indeed be a better pursuit than attempting to find a common ground. LAC RG5 B11, document 80, Letters of Samuel Armour, 29 and 30 May 1826.

20 *Colonial Advocate*, 10 March 1825, 7 April 1825.
21 Ibid., 16 June 1825.
22 It is my interpretation that the "dry and parched soil" metaphor was aimed to appeal to Upper Canada's agrarian population.
23 *Colonial Advocate*, 18 May 1824.
24 Ibid.
25 *Upper Canada Herald*, 25 January 1825.
26 *Kingston Chronicle*, 20 May 1825.
27 John Strachan, *A Sermon Preached at York, Upper Canada, Third of July, 1825, On the death of the Late Lord Bishop of Quebec* (Kingston: James McFarlane, 1826), 26.
28 Ibid., 21.
29 Mills, *The Idea of Loyalty in Upper Canada*, 51.
30 Egerton Ryerson, *Letters from the Reverend Egerton Ryerson to The Hon. And Reverend Doctor Strachan* (Kingston: Herald Office, 1828). The letters originally appeared in the *Colonial Advocate* throughout the spring of 1826.
31 Ibid., 37.
32 Ibid., 39–40.
33 *Upper Canada Herald*, 22 October 1827, reprinted in *Canadian Freeman*, 25 October 1827.
34 By no means, however, were all Methodists united in 1820s Upper Canada. Todd Webb has demonstrated that the complexity of the relationship between the Canadian Methodists and the British Wesleyans would hinder the formation of a unified culture among the Methodists in Upper Canada until the 1850s. Nevertheless, they were in agreement in their opposition to Strachan. See Todd Webb, "How the Canadian Methodists Became British," in Christie, ed., *Transatlantic Subjects*, 159–98.
35 *Colonial Advocate*, 22 July 1828.
36 Ibid., 11 May 1826.
37 *U.E. Loyalist*, 6 June 1828.
38 William Westfall, *Two Worlds: The Protestant Culture of Nineteenth-Century Ontario* (Montreal and Kingston: McGill-Queen's University Press, 1989), 24–5.
39 *U.E. Loyalist*, 3 June 1826; 24 June 1826; 15 July 1826.
40 *Kingston Chronicle*, 7 July 1826.
41 *Colonial Advocate*, 9 March 1828.
42 *U.E. Loyalist*, 15 September 1827.

CHAPTER SIX

1   *Upper Canada Gazette*, 2 March 1826.
2   John Strachan, *An Appeal to the Friends of Religion and Literature, in Behalf of the University of Upper Canada* (London: R. Gilbert, 1827).
3   Ibid., 6.
4   Ibid.
5   John Webster Grant, *A Profusion of Spires: Religion in Nineteenth-Century Ontario* (Toronto: University of Toronto Press, 1988), 90.
6   *Colonial Advocate*, 27 September 1827.
7   *Canadian Freeman*, reprinted in the *Colonial Advocate*, 27 September 1827.
8   *Gore Gazette*, 29 September 1827.
9   *Canadian Freeman*, 11 October 1827.
10   *Gleaner, and Niagara Newspaper*, 29 October 1827.
11   Ibid., 3 December 1827.
12   *Gore Gazette*, 29 September 1827.
13   *Colonial Advocate*, 18 October 1827.
14   14*Canadian Freeman*, 6 October 1827.
15   *Colonial Advocate*, 25 October 1827.
16   *Upper Canada Herald*, reprinted in *Canadian Freeman*, 8 November 1827.
17   LAC, RG5 B11, document 130, "The Petition of His Majesty's Dutiful and Loyal Subjects, the Inhabitants of the Midland District," January 1828.
18   *Colonial Advocate*, 22 November 1827.
19   Ibid., 20 December 1827.
20   *Quebec Gazette*, December 1827, reprinted in *Colonial Advocate*, 27 December 1827.
21   *Kingston Chronicle*, 19 October 1827, reprinted in *Colonial Advocate*, 25 October 1827.
22   *Colonial Advocate*, 25 October 1827.
23   Ibid.
24   Such a clause, in fact, did not exist in the charter, and so Mackenzie either misinterpreted it, or misled his readers on this point.
25   *Colonial Advocate*, 11 October 1827.
26   *Canadian Freeman*, 11 October 1827.
27   *Gleaner, and Niagara Newspaper*, 22 October 1827.
28   *Colonial Advocate*, 8 November 1827.

29 Ibid.
30 *Gleaner, and Niagara Newspaper*, 19 November 1827.
31 *Colonial Advocate*, 20 December 1827.
32 *Gleaner, and Niagara Newspaper*, 19 November 1827.
33 *U.E. Loyalist*, 1 December 1827.
34 *Upper Canada Gazette*, 22 December 1827.
35 Ibid., 26 January 1828.
36 *Journal of the House of Assembly of Upper Canada*, 8 February 1828 to 3 March 1828. A total of forty-six petitions signed by 5,146 inhabitants were presented to the assembly from 8 February 1828 to 3 March 1828. In *DHE*, 1:230–44.
37 *U.E. Loyalist*, 19 April to 17 May 1828; John Strachan, *A Speech of the Venerable John Strachan, D.D., Archdeacon of York, in the Legislative Council, Thursday Sixth March, 1828, on the Subject of the Clergy Reserves* (York: Robert Stanton, 1828).
38 Strachan, *A Speech*, 5.
39 Ibid., 13.
40 Ibid., 14–18.
41 Ibid., 19.
42 Ibid., 20.
43 Ibid., 22.
44 Ibid., 42.
45 *Gleaner, and Niagara Newspaper*, 28 April 1828.
46 Craig, *Upper Canada: The Formative Years*, 175.
47 "Report on the Petition of Christians of all Denominations Against Doctor Strachan's University Charter, Church Monopoly, &c. &c," quoted from the *Gleaner, and Niagara Newspaper*, 19 May 1828.
48 See chapter 4.
49 *Journal of the House of Assembly of Upper Canada*, 20 March 1828. The complete report can be found in *DHE*, 1:245–6. It was also published in its entirety in a series of issues of the *Colonial Advocate* beginning on 31 July 1828.
50 *DHE*, 1:245–6.
51 Ibid.
52 Ibid.
53 Ibid.
54 *Colonial Advocate*, 31 July 1828.
55 Ibid., 7 August 1828.

56 Ibid., 14 August 1828.

57 *U.E. Loyalist*, 20 January 1827.

58 *Gore Gazette*, 3 March 1827.

59 Ibid., 24 March 1827 and 21 April 1827.

60 *Farmers' Journal and Welland Canal Intelligencer*, 26 September 1827.

61 *Brockville Recorder*, 8 July 1828.

62 Quoted in the *Colonial Advocate*, 21 August 1828.

63 *Gore Gazette*, 30 August 1828.

64 Ibid., 4 October 1828.

65 *Colonial Advocate*, 15 March 1828.

CHAPTER SEVEN

1 *Colonial Advocate*, 25 September 1828.

2 Errington, *The Lion, the Eagle, and Upper Canada*, 186.

3 Craig, *Upper Canada: The Formative Years*, 176.

4 Errington, *The Lion, the Eagle, and Upper Canada*, 187.

5 Purdy, "John Strachan's Educational Policies," 58.

6 See, especially, Curtis, *Building the Educational State*.

7 Craig, *Upper Canada: The Formative Years*, 195.

8 "Report of the Select Committee on the Affairs of Upper Canada," reprinted in *Kingston Chronicle*, 30 August 1828.

9 *Kingston Chronicle*, 30 August 1828. See also *Colonial Advocate* 25 September 1828 and 27 November 1828.

10 Craig, *Upper Canada: The Formative Years*, 195.

11 *Canadian Freeman*, 23 October 1828.

12 *Brockville Gazette*, 17 October 1828.

13 *Kingston Chronicle*, 17 January 1829.

14 The debates of the 1820s led to the Reform Act of 1832, which introduced major changes to the electoral system of Britain, including the expansion of the electorate. Historian J.C.D. Clark argues that the late 1820s was a watershed period in which "the cultural hegemony of the old elite" was shattered. J.C.D. Clark, *English Society, 1688–1832: Ideology, Social Structure, and Political Practice during the Ancien Regime* (Cambridge: Cambridge University Press, 1985), 409.

15 See Boyd Hilton, *A Mad, Bad, and Dangerous People? England, 1783–1846* (Oxford: Oxford University Press, 2006). See also Eric J. Evans, *The Forging of the Modern State: Early Industrial Britain, 1783–1846*

(London: Longman, 1983); Frank O'Gorman, *The Long Eighteenth Century: British Political and Social History, 1688–1832* (New York: St Martin's Press, 1997).

16 *Colonial Advocate*, 4 December 1828.

17 *Kingston Chronicle*, 17 January 1829.

18 *Upper Canada Gazette*, 10 January 1829.

19 *Journal of the Legislative Council of Upper Canada*, 14 January 1829, 14–15; Upper *Canada Gazette*, 22 January 1829.

20 *Gore Gazette*, 17 January 1829.

21 Ibid.

22 *Gleaner, and Niagara Newspaper*, 23 January 1830.

23 Ibid.

24 *Journal of the House of Assembly of Upper Canada*, 14, 15, and 16 January 1829, 10–13.

25 Ibid., 17 January 1829, 13–14.

26 On 5 February 1829, this report was presented to the lieutenant governor, who thereafter, on 20 February 1829, forwarded a copy to the House of Assembly.

27 *Upper Canada Gazette*, 20 March 1829.

28 Ibid., 21 January 1830.

29 *Brockville Gazette*, 1 December 1831. This theme would also be picked up on in the Duncombe report of 1836.

30 *Canadian Freeman*, 15 September 1831.

31 Ibid., 6 October 1831.

32 Similar debates concerning the merits of a classical education were in fact also found in Britain itself. The Society for the Diffusion of Useful Knowledge was established in 1826 with the expressed purpose to publish "useful knowledge" aimed at those without the means, or need, to receive a classical education. The movement was closely associated with the establishment of London University in 1826 (later University College London), offering an alternative to the curricula of Oxford and Cambridge. See Negley Harte and John North, *The World of University College London, 1828–1990* (London: Routledge, 1991).

33 *Colonial Advocate*, 17 September 1829.

34 Ibid., 1 October 1829.

35 *Patriot and Farmer's Monitor*, 30 November 1829.

36 Ibid., 12 October 1829.

37 *Colonial Advocate*, 3 November 1829.

38   *Upper Canada Herald*, 25 February 1829.

39   *Kingston Chronicle*, 28 February 1829.

40   *Colonial Advocate*, 3 December 1829.

41   *Kingston Chronicle*, 10 October 1829, 31 October 1829, 7 November 1829, 21 November 1829, 5 December 1829, 19 December 1829.

42   LAC, RG5 B11, document 167, Petition of Robert Addison, Minister of Niagara, 3 January 1829.

43   LAC, RG5 B11, document 146, Petition of William Casgrave, 15 December 1828.

44   A petition from the inhabitants from the Township of West Gillimburg for school funding is interesting in that they make no reference to the Common School Act, nor to their right for school funding under that act. This is one example suggesting that such funding was seen as inadequate altogether, and, indeed, they proclaimed themselves to be "totally without the means of affording to their Children the smallest portion of education." LAC, RG5 B11, document 293, Petition of the Inhabitants of the 8th and 9th Concessions of the Township of Gillimburg," 20 May 1830.

45   See, for example, LAC RG5 B11, document 265, Petition of the Trustees of the Grantham Academy, 28 July 1830; LAC RG5 B11, document 298, Petition of the United Presbytery of Upper Canada, undated, circa 1830.

46   *Kingston Chronicle*, 7 November 1829.

47   Ibid., 19 December 1829.

48   John Strachan, *A Letter, To the Rev. A. N. Bethune, Rector of Cobourg, on the Management of Grammar Schools* (York: R. Stanton, 1829), 3–4.

49   Ibid., 4.

50   Ibid., 8–9.

51   Ibid., 10,

52   *Christian Guardian*, 21 November 1829.

53   Ibid.

54   *Christian Guardian*, 26 December 1829.

CHAPTER EIGHT

1   Albert Fiorino has studied the early foundations of Ryerson's educational thought prior to his appointment as superintendent of education in Canada West. Fiorino does much to contextualize Ryerson's educational philosophy within a transatlantic network of Wesleyan Methodist thought. While Fiorino brings Ryerson's early philosophical principles to

light, he does not link Ryerson's philosophy with either the public or the political context within which Ryerson's ideas were disseminated and developed. See Albert Fiorino, "The Philosophical Roots of Egerton Ryerson's Idea of Education as Elaborated in His Writings Preceding and Including the Report of 1846" (PhD diss., University of Toronto, 1975).

2 William Lyon Mackenzie, *Catechism of Education. Part First* (York: Colonial Advocate Press, 1830).

3 J. George Hodgins considers Mackenzie's pamphlet a "republication" of Hume's essay. See J. George Hodgins, ed., *Ryerson Memorial Volume: Prepared on the Occasion of the Unveiling of the Ryerson Statue in the Grounds of the Education Department on the Queen's Birthday, 1889* (Toronto: Warwick and Sons, 1889), 46. A reading of Mackenzie's pamphlet, however, makes it clear that, whatever the similarities, it was in fact readapted to address circumstances in Upper Canada.

4 Mackenzie, *Catechism of Education*, 4–6.

5 Ibid., 12–13.

6 Ibid., 24–46.

7 Ibid., 32, 36–40.

8 Ibid., 35.

9 Ibid., 24.

10 Ibid., 26.

11 Ibid., 35.

12 Ibid., 36–8.

13 Ibid., 38–40.

14 *Colonial Advocate*, 7 January 1830.

15 *Gleaner, and Niagara Newspaper*, 24 April 1830.

16 *Colonial Advocate*, 9 August 1832.

17 *Christian Guardian*, 16 January 1830.

18 Ibid. This very idea made its way into Duncombe's 1836 *Report upon the Subject of Education*, p. 19: "Hence, *now*, whatever may have been the state of things heretofore, it is criminal to acquire knowledge merely for the sake of knowledge – The man must be disciplined and furnished according to the duties that lie before him."

19 Ibid.

20 Ibid., 30 January 1830.

21 Ibid., 23 April 1831.

22 *Brockville Recorder*, 4 May 1830.

23 Ibid., 11 May 1830.

24 Ibid., 22 June 1830.

25 William Buell, a reform member of the House of Assembly from Leeds, headed a committee on education in early 1830. Also sitting on the committee were Robert Baldwin, Peter Perry, George Rolph, and James Lyon. On 24 February, their proposed bill was voted down, 20 to 19, by a majority of conservatives in the house. See *Journal of the House of Assembly of Upper Canada*, 22 January 1830 to 24 February 1830; and DHE, 1:300–16.

26 *Colonial Advocate*, 4 March 1830. This writer did not explain the use of the pseudonym "Clio," but significantly, she noted that "no new ideas are advanced" in her letter. The idea of extending education to the poor, she thus notes, had a history in Upper Canada.

27 *Christian Guardian*, 12 February 1831.

28 *Upper Canada Herald*, 3 March 1830.

29 *York Observer*, reprinted in *Canadian Freeman*, 26 August 1830.

30 *Canadian Freeman*, 26 August 1830.

31 *Brockville Gazette*, 28 December 1830.

32 *Journal of the House of Assembly of Upper Canada*, 18 November 1831, 23 November 1831, 5 January 1832, 25 January 1832, 8, 14, 76, 122.

33 Ibid., 1 February 1831, 34–5.

34 "Report of Select Committee on School Lands," *Appendix to the Journal of the House of Assembly of Upper Canada*, 1831, 214–15.

35 *Journal of the House of Assembly of Upper Canada*, 13 December 1831, 40.

36 Ibid., 5 January 1832.

CONCLUSION

1 Malcolm Gladwell, *The Tipping Point: How Little Things Can Make a Big Difference* (New York: Little, Brown, and Co., 2000).

2 Patrick Walsh, "Education and the 'Universalist' Idiom of Empire: Irish National School Books in Ireland and Ontario," *History of Education* 37, no. 5 (2008): 645–60; Donald Akenson, *Being Had: Historians, Evidence, and the Irish in North America* (Port Credit: P.D. Meany, 1985), see especially chapter 6, "Mass Schooling in Ontario: The Irish and "English Canadian" Popular Culture; V.E. Parvin, *Authorization of Textbooks for the Schools of Ontario, 1846–1950* (Toronto: University of Toronto Press, 1965).

3 Mackenzie, *Catechism of Education*, 32, 36–40.

4 Ibid., 35.

5 *Kingston Chronicle*, 28 May 1831, 11 June 1831, 9 July 1831.

6 Quoted in Egerton Ryerson, *The Story of My Life*, ed. J. George Hodgins (Toronto: W. Briggs, 1883), 284.

7 Chad Gaffield, *Language, Schooling, and Cultural Conflict: The Origins of the French-Language Controversy in Ontario* (Montreal and Kingston: McGill-Queen's University Press, 1987), 12.

8 Curtis, *Building the Educational State*, 98.

9 *Brockville Gazette*, 5 January 1832.

10 *Canadian Freeman*, 23 February 1832.

11 *Kingston Chronicle*, 10 March 1832.

12 Ibid.

13 Ibid., 17 March 1832.

14 Ibid., 24 March 1832.

15 Ibid.

16 Ibid., 31 March 1832.

17 *Christian Guardian*, 10 May 1832.

18 *Colonial Advocate*, 1 March 1832.

19 See Colborne's reply to the Conference of the Methodist Episcopal Church in Canada, in *Canadian Freeman*, 5 January 1832.

20 *Brockville Recorder*, 12 January 1832.

21 *The Times* (London, UK), 6 June 1836, reprinted in Egerton Ryerson, *The Affairs of the Canadas in a Series of Letters by A Canadian* (London, UK: J. King, College Hill, 1837).

22 Ibid., 30 June 1836; *Affairs* 32–35.

23 I am indebted to Richard Connors for pointing out the idea of Ryerson "making a statement" to the imperial government and for helping me develop this idea further.

24 *Patriot*, 15 November 1836, reprinted in Ryerson, *Affairs of the Canadas*, iii.

25 Ibid., 15 November 1836, reprinted in Ryerson, *Affairs of the Canadas*, iii.

26 *Montreal Gazette*, 19 November 1836, reprinted in Ryerson, *Affairs of the Canadas*, iii.

27 *Kingston Chronicle*, 30 November 1836, reprinted in Ryerson, *Affairs of the Canadas Affairs*, iv.

28 *Christian Guardian*, 16 January 1830.

29 Garth R. Lambert, *Dethroning Classics and Inventing English: Liberal Education and Culture in Nineteenth-Century Ontario* (Toronto: James Lorimer, 1995).

30 Indeed, focusing on Ryerson's writing alone has proven to be as frustrating as it has been revealing. Consider, for example, how he opposed the idea of separate schooling his entire life while sending his own daughter to a Catholic convent school in Quebec.

31 Catherine Hall, "Making Colonial Subjects: Education in the Age of Empire," *History of Education* 37, no. 6 (2008): 773–87.

Bibliography

PRIMARY SOURCES

Archival Collections

Library and Archives Canada, RG5-A1, Upper Canada Sundries
Library and Archives Canada, RG5-B3, Civil Secretary, Petitions and
  Addresses, Upper Canada, Volumes 6 to 9
Library and Archives Canada, RG5-B11, Upper Canada and Canada West:
  Civil Secretary, Records Relating to Education
Library and Archives Canada, MG24-J1, John Strachan Fonds

Newspapers

The Brockville Gazette, Brockville (1828–32)
Brockville Recorder, Brockville (1830–40, 1843–55)
Canada Constellation, Niagara (1799–1800)
The Canadian Casket, Hamilton (1831)
Canadian Correspondent, York/Toronto (1832–34)
Canadian Emigrant and Western District Advertiser, Sandwich (1831–34)
Canadian Freeman, York/Toronto (1825–34)
The Christian Guardian, York/Toronto (1829–44)
The Christian Recorder, York (1819–21)
The Cobourg Star, Cobourg (1831–44)
Colonial Advocate, Queenston and York/Toronto (1824–34)
The Courier of Upper Canada, York/Toronto (1830–36)

The Farmers' Journal and Welland Canal Intelligencer, St Catharines
   (1826–35)
The Gleaner, and Niagara Newspaper, Niagara (1818–37)
The Gore Gazette, Ancaster (1827–29)
Hallowell Free Press, Hallowell (1830–34)
The Kingston Gazette, Kingston (1810–18)
The Kingston Chronicle/The Chronicle and Gazette, Kingston (1819–44)
Niagara Herald, Niagara (1801–02)
The Niagara Spectator, Niagara (1816–20)
The Patriot, Kingston and Toronto (1828–75)
The Reformer, Cobourg (1832–35)
St Thomas Liberal, St Thomas (1832–33)
Spirit of the Times, Niagara (1830–31)
The Times, London, England (1785–)
Weekly Register, York (1822–25)
Western Mercury, Hamilton (1831–34)
The United Empire Loyalist/The Loyalist, York (1826–28)
Upper Canada Gazette/York Gazette, Newark and York/Toronto
   (1793–1842)
Upper Canada Guardian, or, Freeman's Journal, Niagara (1807–12)
The Upper Canada Herald, Kingston (1819–40)
York Weekly Post, York (1821)

                              Pamphlets

Anonymous. *A Tour Through Upper and Lower Canada. By a Citizen of
   the United States. Containing, A View of the present State of Religion,
   Learning, Commerce, Agriculture, Colonization, Customs and Manners,
   among the English, French, and Indian Settlements.* Litchfield, 1799.
Anonymous. *To the Right Honourable Lord Castlereagh one of His
   Majesty's Principle Secretaries of State.* Quebec, 1809.
Bidwell, Marshall S. *Mr. Bidwell's Speech on the Intestate Estate Bill, in
   the Provincial Assembly of Upper Canada, January 24, 1831.* York,
   1831.
– *Substance of Mr. Bidwell's Speech on the second reading of his Intesttne
   [sic]Estates Bill, in the Session of 1832.* York, 1832.
Boulton, D'arcy. *Sketch of His Majesty's Province of Upper Canada.* Lon-
   don: C. Rickaby, 1805.

Bridges, John George. *A Digest of British Constitution; Compiled by Dr. Bridges, and Delivered by Him as a Lecture at Many of the Principal Towns in Upper Canada.* Montreal: John Lovell, 1839.

– *The Every Boy's Book, or a Digest of the British Constitution. Compiled and Arranged for the Use of Schools and Private Families.* Ottawa: Ottawa Advocate Office, 1842.

Buchanan, Isaac. *First Series of Five Letters, Against the Baldwin Faction, by An Advocate of Responsible Government, and of the New College Bill.* Toronto: British Colonist Office, 1844.

Burns, Rev. John. *True Patriotism: A Sermon, Preached in the Presbyterian Church in Stanford, Upper Canada, on the 3rd day of June 1814.* Montreal: Nahum Mower, 1814.

Cartwright, Richard. *Letters from an American Loyalist in Upper-Canada to His Friend in England.* Halifax, 1810.

Davis, Robert. *The Canadian Farmer's Travels In the United States of America, in which remarks are made on The Arbitrary Colonial Policy Practiced in Canada and the Free and Equal Rights, And Happy Effects of the Liberal Institutions and Astonishing Enterprise of the United States.* Buffalo: Steele's Press, 1837.

Declaration of the Views and Objects, of the British Constitutional Society, on its Re-organization. Addressed to their Fellow Subjects in Upper Canada. Toronto, 1836.

Dunbar, Ross [pseudo. Zeno]. *The 'Crise' Metcalfe and The Lafontaine-Baldwin Cabinet Defended. Letter of Zeno to the Legislative Assembly of Canada.* Quebec: W. Cowan & Son, 1844.

First Report of the Central Committee of the Inhabitants of Upper Canada. York: William Lyon Mackenzie, 1827.

First Report on the State of the Representation of the People of Upper Canada in the Legislature of that Province. York: Colonial Advocate, 1831.

Fuimus [?]. *Letter to His Excellency the Right Honourable Lord Elgin, On Responsible Government, As applied simply to the Province of Canada; Together with his Lordship's Celebrated Speech Delivered in the House of Commons as Lord Bruce, in 1841, Deprecating in the Strongest Terms, All Appointments to Office by a Tottering Ministry, Not Enjoying the Confidence of the People.* Montreal: Donoghue & Mantz, 1847.

Gourlay, Robert. *A Constitutional Conversation with a Conscientious Colonist; or Truth as Error.* Np, nd.

– *General Introduction to a Statistical Account of Upper Canada*. London: Simpkin and Marshall, 1822.
– *Statistical Account of Upper Canada*. 2 vols. London: Simpkin and Marshall, 1922. Reprint, New York: Johnson Reprint Corp., 1966.
Gowan, Lieutenant-Colonel. *An Important Letter on Responsible Government*. Toronto: Examiner Office, 1839.
Grant, James Charles. *A Letter from J. C. Grant, Esquire, of Montreal, in Reply to the Honorable and Venerable John Strachan, D. D., LL.D., Archdeacon of York*. Kingston: Upper Canada Herald Office, 1830.
Great Britain, Sovereign, Queen Victoria. *Letters Patent Under the Great Seal of the United Kingdom of Great Britain and Ireland, Erecting the Province of Upper Canada into the Bishopric of Toronto, and Appointing John Strachan, D.D., Archdeacon of York, Bishop of Toronto, dated 27th July, 1839*. Toronto: H. and W. Rowsell, 1842.
Head, Sir Francis Bond. *A Narrative with notes by William Lyon Mackenzie, 1939*. Edited by S.F. Wise. Toronto: McClelland and Stewart, 1969.
Hincks, Francis. *Address of the Honourable Francis Hincks, to the Reformers of Frontenac*. Toronto: Reform Association of Canada, 1844.
Howison, John. *Sketches of Upper Canada, Domestic, Local, and Characteristic: to which are added, Practical Details for the Information of Emigrants of every class; and some recollections of the United States of America*. East Ardsley: R.R. Publishers, 1821; reprint, Toronto: Johnson Reprint Corp., 1965.
J.K. *Plain Reasons for Loyalty: Addressed to Plain People*. Cobourg: R.D. Catterton, 1838.
Jackson, John Mills. *A View of the Political Situation of the Province of Upper Canada, in North America in which her physical capacity is stated; the means of diminishing her burden, encreasing her value, and securing her connection to Great Britain are fully considered, with an appendix*. London: W. Earle, 1809.
McDonald, Archibald. *Reply to the Letter, Lately Addressed to the Right Honorable the Earl of Selkirk, by the Hon. and Rev. John Strachan, D.D., rector of York, in Upper Canada. Being Four Letters (Re-Printed from the Montreal Herald) Containing a Statement of Facts, Concerning the Settlement on Red-River in the District of Ossiniboia, Territory of the Honble. Hudson's Bay Company, properly called Rupert's Land*. Montreal: W. Gray, 1816.
MacGill, Robert. *The Love of Country, A Discourse*. Niagara, 1838.

Mackenzie, William Lyon. *Catechism of Education. Part First*. York: Colonial Advocate Press, 1830.

– "Draft Constitution." In H.D. Forbes, ed., *Canadian Political Thought*, 38–42. Toronto: Oxford University Press, 1985.

– *Sketches of Canada and the United States*. London: Effingham Wilson, 1833.

Morris, William. *Reply of William Morris, Member of the Legislative Council of Upper Canada to Six Letters Addressed to Him by John Strachan, D.D., Archdeacon of York*. Toronto: Scotsman, 1838.

Patton, Henry. *A Sermon on the Life, Labours, and Character of the Late Honourable and Right-Reverend John Strachan, D.D., LL.D., Lord Bishop of Toronto, and in Connection with the Bishop Strachan Memorial Church, Cornwall*. Montreal: J. Lovell, 1868.

The Reform Alliance Society to their Brother Reformers in Upper Canada. Toronto, 1836.

Reform Association of Canada. *'The Globe' Extra. Proceedings at the First General Meeting of the Reform Association of Canada, Held at the Rooms of the Association, Toronto, on Monday, 25th March, 1844*. Toronto: The Globe, 1844.

– *Address to the People of Canada by the Reform Association; Adopted at a General Meeting, held at the Association Rooms, at Toronto, the 16th Day of May, 1844*. Toronto: Examiner Office, 1844.

Russell, Lord John. *An Essay on the History of English Government and Constitution, From the Reign of Henry VII To the Present Time*. London: Longman, Hurst, Rees, Orme, and Brown, 1823.

Ryerson, Egerton. "Letters From the Reverend Egerton Ryerson to the Hon. And Reverend Doctor Strachan." These letters were originally printed in the *Upper Canadian Herald* and then published as a collection by The Herald Office in 1828.

– "Wesleyan Methodism in Upper Canada: A Sermon Preached Before the Conference of Ministers of the Wesleyan-Methodist Church in Canada." Printed in Toronto at the Conference Office by J.H. Lawrence, 1837.

– [A Canadian]. *The Affairs of the Canadas in a Series of Letters by a Canadian*. London: J. King, College Hill, 1837.

– *Civil Government – The Late Conspiracy. A Discourse, Delivered in Kingston, U.C. December 31, 1837*. Toronto: Conference Office, 1838.

– *Petition of the Rev. E. Ryerson to the House of Assembly, Together with a Message from His Excellency the Lieut. Governor, and*

Correspondence Between the Right Hon. Lord Glenelg, His Excellency, and Mr. Ryerson, Relating to the Upper Canada Academy. Toronto: J.H. Lawrence, 1838.

– [A United Empire Loyalist]. *Sir F.B. Head and Mr. Bidwell. The Cause and Circumstances of Mr. Bidwell's Banishment.* Kingston: T.H. Bentley, 1838.

– *The Clergy Reserve Question: As a Matter of History – A Question of Law – And a Subject of Legislation; In a series of Letters to the Hon. W.H. Draper, M.P.P.* Toronto: J.H. Lawrence, 1839.

– , ed. *Wesleyan Methodist Conference; Official Proceedings.* London: Thomas Tegg, 1840.

– *Some Remarks upon Sir Charles Bagot's Canadian Government.* Kingston: Desbarats and Derbishire, 1843.

– *Sir Charles Metcalfe Defended Against the Attacks of His Late Counsellors.* Toronto: British Colonial Office, 1844.

Simpson, John. *Essay on Modern Reformers; Addressed to the People of Upper Canada to which is added A Letter to Mr. Robert Gourlay.* Kingston: Stephen Miles, 1818.

Smith, Michael. *A Geographical View of the Province of Upper Canada.* Philadelphia: Thomas and Robert Desliver, 1813.

Strachan, James. *A Visit to the Province of Upper Canada, in 1819.* Aberdeen: D. Chalmers & Co., 1820.

Strachan, John. *The Christian Religion Recommended in a Letter to His Pupils.* Montreal: Nahum Mower, 1807.

– *A Concise Introduction to Practical Arithmetic for the use of Schools.* Montreal: N. Mower, 1809.

– *A Discourse on the Character of King George the Third: Address to the Inhabitants of British America.* Montreal: Nahum Mower, 1810.

– *A Sermon on the Death of the Rev. John Stuart, D.D., Preached at Kingston, 25th August, 1811 by the Rev. John Strachan, D.D., and Published at the Request of the Congregation.* Kingston: Charles Kendall, 1811.

– *A Sermon Preached at York before the Legislative Council and House of Assembly, August 2nd, 1812.* York: John Cameron, 1812.

– *A Sermon Preached at York, Upper Canada, on the Third of June, being the day appointed for a general thanksgiving.* Montreal: W. Gray, 1814.

– *A Sermon on the Death of the Honorable Richard Cartwright, With a Short Account of His Life. Preached at Kingston, on the 3rd of September, 1815.* Montreal: W. Gray, 1816.

- *A Letter to the Right Honourable the Earl of Selkirk, on his Settlement at the Red River, Near Hudson's Bay.* London: Longman, Hurst, Rees, Orme, and Brown; Edinburgh: W. Turnbull; Glasgow: A. Brown and Company and John Strachan, Aberdeen, 1816.
- *A Sermon Preached at York, Upper Canada, Third of July, 1825, on the Death of the Late Lord Bishop of Quebec.* Kingston: J. Macfarlane, 1826.
- *An Appeal to the Friends of Religion and Literature, on Behalf of the University of Upper Canada.* London: R. Gilbert, 1827.
- *Observations on the Provision made for the maintenance of a Protestant Clergy, in the Provinces of Upper and Lower Canada, Under the 31st Geo. III. Cap. 31.* London: R. Gilbert, 1827.
- *Remarks on the Emigration from the United Kingdom by John Strachan, D.D., Archdeacon of York, Upper Canada: Addressed to Robert Wilmot Horton, Esq., M.P., Chairman of the Select Committee of Emigration in the last Parliament.* London: J. Murray, 1827.
- *A Speech of the Venerable John Strachan, D.D., Archdeacon of York, in the Legislative Council, Thursday, sixth March, 1828, on the Subject of the Clergy Reserves.* York/Toronto: R. Stanton, 1828.
- *A Letter to Rev. A.N. Bethune on the Management of Grammar Schools.* York, 1829.
- *A Letter to the Right Honorable Thomas Frankland Lewis.* York/Toronto: R. Stanton, 1830.
- *Church Fellowship: A Sermon Preached on Wednesday, September 5, 1832, at the Visitation of the Honorarle [sic] and Right Rev. Charles James, Lord Bishop of Quebec.* York/Toronto: R. Stanton, 1832.
- *A Letter to the Rev. Thomas Chalmers, D.D., Professor of Divinity in the University of Edinburgh, on the Life and Character of the Right Reverend Dr. Hobart, Bishop of New-York, North-America.* New York: Swords, Stanford, 1832.
- *A Letter to the Congregation of St. James' Church, York, U. Canada, Occasioned by the Hon. John Elmsley's Publication of the Bishop of Strasbourg's Observations on the 6th Chapter of St. John's Gospel.* York/Toronto: R. Stanton, 1834.
- *The Poor Man's Preservative Against Popery: Part 1. Containing an Introduction on the Character and Genius of the Roman Catholic Religion, and the Substance of a Letter to the Congregation of St. James' Church, U.C., Occasioned by the Hon. J. Elmsley's Publication of the*

Bishop of Strasbourg's Observations on the 6th Chapter of St. John's Gospel. Toronto: G.P. Bull, 1834.

– *The Church of the Redeemed: A Sermon Preached on Wednesday, 5th October, 1836, at a Meeting of the Clergy of the Established Church of Upper Canada, Under their Archdeacons Assembled.* Toronto: R. Stanton, 1836.

– *Address to the Clergy of the Archdeaconry of York.* Toronto, 1837.

– *Letters to the Honorable William Morris: being strictures on the correspondence of that gentleman with the Colonial Office, as a delegate from the Presbyterian body in Canada.* Cobourg: R.D. Chatterton, 1838.

– *A Charge Delivered to the Clergy of the Diocese of Toronto, at the Primary Visitation Held in the Cathedral Church of St. James, Toronto, on the 9th September, 1841.* Toronto: H. and W. Rowsell, 1841.

– *A Sermon Preached in the Cathedral Church of St. James Toronto, Canada, on the 15th Day of May, 1842 by the Honourable and Right Reverend the Lord Bishop of Toronto on the Death of Elizabeth Emily, Wife of the Honourable Mr. Justice Hagerman.* Toronto: H. and W. Rowsell, 1842.

– *A Charge, Delivered to the Clergy of the Diocese of Toronto, at the Triennial Visitation, Held in the Cathedral Church of St. James, Toronto, on the 6th June, 1844.* Cobourg: Diocesan Press, 1844.

– *Circular, Addressed to the Poorer Families of the United Church of England and Ireland Residing in Toronto.* Toronto: United Church of England and Ireland, Diocese of Toronto, 1847[?].

– *Pastoral Letter to the Clergy and Laity of the Diocese of Toronto, on the Subject of the Cholera.* Toronto: Diocesan Press, 1848.

– *Secular State of the Church in the Diocese of Toronto, Canada West.* Toronto: Diocesan Press, 1849[?].

– *Pastoral Letter to the Clergy and Laity of the Diocese of Toronto, on the Subject of the University.* Toronto: printed for the Diocesan Press by A.F. Plees, 1850.

– *Thoughts on the Rebuilding of the Cathedral Church of St. James.* Toronto: Diocesan Press, 1850.

– *Pastoral Letter to the Clergy and Laity of the Diocese of Toronto: Having Been Prevented, by Necessary Absence in England, From Holding the Triennial Visitation of My Clergy Last Summer.* Toronto: unknown, 1851[?].

- *Pastoral Letter to the Clergy and Laity of the Diocese of Toronto.* Toronto: 1852[?].
- *A Charge Delivered to the Clergy of the Diocese of Toronto at the Visitation on Wednesday Oct. 12, 1853, by John, Lord Bishop of Toronto.* Toronto: H. Rowsell, 1853.
- *A Pastoral Letter to the Clergy and Laity of the Diocese of Toronto.* Toronto: 1861.

Strachan, John, Henry James Grasett, and William Buell Richards. *In the Court of Error and Appeal, Between the Honorable William Buell Richards, Attorney General of Upper Canada, on Behalf of Her Majesty, Appellant, and the Reverend Henry James Grasett, the Honorable and Right Reverend John Strachan, Lord Bishop of Toronto, and the Church Society of the Diocese of Toronto, Respondents. An Appeal From the Court of Chancery, Joint Case.* Toronto: Thompson and Company, 185[?].

Sullivan, R.B. *Letters on Responsible Government.* Toronto: Examiner Office, 1844.

Talbot, Edward Allan. *Five Years' Residence in the Canadas.* East Ardsley: S.R. Publishers, 1824; Toronto: Johnson Reprint Corp., 1968.

Taylor, Fennings. *The Last Three Bishops Appointed by the Crown, for the Anglican Church in Canada: Notices, Opinions, and Criticisms of the Press.* Montreal: J. Lovell, 1870.

United Church of England and Ireland, Diocese of Toronto. *Extracts From a Charge Delivered to the Clergy of the Diocese of Toronto at the Primary Visitation, on the 9th Sept. 1841.* London: R. Clay, 1841.

Government Publications and Published Reports

The Constitution of the Canadas, Adopted by the Imperial Parliament in the Thirty-First Year of the Reign of His Majesty, George III, and, in the Year of Our Lord, 1791. Together with the Debates Thereon. Hallowell: Joseph Wilson, 1833.

Doughty, Arthur G., and Adam Shortt, eds. *Documents Relating to the Constitutional History of Canada, 1759–1791.* Ottawa: J. de L. Taché, 1918.

Duncombe, Charles. *Report of the Select Committee to which was Referred the Petition of David Burns, and others, Inhabitants of the*

County of Oxford, and Draft of an Address to His Majesty on the Subject of Lands for Common Schools Founded on the Same. 1830.

– *Doctor Charles Duncombe's Report upon the Subject of Education: Made to the Parliament of Upper Canada, 25th February, 1836, through the commissioners, Doctors Morrison and Bruce, appointed by a resolution of the House of Assembly in 1835, to obtain information upon the subject of education, &c.* Toronto: M. Reynolds, 1836.

Hodgins, J. George, ed. *Ryerson Memorial Volume: Prepared on the Occasion of the Unveiling of the Ryerson Statue in the Grounds of the Education Department on the Queen's Birthday, 1889.* Toronto: Warwick and Sons, 1889.

– *Documentary History of Education in Upper Canada, from the Passing of the Constitutional Act of 1791 to the Close of the Reverend Doctor Ryerson's Administration of the Education Department in 1876.* 28 vols. Toronto: L.K. Cameron, 1894–1910.

– *The Establishment of Schools and Colleges in Ontario, 1792–1910.* Toronto: L.K. Cameron, 1910.

– *Historical and Other Papers and Documents Illustrative of the Educational System of Ontario, 1792–1871.* Toronto: L.K. Cameron, 1911–12.

Journal of the House of Assembly of Upper Canada. Canadian Institute for Historical Microreproductions (CIHM) collection.

Journal of the Legislative Council of Upper Canada. Canadian Institute for Historical Microreproductions (CIHM) collection.

Report of a Committee of the Council on the Subject of Promoting the Means of Education/Rapport du comité du conseil sur l'objet d'augmenter les moiens d'éducation. Quebec: Samuel Neilson, 1789.

Report of the Legislative Council on the Civil Rights of Certain Inhabitants. 1825–26.

Ryerson, Egerton. *Report on a System of Elementary Instruction.* Montreal: Lovell and Gibson, 1846.

Strachan, John. "Report on Education," 1815. Library and Archives Canada, MG24-J1, John Strachan Fonds, Letterbooks and Miscellaneous Papers.

SECONDARY SOURCES

Aitchison, J.H. "The Development of Local Government in Upper Canada, 1783–1850." PhD diss., University of Toronto, 1953.

Akenson, Donald H. *The Irish Education Experiment: The National System of Education in the Nineteenth Century*. London: Routledge and Kegan Paul, 1970.

– *The Irish in Ontario: A Study in Rural History*. Montreal and Kingston: McGill-Queen's University Press, 1984.

– *Being Had: Historians, Evidence, and the Irish in North America*. Port Credit, ON: P.D. Meany, 1985.

Anderson, Benedict. *Imagined Communities: Reflections on the Origins and Spread of Nationalism*. New York: Verso, 2006.

Angrave, James. "John Strachan and Scottish Influence in the Charter of King's College, York, 1827." *Journal of Canadian Studies* 11 (1976): 60–8.

Armitage, David. *The Ideological Origins of the British Empire*. Cambridge, UK: Cambridge University Press, 2000.

Armstrong, F.H. "The York Riots of March 23, 1832." *Ontario History* 55 (1963): 61–72.

Axelrod, Paul. "Historical Writing and Canadian Education from the 1970s to the 1990s." *History of Education Quarterly* 36 (1996): 19–38.

– *The Promise of Schooling: Education in Canada, 1800–1914*. Toronto: University of Toronto Press, 1997.

Bailyn, Bernard. *Education in the Forming of American Society*. New York: Vintage Books, 1960.

Bailyn, Bernard, and Philip D. Morgan, eds. *Strangers within the Realm: Cultural Margins of the First British Empire*. Chapel Hill: University of North Carolina Press, 1991.

Baker, G. Blaine. "The Juvenile Advocate Society, 1821–1826: Self-Proclaimed Schoolroom for Upper Canada's Governing Class." *Canadian Historical Association: Historical Papers*, 1985, 74–101.

Banfield, Paul Anthony. "The Well Regulated Family: John Strachan and the Role of the Family in Early Upper Canada, 1800–1812." MA thesis, Queen's University, 1985.

Barker, Hannah, and Simon Burrows, eds. *Press, Politics and the Public Sphere in Europe and North America, 1760–1820*. Cambridge, UK: Cambridge University Press, 2002.

Baskerville, P.A. "Entrepreneurship and the Family Compact: York-Toronto, 1822–1855." *Urban History Review* 9 (1981): 15–34.

Bayly, Christopher A. *Imperial Meridian: The British Empire and the World, 1780–1830*. New York: Longman, 1989.

Beadie, Nancy. "Tuition Funding for Common Schools: Education Markets and Market Regulation in Rural New York, 1815–1850." *Social Science History* 32, no. 1 (2008): 107–33.

– "Toward a History of Education Markets in the United States: An Introduction." *Social Science History* 32, no. 1 (2008): 47–73.

– "Education and the Creation of Capital: Or What I Have Learned from Following the Money." *History of Education Quarterly* 48, no. 1 (2008): 1–29.

– "Education, Social Capital and State Formation in Comparative Historical Perspective: Preliminary Investigations." *Paedagogica Historica* 46, nos 1–2 (2010): 15–32.

– *Education and the Creation of Capital in the Early American Republic.* New York: Cambridge University Press, 2010.

Bell, David V.J. "The Loyalist Tradition in Canada," *Journal of Canadian Studies,* 5, no. 2 (1970): 22–33.

Benn, Carl. "The Upper Canadian Press, 1793–1815." *Ontario History* 70 (1978): 91–114.

Berger, Carl. *The Sense of Power: Studies in the Ideas of Canadian Imperialism, 1867–1914.* Toronto: University of Toronto Press, 1971.

Bethune, A.N. *Memoir of the Right Reverend John Strachan, First Bishop of Toronto.* Toronto: Henry Rowsell, 1870.

Black, Jeremy. *The English Press, 1621–1861.* Stroud, UK: Sutton Publishing, 2001.

– "The Press and Politics in the Eighteenth Century." *Media History* 8, no. 2 (2002): 175–82.

Boorman, Sylvia. *John Toronto: A Biography of Bishop Strachan.* Toronto: Clarke, Irwin, 1969.

Bowler, Reginald Arthur. "Propaganda in Upper Canada: A Study of Propaganda Directed at the People of Upper Canada during the War of 1812." MA thesis, Queen's University, 1964.

Bowsfield, Hartwell. "Upper Canada in the 1820's: The Development of a Political Consciousness." PhD diss., University of Toronto, 1976.

Bradley, A.G. *The United Empire Loyalists: Founders of British Canada.* London: Thornton Butterworth, 1932.

Brown, George W. "The Early Methodist Church and the Canadian Point of View." *Canadian Historical Association Annual Report,* 1938, 79–96.

– "The Durham Report and the Upper Canadian Scene." *Canadian Historical Review* 20 (1939): 136–60.

Brown, Wallace, and Hereward Senior. *Victorious in Defeat: The Loyalists in Canada*. Toronto: Methuen, 1984.

Buckner, Philip. *The Transition to Responsible Government: British Policy in British North America, 1815–1850*. Westport, CT: Greenwood Press, 1985.

– , ed. *Canada and the British Empire*. Toronto: Oxford University Press, 2008.

Bumsted, J.M. "Loyalists and Nationalists: An Essay on the Problem of Definitions." *Canadian Review of Studies in Nationalism* 6 (Spring 1979): 218–32.

Burnet, Jean R. *Ethnic Groups in Upper Canada*. Toronto: Ontario Historical Society, 1972.

Burns, R. "God's Chosen People: The Origins of Toronto Society, 1793–1818." *Canadian Historical Association: Historical Papers*, 1973, 213–28.

Burroughs, Peter. *The Colonial Reformers and Canada, 1830–1849*. Toronto: McClelland and Stewart, 1969.

– , ed. *British Attitudes toward Canada, 1822–1849*. Scarborough: Prentice-Hall of Canada, 1971.

Burwash, Nathanael. *Egerton Ryerson*. Toronto: G.N. Morang, 1903.

Calhoon, R.M. "The Loyalist Perception." *Acadiensis* 2 (1973): 3–15.

Calhoun, Craig, ed. *Habermas and the Public Sphere*. Cambridge, MA: MIT Press, 1992.

Cameron, Richard M. *Methodism and Society in Historical Perspective*. New York: Abingdon Press, 1961.

Careless, J.M.S. "Frontierism, Metropolitanism, and Canadian History." *Canadian Historical Review* 35 (1954): 1–21.

– *The Union of the Canadas: The Growth of Canadian Institutions, 1841–1857*. Toronto: McClelland and Stewart, 1967.

– *Colonists and Canadians, 1763–1867*. Toronto: Macmillan of Canada, 1971.

Carruthers, John. *Retrospect of Thirty-Sex Years' Residence in Canada West: Being a Christian Journal and Narrative*. Hamilton: T.L. M'Intosh, 1861.

Cell, J.W. *British Colonial Administration in the Mid-Nineteenth Century: The Policy-Making Process*. New Haven, CT: Yale University Press, 1970.

Cheal, David J. "Ontario Loyalism: A Socio-Religious Ideology in Decline." *Canadian Ethnic Studies* 13 (1981): 40–51.

Christie, Nancy. "'On the threshold of manhood': Working-Class Religion and Domesticity in Victorian Britain and Canada." *Histoire Sociale/ Social History* 36, no. 71 (2003): 145–75.

– , ed. *Transatlantic Subjects: Ideas, Institutions, and Social Experience in Post-Revolutionary British North America.* Montreal and Kingston: McGill-Queen's University Press, 2008.

Christie, Nancy, and Michael Gauvreau. "Modalities of Social Authority: Suggesting an Interface for Religious and Social History." *Histoire Sociale/Social History* 36, no. 71 (2003): 1–30.

Clark, S.D. *Church and Sect in Canada.* Toronto: University of Toronto Press, 1948.

– *Movements of Political Protest in Canada, 1640–1840.* Toronto: University of Toronto Press, 1959.

Clarke, Brian P. *Piety and Nationalism: Lay Voluntary Associations and the Creation of an Irish-Catholic Community in Toronto, 1850–1895.* Montreal and Kingston: McGill-Queen's University Press, 1993.

Clarke, J.C.D. *English Society, 1688–1832: Ideology, Social Structure, and Political Practice during the Ancien Regime.* Cambridge, UK: Cambridge University Press, 1985.

Clarke, John. *Land, Power, and Economics on the Frontier of Upper Canada: An Examination of Ontario's Formative Years, Focusing on Essex County from 1788 to 1850.* Montreal and Kingston: McGill-Queen's University Press, 2000.

Codell, Julie F., ed. *Imperial Co-Histories: National Identities and the British Colonial Press.* Madison, NJ: Fairleigh Dickinson University Press, 2003.

Colley, Linda. *Britons: Forging the Nation, 1707–1837.* New Haven, CT: Yale University Press, 1992.

Colombo, John Robert, and William Kilbourn. *John Toronto: New Poems.* Ottawa: Oberon Press, 1969.

Constant, Jean-François, and Michel Ducharme. *Liberalism and Hegemony: Debating the Canadian Liberal Revolution.* Toronto: University of Toronto Press, 2009.

Cook, Terry. "John Beverley Robinson and the Conservative Blueprint for the Upper Canadian Community." *Ontario History* 64 (1972): 79–94.

Corey, Albert B. *The Crisis of 1830–1842 in Canadian-American Relations.* New York: Russell and Russell, 1941.

Craig, Gerald M. "The American Impact on the Upper Canadian Reform Movement before 1837." *Canadian Historical Review* 29 (1948): 333–52.

– "Comments on Upper Canada in 1836 by Thomas Carr." *Ontario History* 47 (1955): 171–9.

– *Upper Canada: The Formative Years, 1784–1841.* Toronto: McClelland and Stewart, 1963.

–, ed. *Lord Durham's Report.* Toronto: McClelland and Stewart, 1969.

– "Two Contrasting Upper Canadian Figures: John Rolph and John Strachan." *Transactions of the Royal Society of Canada*, series 4, 12 (1974): 237–48.

–, ed. *Discontent in Upper Canada.* Toronto: Copp Clark, 1974.

Cross, M.S., and R.L. Fraser. "'The Waste That Lies before Me': The Public and Private Worlds of Robert Baldwin." *Canadian Historical Association: Historical Papers*, 1983, 164–83.

Curtis, Bruce. "The Political Economy of Elementary Educational Development: Comparative Perspectives on State Schooling in Upper Canada." PhD diss., University of Toronto, 1980.

– "Schoolbooks and the Myth of Curricular Republicanism: The State and the Curriculum in Canada West, 1820–1850." *Histoire Sociale/ Social History* 16 (November 1983): 305–30.

– "Preconditions of the Canadian State: Educational Reform and the Construction of a Public in Upper Canada, 1837–1846." *Studies in Political Economy* 10 (Winter 1983): 99–121.

– *Building the Educational State: Canada West, 1836–1871.* London: Althouse Press, 1988.

– "Some Recent Work on the History of Literacy in Canada." *History of Education Quarterly* 30, no. 4 (1990): 613–24.

– *True Government by Choice Men? Inspection, Education, and State Formation in Canada West.* Toronto: University of Toronto Press, 1992.

Davey, Ian E. "School Reform and School Attendance: The Hamilton Central School, 1853–1861." MA thesis, University of Toronto, 1972.

– "Educational Reform and the Working Class: School Attendance in Hamilton, Ontario, 1851–1891." PhD diss., University of Toronto, 1975.

– "Rethinking the Origins of British Colonial Schools Systems." *Historical Studies in Education* 1 (1989): 149–59.

Davies, Gwendolyn. "Consolation to Distress: Loyalist Literary Activity in the Maritimes." *Acadiensis* 16, no. 2 (1987): 51–68.

de Kerckhove, Derrick. "McLuhan and the 'Toronto School of Communication." *Canadian Journal of Communication*, 1989, 73–39.

Dent, J.C. *The Story of the Upper Canadian Rebellion.* 2 vols. Toronto: C. Blackett Robinson, 1885.

Di Mascio, Anthony. "Forever Divided? Assessing the 'National' Question and the Governance in Education through a Reexamination of Québec's 1789 Report on Education." *McGill Journal of Education/Revue des sciences de l'éducation de McGill* 42, no. 3 (2007): 463–72.

– "Educational Discourse and the Making of Educational Legislation in Early Upper Canada." *History of Education Quarterly* 50, no. 1 (2010): 34–54.

Dufour, Andrée. *Histoire de l'éducation au Québec.* Montreal: Boréal, 1997.

Dunae, Patrick. *Gentleman Emigrants: From the British Public Schools to the Canadian Frontier.* Vancouver: Douglas and McIntyre, 1981.

Dunham, Aileen. *Political Unrest in Upper Canada, 1815–1836.* Toronto: McClelland and Stewart, 1971.

Earl, D.W.L. "British Views of Colonial Upper Canada, 1791–1841." *Ontario History* 53 (1961): 117–36.

– *The Family Compact: Aristocracy or Oligarchy?* Toronto: Copp Clark Publishing, 1967.

Elgee, W.H. *The Social Teachings of the Canadian Churches: Protestant. The Early Period, before 1850.* Toronto: Ryerson Press, 1964.

Errington, Elizabeth Jane. "A Developing Upper Canadian Identity: Kingston's View of the United States and Great Britain, 1810–1815." MA thesis, Queen's University, 1982.

– *The Lion, the Eagle, and Upper Canada: A Developing Colonial Ideology.* Montreal and Kingston: McGill-Queen's University Press, 1987.

– "Ladies and Schoolmistresses: Educating Women in Early Nineteenth-Century Upper Canada." *Historical Studies in Education* 6, no. 1 (1994): 71–96.

– *Wives and Mothers, School Mistresses and Scullery Maids: Working Women in Upper Canada, 1790–1840.* Montreal and Kingston: McGill-Queen's University Press, 1995.

– *Emigrant Worlds and Transatlantic Communities: Migration to Upper Canada in the First Half of the Nineteenth Century.* Montreal and Kingston: McGill-Queen's University Press, 2007.

Errington, Elizabeth Jane, and George Rawlyk. "The Loyalist-Federalist Alliance of Upper Canada." *American Review of Canadian Studies* 14 (Summer 1984): 157–76.

Evans, Eric J. *The Forging of the Modern State: Early Industrial Britain, 1783–1846.* London: Longman, 1983.

Fahey, Curtis. "A Troubled Zion: The Anglican Experience in Upper Canada, 1791–1854." PhD diss., Carleton University, 1981.

– *In His Name: The Anglican Experience in Upper Canada, 1791–1854.* Ottawa: Carleton University Press, 1991.

Fairley, Margaret, ed. *The Selected Writings of William Lyon Mackenzie, 1824–1837.* Toronto: Oxford University Press, 1960.

Fiorino, Albert F. "The Philosophical Roots of Egerton Ryerson's Idea of Education as Elaborated in His Writings Preceding and Including the Report of 1846." PhD diss., University of Toronto, 1975.

Firth, Edith. *Early Toronto Newspapers, 1793–1867.* Toronto: McClelland and Stewart, 1961.

– , ed. *Profiles of a Province: Studies in the History of Ontario.* Toronto: Ontario Historical Society, 1967.

Fleming, Patricia Lockhart, Gilles Gallichan, and Yvan Lamonde, eds. *History of the Book in Canada.* 3 vols. Toronto: University of Toronto Press, 2004.

Flint, David. *John Strachan, Pastor and Politician.* Toronto: Oxford University Press, 1971.

Fraser, R.L. "Like Eden in Her Summer Dress: Gentry, Economy and Society: Upper Canada, 1812–1840." PhD diss., University of Toronto, 1979.

French, Goldwin. *Parsons and Politics: The Role of the Wesleyan Methodists in Upper Canada and the Maritimes from 1780 to 1855.* Toronto: Ryerson Press, 1962.

Friesen, Gerald. *Citizens and Nation: An Essay on History, Communication, and Canada.* Toronto: University of Toronto Press, 2000.

Gaffield, Chad. "Cultural Challenge in Eastern Ontario: Land, Family, and Education in the Nineteenth Century." PhD diss., University of Toronto, 1978.

– "Schooling, the Economy, and Rural Society in Nineteenth Century Ontario." In Joy Parr, ed., *Childhood and Family in Canadian History,* 69–92. Toronto: McClelland and Stewart, 1982.

– "Wage Labour, Industrialization, and the Origin of the Modern Family."
   In Maureen Baker, ed., *The Family: Changing Trends in Canada*, 21–34.
   Toronto: McGraw-Hill, 1984.
– "Back to School: Towards a New Agenda for the History of Education."
   Acadiensis 15, no. 2 (1986): 169–90.
– "Coherence and Chaos in Educational Historiography." *Interchange* 17,
   no. 2 (1986): 112–21.
– *Language, Schooling, and Cultural Conflict: The Origins of the French-
   Language Controversy in Ontario.* Montreal and Kingston: McGill-
   Queen's University Press, 1987.
– "Schooling, Children, and Family Reproduction in Nineteenth-Century
   Ontario." *Canadian Historical Review* 72, no. 2 (1991): 157–91.
– "Canadian Families in Cultural Context: Hypotheses from the Mid-
   Nineteenth Century." In Bettina Bradbury, ed., *Canadian Family Hist-
   ory: Selected Readings*, 135–57. Toronto: Copp Clark, 1992.
– "Two Steps Back: Reflections on the Search for Synthesis." *Historical
   Studies in Education* 5, no. 1 (1993): 117–21.
Gaffield, Chad, and Gerard Bouchard. "Literacy, Schooling, and Family
   Reproduction in Rural Ontario and Quebec." *Historical Studies in Edu-
   cation* 1, no. 2 (1989): 201–18.
Gates, L.F. "The Decided Policy of William Lyon Mackenzie." *Canadian
   Historical Review* 40 (1959): 185–208.
– "W.L. Mackenzie's 'Volunteer' and the First Parliament of United
   Canada." *Ontario History* 59 (1967): 163–83.
Gauvreau, Michael. *The Evangelical Century: College and Creed in
   English Canada from the Great Revival to the Great Depression.* Mont-
   real and Kingston: McGill-Queen's University Press, 1991.
– "Covenanter Democracy: Scottish Popular Religion, Ethnicity, and the
   Varieties of Politico-religious Dissent in Upper Canada, 1815–1841."
   Histoire Sociale/Social History 36, no. 71 (2003): 55–83.
Gidney, R.D. "Education and Society in Upper Canada, 1791–1850."
   MPhil thesis, University of London, 1969.
– "Centralization and Education: The Origins of an Ontario Tradition."
   Journal of Canadian Studies 7 (1972): 33–48.
– "Upper Canadian Public Opinion and Common School Improvement in
   the 1830s." *Histoire Sociale/Social History* 5, no. 9 (1972): 48–60.
– "Elementary Education in Upper Canada: A Reassessment." *Ontario
   History* 65, no. 3 (1973): 169–85.

- "Making Nineteenth-Century School Systems: The Upper Canadian Experience and Its Relevance to English Historiography." *History of Education* 9 (1980): 101–16.
Gidney, R.D., and Douglas Lawr. "The Development of an Administrative System for the Public Schools: The First Stage, 1841–50." In Neil McDonald and Alf Chaiton, eds, *Egerton Ryerson and His Times*, 160–84. Toronto: Macmillan of Canada, 1978.
- "Egerton Ryerson and the Origins of the Ontario Secondary School." *Canadian Historical Review* 60 (1979): 442–65.
- "Bureaucracy vs. Community? The Origins of Bureaucratic Procedure in the Upper Canadian School System." *Journal of Social History* 13, no. 3 (1980): 438–57.
Gidney, R.D., and W.P.J. Millar. "From Voluntarism to State Schooling: The Creation of the Public School System in Ontario." *Canadian Historical Review* 66, no. 4 (1985): 443–73.
- *Inventing Secondary Education: The Rise of the High School in Nineteenth-Century Ontario.* Montreal and Kingston: McGill-Queen's University Press, 1990.
Gladwell, Malcolm. *The Tipping Point: How Little Things Can Make a Big Difference.* New York: Little, Brown, and Co., 2000.
Gould, Eliga H. "America's Independence and Britain's Counter-Revolution." *Past and Present* 154 (1997): 107–41.
- "A Virtual Nation: Greater Britain and the Imperial Legacy of the American Revolution." *American Historical Review* 87, no. 2 (1999): 476–89.
Graff, Harvey. "Toward a Meaning of Literacy: Literacy and Social Structure in Hamilton, Ontario, 1861." *History of Education Quarterly* 13, no. 3 (1972): 411–31.
- "Literacy and Social Structure in Elgin County, Canada West: 1861." *Histoire Sociale/Social History* 6, no. 11 (1973): 25–48.
- "Literacy and Social Structure in the Nineteenth-Century City." PhD diss., University of Toronto, 1975.
- "The Reality behind the Rhetoric: The Social and Economic Meanings of Literacy in the Mid-Nineteenth Century: The Example of Literacy and Criminality." In Neil McDonald and Alf Chaiton, eds, *Egerton Ryerson and His Times*, 187–220. Toronto: Macmillan of Canada, 1978.

– *The Literacy Myth: Cultural Integration and Social Structure in the Nineteenth Century*. Vancouver: University of British Columbia Press, 1991.

Grant, John Webster. *A Profusion of Spires: Religion in Nineteenth-Century Canada*. Toronto: University of Toronto Press, 1988.

Greer, Allan. "The Sunday Schools of Upper Canada." *Ontario History* 67 (September 1975): 169–84.

Guest, Harry H. "Baldwin of Spadina: The Life of William Warren Baldwin, Central Figure in the Movement for Responsible Government in Upper Canada." MA thesis, University of Manitoba, 1961.

– "Upper Canada's First Political Party." *Ontario History* 54 (1962): 275–96.

Habermas, Jurgen. *The Structural Transformation of the Public Sphere: An Inquiry into a Category of Bourgeois Society*. Cambridge, MA: MIT Press, 1991.

Hall, Catherine. "Making Colonial Subjects: Education in the Age of Empire." *History of Education* 37, no. 6 (2008): 773–87.

Hall, J. Geoffrey. "The Educational Policy of Egerton Ryerson, Superintendent of Education for Upper Canada and Some Contemporary Criticisms of the Policy." MA thesis, McGill University, 1976.

Harris, R.C., and J. Warkentin. *Canada before Confederation*. Toronto: Oxford University Press, 1974.

Harris, Robin S. "Egerton Ryerson." In R.L. McDougall, ed., *Our Living Tradition*, 244–67. Toronto: University of Toronto Press, 1959.

Heap, Ruby, and Alison Prentice. *Gender and Education in Ontario: An Historical Reader*. Toronto: Canadian Scholars' Press, 1991.

Hempton, David. *Methodism and Politics in British Society, 1750–1850*. Stanford, CA: Stanford University Press, 1984.

Henderson, J.L.H. *John Strachan, 1778–1867*. Toronto: University of Toronto Press, 1969.

– , ed. *John Strachan: Documents and Opinions*. Toronto: McClelland and Stewart, 1969.

Hilton, Boyd. *A Mad, Bad, and Dangerous People? England, 1783–1846*. Oxford: Oxford University Press, 2006.

Horowitz, Gad. "Conservatism, Liberalism and Socialism in Canada: An Interpretation." *Canadian Journal of Economics and Political Science* 32 (1966): 147–71.

Houston, Susan. "Politics, Schools, and Social Change in Upper Canada." *Canadian Historical Review* 53 (1972): 249–71.

- "Victorian Origins of Juvenile Delinquency: A Canadian Experience." *History of Education Quarterly* 12 (1972): 254–80.
- "Impetus to Reform: Urban Crime, Poverty, and Ignorance in Ontario, 1850–1875." PhD diss., University of Toronto, 1974.
- "Social Reform and Education: The Issue of Compulsory Schooling, Toronto, 1851–1871." In Neil McDonald and Alf Chaiton, eds, *Egerton Ryerson and His Times*, 254–76. Toronto: Macmillan of Canada, 1978.

Houston, Susan E., and Alison Prentice. *Schooling and Scholars in Nineteenth-Century Ontario*. Toronto: University of Toronto Press, 1988.

Innis, Harold. *Empire and Communications*. Oxford: Oxford University Press, 1950; reprint, Toronto: Dundurn Press, 2007.
- *The Bias of Communication*. Toronto: University of Toronto Press, 1951.

Jackman, S.W.A. *Galloping Head: The Life of the Right Honourable Sir Francis Bond Head, Bart., P.C., 1793–1875, Late Lieutenant-Governor of Upper Canada*. London: Phoenix House, 1958.

Jackson, Eric. "The Organization of Upper Canadian Reformers, 1818–1867." *Ontario History* 53 (1961): 95–115.

Johnson, J.K. "The Upper Canada Club and the Upper Canadian Elite, 1837–1840." *Ontario History* 69 (1977): 151–68.

Johnson, Jennifer R. "The Availability of Reading Material for the Pioneer in Upper Canada: Niagara District, 1792–1842." MA thesis, University of Western Ontario, 1982.
- *Becoming Prominent: Regional Leadership in Upper Canada, 1791–1841*. Montreal and Kingston: McGill-Queen's University Press, 1989.
- , ed. *Historical Essays on Upper Canada: New Perspectives*. Ottawa: Carleton University Press, 1989.

Kaestle, Carl. *Pillars of the Republic: Common Schools and American Society, 1780–1860*. Toronto: HarperCollins Canada, 2001.

Katz, Michael B. *The Irony of Early School Reform: Educational Innovation in Mid-Nineteenth Century Massachusetts*. Cambridge, MA: Harvard University Press, 1968; reprint, New York: Teacher's College Press, 2001.

Katz, Michael B., and Paul H. Mattingly, eds. *Education and Social Change: Themes from Ontario's Past*. New York: New York University Press, 1975.

- "The Origins of Public Education: A Reassessment." *History of Educational Quarterly*, 16, no. 4 (1976): 381–408.

Kaye, J.W. *The Life and Correspondence of Charles, Lord Metcalfe.* 2 vols. London: R. Bentley, 1854.

Kilbourn, William. *The Firebrand: William Lyon Mackenzie and the Rebellion in Upper Canada.* Toronto: Clarke, Irwin, 1964.

Knaplund, Paul, ed. *Letters from Lord Sydenham, Governor-General of Canada, 1839 1841, to Lord John Russell.* New Jersey: Augustus M. Kelley, 1973.

Lambert, Garth R. *Dethroning Classics and Inventing English: Liberal Education and Culture in Nineteenth-Century Ontario.* Toronto: James Lorimer, 1995.

Lawr, D.A., and R.D. Gidney, "Who Ran the Schools? Local Influence on Education Policy in Nineteenth-Century Ontario." *Ontario History* 72, no. 3 (1980): 131–43.

Leacock, Stephen. *Baldwin, LaFontaine, Hincks: Responsible Government.* Toronto: Morang and Co., 1910.

Longley, R.S. *Sir Francis Hincks: A Study of Canadian Politics, Railways, and Finance in the Nineteenth Century.* Toronto: University of Toronto Press, 1943.

Love, James H. "Social Stress and Education Reform in Mid-Nineteenth Century Upper Canada." PhD diss., University of Toronto, 1978.

- "Cultural Survival and Social Control: The Development of a Curriculum for Upper Canada's Common Schools in 1846." *Histoire Sociale/Social History* 15, no. 30 (1982): 359–60.

Lowe, Roy, ed. *History of Education: Major Themes.* New York: Routledge, 2000.

Lower, A.R.M. "Religion and Religious Institutions." In W.H. Heick, ed., *History and Myth: Arthur Lower and the Making of Canadian Nationalism,* 75–96. Vancouver: University of British Columbia Press, 1975.

Lucas, Sir Charles P., ed. *Lord Durham's Report on the Affairs of British North America.* 3 vols. Oxford: Clarendon Press, 1912.

McCalla, Douglas. "The Loyalist Economy of Upper Canada, 1784–1806." *Histoire Sociale/Social History* 32 (November 1983): 279–304.

- *Planting the Province: The Economic History of Upper Canada, 1784–1870.* Toronto: University of Toronto Press, 1993.

McCullock, Gary, ed. *The RoutledgeFalmer Reader in History of Education*. New York: Routledge, 2005.

McDermott, Mark Charles. "The Theology of Bishop John Strachan: A Study in Anglican Identity." PhD diss., University of Toronto, 1983.

McDonald, Neil, and Alf Chaiton, eds. *Egerton Ryerson and His Times*. Toronto: Macmillan of Canada, 1978.

McGowan, Mark. *The Waning of the Green: Catholics, the Irish, and Identity in Toronto, 1887–1922*. Montreal and Kingston: McGill-Queen's University Press, 1999.

Mackay, R.A. "The Political Ideas of William Lyon Mackenzie." *Canadian Journal of Economics and Political Science* 3 (1937): 1–22.

McKillop, A.B. "Nationalism, Identity and Canadian Intellectual History." *Queen's Quarterly* 81 (Winter 1974): 533–50.

– , ed. *W.D. LeSueru's William Lyon Mackenzie: A Reinterpretation*. Toronto: Macmillan of Canada, 1979.

– *Matters of Mind: The University in Ontario, 1791–1951*. Toronto: University of Toronto Press, 1994.

McLuhan, Marshall. *The Gutenberg Galaxy: The Making of Typographic Man*. Toronto: University of Toronto Press, 1962.

– *Understanding Media: The Extensions of Man*. Toronto: McGraw-Hill, 1964; reprint Cambridge, MA: MIT Press, 1994.

McNairn, Jeffrey L. "Publius of the North: Tory Republicanism and the American Constitution in Upper Canada, 1848–54." *Canadian Historical Review* 77, no. 4 (1996): 504–37.

– "Towards Deliberative Democracy: Parliamentary Intelligence and the Public Sphere in Upper Canada, 1791–1840." *Journal of Canadian Studies* 33, no. 1 (1998): 39–60.

– *The Capacity to Judge: Public Opinion and Deliberative Democracy in Upper Canada, 1791–1854*. Toronto: University of Toronto Press, 2000.

McRae, K.D., ed. "An Upper Canada Letter of 1829 on Responsible Government." *Canadian Historical Review* 31 (1950): 288–96.

– "The Structure of Canadian Society." In Louis Hartz, ed., *The Founding of New Societies*, 219–74. New York: Harcourt, Brace & World, 1964.

MacRae, Norma J. "The Religious Foundation of John Strachan's Social and Political Thought as Contained in His Sermons, 1803–1866." MA thesis, McMaster University, 1978.

Mangan, J.A., ed. *"Benefits Bestowed"? Education and British Imperialism.* Manchester: Manchester University Press, 1988.

Manning, H.T. "The Colonial Policy of the Whig Ministers, 1830–1837." *Canadian Historical Review* 31 (1950): 288–96.

Martin, Chester. *Empire and Commonwealth: Studies in Governance and Self-Government in Canada.* Oxford: Clarendon Press, 1929.

– *Foundations of Canadian Nationhood.* Toronto: University of Toronto Press, 1955.

Martin, Ged. *The Durham Report and British Policy: A Critical Essay.* Cambridge, UK: Cambridge University Press, 1972.

Mealing, S.R., ed. *Robert Gourlay's Statistical Account of Upper Canada.* Toronto: McClelland and Stewart, 1974.

Metcalf, George. "Draper Conservatism and Responsible Government in the Canadas, 1836–1847." *Canadian Historical Review* 42 (1961): 300–24.

Milani, Lois Darroch. *Robert Gourlay, Gadfly: The Biography of Robert Fleming Gourlay, 1778–1863, Forerunner of the Rebellion in Upper Canada, 1837.* Thornhill, ON: Ampersand Press, 1971.

Miller, J.R. "Anti-Catholic Thought in Victorian Canada." *Canadian Historical Review* 66 (1985): 474–94.

Miller, Marilyn G. "The Political Ideas of the Honourable Richard Cartwright, 1759–1815." MA thesis, Queen's University, 1975.

Miller, Pavla. "Education and the State: The Uses of Marxist and Feminist Approaches in the Writing of Histories of Schooling." *Historical Studies in Education* 1 (1989): 283–306.

Mills, David. *The Idea of Loyalty in Upper Canada, 1784–1850.* Montreal and Kingston: McGill-Queen's University Press, 1988.

Moir, John S. "The Origins of the Separate School Question in Ontario." *Canadian Journal of Theology* 5 (1959): 105–18.

– , ed. *Church and State in Canada, 1627–1867.* Toronto: McClelland and Stewart, 1967.

– "The Upper Canadian Roots of Church Disestablishment." *Ontario History* 60 (1968): 247–58.

– *The Church in the British Era: From the British Conquest to Confederation.* Toronto: McGraw-Hill Ryerson, 1972.

– "John Strachan and Presbyterianism." *Journal of the Canadian Church Historical Society* 41 (1999): 81–97.

Moore, Christopher. *The Loyalists: Revolution, Exile, Settlement.* Toronto: Macmillan of Canada, 1984.

Morgan, Cecilia Louise. *Public Men and Virtuous Women: The Gendered Languages of Religion and Politics in Upper Canada, 1791–1850.* Toronto: University of Toronto Press, 1996.

Morton, W.L. "The Local Executive in the British Empire, 1763–1828." *English Historical Review* 78 (1963): 436–57.

– "Strachan in the Round." *Journal of Canadian Studies* 4 (1969): 46–50.

Murray, Heather. *Come, Bright Improvement! The Literary Societies of Nineteenth-Century Ontario.* Toronto: University of Toronto Press, 2002.

Nelles, H.V. "Loyalism and Local Power: The District of Niagara, 1792–1837." *Ontario History* 63 (1966): 99–114.

New, Chester. *Lord Durham's Mission to Canada.* Edited by H.W. McCready. Toronto: McClelland and Stewart, 1968.

O'Gorman, Frank. *The Long Eighteenth Century: British Political and Social History, 1688–1832.* New York: St Martin's Press, 1997.

Ormsby, W.G., ed. *Crisis in the Canadas, 1838–1839: The Grey Journals and Letters.* Toronto: Macmillan of Canada, 1964.

– *The Emergence of the Federal Concept in Canada, 1839–1845.* Toronto: University of Toronto Press, 1969.

Osmond, Oliver. "The Churchmanship of John Strachan." *Journal of the Canadian Church Historical Society* 16 (1974): 46–59.

Owram, Douglas. "Strachan and Ryerson: Guardians of the Future." *Canadian Literature* 83 (Winter 1979): 21–9.

Pammett, Jon H., and M.S. Whittington, eds. *Foundations of Political Culture: Political Socialization in Canada.* Toronto: Macmillan of Canada, 1976.

Parr, Joy, ed. *Childhood and Family in Canadian History.* Toronto: University of Toronto Press, 1982.

Parvin, V.E. *Authorization of Textbooks for the Schools of Ontario, 1846–1950.* Toronto: University of Toronto Press, 1965.

Patterson, Graeme H. "Studies in Elections and Public Opinion in Upper Canada." PhD diss., University of Toronto, 1969.

– "Whiggery, Nationality, and the Upper Canadian Reform Tradition." *Canadian Historical Review* 56 (1975): 25–44.

– "An Enduring Canadian Myth: Responsible Government and the Family Compact." *Journal of Canadian Studies* 12 (Spring 1977): 3–16.

Pearce, Colin. "Egerton Ryerson's Canadian Liberalism." *Canadian Journal of Political Science* 21 (1988): 771–93.

Phillips, C.E. *The Development of Education in Canada*. Toronto: W.J. Gage, 1957.

Pocock, J.G.A. *The Discovery of Islands: Essays in British History*. Cambridge, UK: Cambridge University Press, 2005.

Prentice, Alison. *The School Promoters: Education and Social Class in Mid-Nineteenth Century Upper Canada*. Toronto: McClelland and Stewart, 1977.

Prentice, Alison, and Susan Houston, eds. *Family, School, and Society in Nineteenth-Century Canada*. Toronto: Oxford University Press, 1975.

Prentice, Alison, and Marjorie R. Theobald, eds. *Women Who Taught: Perspectives on the History of Women and Teaching*. Toronto: University of Toronto Press, 1991.

Purdy, J.D. "John Strachan and Education in Canada, 1800–1851." PhD diss., University of Toronto, 1962.

– "John Strachan's Educational Policies, 1815–1841." *Ontario History* 64 (1972): 45–64.

Putnam, J. Harold. *Egerton Ryerson and Education in Upper Canada*. Toronto: William Briggs, 1912.

Quealey, F.M. "The Administration of Sir Peregrine Maitland, Lieutenant Governor of Upper Canada, 1818–1820." PhD diss., University of Western Ontario, 1968.

Rea, J.E. *Bishop Alexander Macdonell and the Politics of Upper Canada*. Toronto: Ontario Historical Society, 1974.

Read, Colin. "The Duncombe Rising, the Aftermath, Anti-Americanism, and Sectarianism." *Histoire Sociale/Social History* 9 (1976): 47–69.

– *The Rising in Western Upper Canada*. Toronto: University of Toronto Press, 1982.

– *The Rebellion of 1837 in Upper Canada*. Ottawa: Canadian Historical Association, 1988.

– "Conflict to Consensus: The Political Culture of Upper Canada." *Acadiensis* 19, no. 2 (1990): 169–85.

Read, Colin, and R.J. Stagg, eds. *The Rebellion of 1837 in Upper Canada*. Ottawa: Champlain Society with Carleton University Press, 1985.

Riddell, R.G. "Egerton Ryerson's Views on the Government of Upper Canada in 1836." *Canadian Historical Review* 19 (1938): 402–10.

Roberton, Thomas Beattie. *The Fighting Bishop, John Strachan, First Bishop of Toronto, and Other Essays in His Times*. Ottawa: Laurentian Press Syndicate, 1932.

Roberts, Julia. "'A Mixed Assemblage of Persons': Race and Tavern Space in Upper Canada." *Canadian Historical Review* 83, no. 1 (2002): 1–28.

– *In Mixed Company: Taverns and Public Life in Upper Canada*. Vancouver: University of British Columbia Press, 2009.

Romney, Paul. "A Conservative Reformer in Upper Canada: Charles Fothergill, Responsible Government and the British Party." *Canadian Historical Association: Historical Papers*, 1985, 42–62.

Rousmaniere, Kate, Kari Dehli, and Ning de Coninck-Smith, eds. *Discipline, Moral Regulation, and Schooling: A Social History*. New York: Garland Publishing, 1997.

Russell, P.A. "Church of Scotland Clergy in Upper Canada: Culture Shock and. Conservatism on the Frontier." *Ontario History* 73 (1981): 88–111.

Ryerson, Egerton. *The Story of My Life*. Edited by J. George Hodgins. Toronto: W. Briggs, 1883.

Sanderson, J.E. *The First Century of Methodism in Canada*. 2 vols. Toronto: William Briggs, 1908–10.

Saunders, R.E. "What Was the Family Compact?" *Ontario History* 49 (1957): 165–78.

Schweizer, Kark W. "Introduction. Parliament and the Press: A Case for Synergy." *Parliamentary History* 25, no. 1 (2006): 1–8.

Semple, Neil. *The Lord's Dominion: The History of Canadian Methodism*. Montreal and Kingston: McGill-Queen's University Press, 1996.

Sheppard, George. *Plunder, Profit, and Paroles: A Social History of the War of 1812 in Upper Canada*. Montreal and Kingston: McGill-Queen's University Press, 1994.

Sissons, C.B. *Egerton Ryerson: His Life and Letters*. 2 vols. Toronto: Clarke, Irwin, 1937–47.

– "Four Early Letters of Egerton Ryerson." *Canadian Historical Review* 23 (1942): 58–64.

– "Ryerson and the Elections of 1844." *Canadian Historical Review* 23 (1942): 157–76.

– "Canadian Methodism in 1828: A Note on an Early Ryerson Letter." *Douglas Library Notes* (Kingston) 12 (Spring 1963): 2–6.

Smaller, Harry. "Teachers and Schools in Early Ontario." *Ontario History* 85, no. 4 (1993): 291–308.

Smith, Alison. "John Strachan and Early Upper Canada, 1799–1814." *Ontario History* 52 (1960): 159–73.

Smith, Allan Charles. "The Imported Image: American Publications and American Ideas in the Evolution of the English Canadian Mind, 1820–1900." PhD diss., University of Toronto, 1972.

Smith, Brian P. "The Political Ideas and Attitudes of William Henry Draper." MA thesis, Queen's University, 1978.

Smith, Goldwin. *Canada and the Canadian Question*. Toronto: University of Toronto Press, 1971.

Spragge, G.W. "The Upper Canada Central School." *Ontario History* 32 (1937): 171–91.

– "John Strachan's Contribution to Education, 1800–1823." *Canadian Historical Review* 22 (1941): 147–58.

– "John Strachan's Connexion with Early Proposals for Confederation." *Canadian Historical Review* 23 (1942): 363–73.

– "The Cornwall Grammar School under John Strachan, 1803–1812." *Ontario History* 34 (1942): 63–84.

– , ed. *The John Strachan Letter Book, 1812–1834*. Toronto: Ontario Historical Society, 1946.

– "Elementary Education in Upper Canada." *Ontario History* 43 (1951): 107–22.

Stagg, Ronald John. "The Yonge Street Rebellion of 1837: An Examination of the Social Background and a Re-assessment of the Events." PhD diss., University of Toronto, 1976.

Stewart, Gordon. *The Origins of Canadian Politics: A Comparative Approach*. Vancouver: University of British Columbia Press, 1986.

Stewart, W.S., ed. *Mackenzie's Narrative of the Rebellion with Notes*. Toronto: Rous and Mann, 1937.

Talman, J.J. "The Position of the Church of England in Upper Canada, 1791–1840." *Canadian Historical Review* 15 (1934): 361–75.

– , ed. *Loyalist Narratives from Upper Canada*. Toronto: Champlain Society, 1946.

Temperley, Howard. "Frontierism, Capital and the American Loyalists in Canada." *Journal of American Studies* 13 (1977): 5–27.

Thomas, Jonathan Paul. *The Sense of the People: Politics, Culture, and Imperialism in England, 1715–1785*. Cambridge, UK: Cambridge University Press, 1995.

Tilly, Charles. *Popular Contention in Great Britain, 1758–1834*. Cambridge, MA: Harvard University Press, 1998.

Tolley, Kim, and Nancy Beadie. "Socioeconomic Incentives to Teach in New York and North Carolina: Toward a More Complex Model of Teacher Labor Markets, 1800–1850." *History of Education Quarterly* 46, no. 1 (2006): 36–72.

Underhill, Frank. *In Search of Canadian Liberalism*. Toronto: Macmillan of Canada, 1975.

University of Toronto. *Memorials of Chancellor W. H. Blake, Bishop John Strachan, Professor H.H. Croft, and Professor G.P. Young: Presented to the University of Toronto in the University Library, January 13th, 1894*. Toronto: Rowsell and Hutchison, 1894.

Upton, L.F.S. *The United Empire Loyalists: Men and Myths*. Toronto: Copp Clark, 1967.

Urban, Wayne. "Marshall McLuhan and the Book: A Reconsideration." *Historical Studies in Education* 16, no. 1 (2004): 139–54.

Vance, Bruce. *Reverend Doctor John Strachan, Reverend Samuel Armour and the Old Blue School, 1812–1825*. Toronto: Sesquicentennial Museum and Archives, Toronto Board of Education, 1995.

Vance, Jonathan. *A History of Canadian Culture*. Toronto: Oxford University Press, 2009.

Walker, Audrey N.B. "History of Education in Ontario, 1791–1841." MA thesis, Bishop's University, 1946.

Walker, Franklin A. *Catholic Education and Politics in Upper Canada: A Study of the Documentation Relative to the Origin of Catholic Elementary Schools in the Ontario School System*. Toronto: J.M. Dent and Sons, 1955.

Wallace, W.S. *The United Empire Loyalists: A Chronicle of the Great Migration*. Toronto: Glasgow, Brook, and Company 1914.

– *The Family Compact: A Chronicle of the Rebellion in Upper Canada*. Toronto: Glasgow, Brook, and Company, 1915.

– *John Strachan*. Toronto: Ryerson Press, 1930.

Walsh, Patrick. "Education and the 'Universalist' Idiom of Empire: Irish National School Books in Ireland and Ontario." *History of Education* 37, no. 5 (2008): 645–60.

Walton, J.B. "An End to All Order: A Study of the Upper Canadian Conservative Response to Opposition, 1805–1810." MA thesis, Queen's University, 1977.

Ward, John Manning. *Colonial Self-Government: The British Experience, 1759–1856*. Toronto: University of Toronto Press, 1976.

Wearmouth, Robert F. *Methodism and the Common People of the Eighteenth Century*. London: Epworth Press, 1957.

Westfall, William. "The Sacred and the Secular: Studies in the Cultural History of Protestant Ontario in the Victorian Period." PhD diss., University of Toronto, 1976.

– "The Dominion of the Lord: An Introduction to the Cultural History of Protestant Ontario in the Victorian Period." *Queen's Quarterly* 83 (1976): 47–70.

– "Order and Experience: Patterns of Religious Metaphor in Early Nineteenth Century Upper Canada." *Journal of Canadian Studies* 20 (Spring 1985): 5–24.

– *Two Worlds: The Protestant Culture of Nineteenth-Century Ontario*. Montreal and Kingston: McGill-Queen's University Press, 1989.

Whelchel, Aaron David. "'The Schoolmaster Is Abroad': The Diffusion of Educational Innovations in the Nineteenth Century British Empire." PhD diss., Washington State University, 2011.

Wilson, Alan. *The Clergy Reserves of Upper Canada: A Canadian Mortmain*. Toronto: University of Toronto Press, 1968.

Wilson, Bruce. *As She Began: Al Illustrated Introduction to Loyalist Ontario*. Toronto: Dundurn Press, 1981.

Wilson, Catharine Anne. *Tenants in Time: Family Strategies, Land, and Liberalism in Upper Canada, 1799–1871*. Montreal and Kingston: McGill-Queen's University Press, 2008.

Wilson, J. Donald. "Foreign and Local Influences on Popular Education in Upper Canada, 1815–1844." PhD diss., University of Western Ontario, 1971.

– "From Social Control to Family Strategies: Some Observations on Recent Trends in Canadian Educational History." *History of Education Review* 13 (1984): 1–13.

Wilson, J. Donald, Robert M. Stamp, and Louis-Philippe Audet, eds. *Canadian Education: A History*. Toronto: Prentice Hall, 1970.

Wilson, Kathleen. *The Sense of the People: Politics, Culture, and Imperialism in England, 1715–1785*. Berkeley: University of California Press, 2002.

Wilton, Carol. "Administrative Reform: A Conservative Alternative to Responsible Government." *Ontario History* 78 (1986): 105–26.

– *Popular Politics and Political Culture in Upper Canada, 1800–1850*. Montreal and Kingston: McGill-Queen's University Press, 2000.

Wise, S.F. "The Origins of Anti-Americanism in Canada." In F.J. Boland, *Fourth Seminar on Canadian-American Relations*. Proceedings. Windsor: Assumption University, 1962.

– , ed. *Sir Francis Bond Head: A Narrative*. Toronto: McClelland and Stewart, 1969.

– *God's Peculiar Peoples: Essays on Political Culture in Nineteenth-Century Canada*. Edited by A.B. McKillop and Paul Romney. Ottawa: Carleton University Press, 1988.

Wise, S.F., et al., eds. *"None was ever better ...": The Loyalist Settlement of Ontario*. Cornwall, ON: Stormont, Dundas, and Glengarry Historical Society, 1984.

Yates, David Ross Allen. "Bred in the Bone: Egerton Ryerson, Methodist Polity, and Educational Administration, 1844–1850." MEd thesis, University of Western Ontario, 1995.

Index